BTEC
NATIONAL

Book 1

Sport
Development, Coaching and Fitness

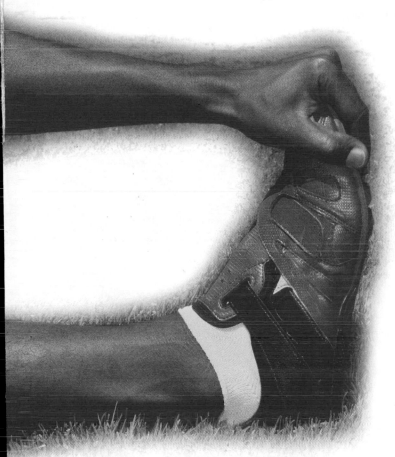

John Honeybourne

Nelson Thornes
a Wolters Kluwer business

First edition published in 2003

Second edition published in 2007 by:
Nelson Thornes Ltd
Delta Place
27 Bath Road
CHELTENHAM
GL53 7TH
United Kingdom

07 08 09 10 11 / 10 9 8 7 6 5 4 3 2 1

A catalogue record for this book is available from the British Library

ISBN 978 0 7487 8164 5

Page make-up by Pantek Arts, Maidstone, Kent

Printed and bound in Slovenia by Korotan

Contents

Introduction

Sport is such an important aspect in our world today. A significant number of people watch, take part in or work in sport. Millions of pairs of eyes will be on London in the summer of 2012, watching the Olympic Games. Thousands of people each week watch football, rugby and athletics events in the UK. Many compete in sports at different levels, from Sunday morning club games to the elite athletes who train many hours each day to achieve high standards in performance. There is a thriving industry supporting sport, with a range of related jobs from sports hall supervisors to events organisers, to top performance coaches. Should you want to be part of the sports industry, a BTEC National Diploma in Sport is an important step in your sports education.

How do you use this book?

Covering all 8 core units of the new 2007 specification and 2 specialist units, this book has everything you need if you are studying BTEC National Certificate or Diploma in Sport (Development, Coaching and Fitness). Simple to use and understand, it is designed to provide you with the skills and knowledge you need to gain your qualification. We guide you step by step toward your qualification, through a range of features that are fully explained over the page.

Which units do you need to complete?

BTEC National Sport Book 1 provides coverage of 10 units for the BTEC National Diploma in Sport (Development, Coaching and Fitness). To achieve the Diploma, you are required to complete 7 core units plus 11 specialist units that provide for a combined total of 1080 guided learning hours (GLH). *BTEC National Sport Book 1* provides you with coverage of the following:

Core Units	Specialist Units
Unit 1 **The Body in Action**	Unit 11 **Sport and Society**
Unit 2 **Health and Safety in Sport**	Unit 16 **Psychology for Sports Performance**
Unit 3 **Training and Fitness for Sport**	
Unit 4 **Sports Coaching**	
Unit 5 **Sports Development**	
Unit 6 **Fitness Testing for Sport and Exercise**	
Unit 7 **Practical Team Sports***	
Unit 8 **Practical Individual Sports***	

* Learners must select one of these units (Unit 7 or Unit 8) as a core unit, and may select the other as a specialist unit

Is there anything else you need to do?

1 Find out about sport and leisure in your area – check local newspapers, TV and radio.
2 Get as much experience as you can in the sports industry, for example at local clubs or leisure centres.
3 Keep yourself fit and healthy by participating in sport.
4 Read national newspapers, including the broadsheets, to gain a wider knowledge of sport.
5 Talk to people who are involved in the sports industry, ask them how they got their position and what qualifications/experience they needed.

We hope you enjoy your BTEC course – Good Luck!

Turn over now for your guide to the features of this book.

Features of this book

Learning Objectives

At the beginning of each Unit there will be a bulleted list letting you know what material is going to be covered. They specifically relate to the learning objectives within the specification.

Grading Criteria

The table of Grading Criteria at the beginning of each unit identifies achievement levels of pass, merit and distinction, as stated in the specification.

To achieve a **pass**, you must be able to match each of the 'P' criteria in turn.

To achieve **merit** or **distinction**, you must increase the level of evidence that you use in your work, using the 'M' and 'D' columns as reference. For example, to achieve a distinction you must fulfil all the criteria in the pass, merit and distinction columns. Each of the criteria provides a specific page number for easy reference.

UNIT 1

The body in action

This unit covers:

This unit covers the following objectives:

- The structure and function of the skeletal system and how it responds to exercise.
- The structure and function of the muscular system and how it responds to exercise.
- The structure and function of the cardiovascular system and how it responds to exercise.
- The structure and function of the respiratory system and how it responds to exercise.
- The different energy systems and their use in sport and exercise.

This chapter will provide information about how the body responds and adapts to exercise. The structure of the skeletal and muscular systems will be covered and their role in producing movement related to sport. There is also a section on the structure and function of the cardio-vascular and respiratory systems. This chapter also includes the necessary information on different energy systems and their uses in sport and exercise.

grading criteria

To achieve a **Pass** grade the evidence must show that the learner is able to:	To achieve a **Merit** grade the evidence must show that the learner is able to:	To achieve a **Distinction** grade the evidence must show that the learner is able to:
P1 describe the structure and function of the axial and appendicular skeleton, including all the major bones, and the different classifications of joints and the range of movements at each p1	**M1** explain why different classifications of joints allow different ranges of movement p3	**D1** analyse how the skeletal system responds to exercise p7
P2 describe how the skeletal system responds to exercise p5	**M2** explain how the skeletal system responds to exercise p5	**D2** analyse how the muscular system responds to exercise p14
P3 describe the muscular system, including all the major muscles, and how muscles move p9	**M3** explain how the muscular system responds to exercise p10	**D3** analyse how the cardiovascular system responds to exercise p25
P4 describe how the muscular system responds to exercise p10	**M4** explain the function of the cardiovascular system and how it responds to exercise p22	**D4** analyse how the respiratory system responds to exercise p36
P5 describe the structure and function of the cardiovascular system p17	**M5** explain the function of the respiratory system, including the mechanisms of breathing, and how it responds to exercise p35	
P6 describe how the cardiovascular system responds to exercise p20	**M6** explain the different energy systems and their use in sport and exercise activities p39	

activity
GROUP WORK

P1

Write the following major bones on separate sticky notes:
Cranium, clavicle, ribs, sternum, humerus, radius, ulna, scapula, ilium, pubis, ischium, carpals, metacarpals, phalanges, femur, patella, tibia, fibula, tarsals, metatarsals, vertebral column, cervical vertebrae, thoracic vertebrae, lumbar vertebrae, sacrum, coccyx.

In pairs, take it in turns to stick the post-its on an appropriate area of your partner to indicate the position of each bone and tell your partner what type of bone it is (e.g. long bone). Check with the diagram in figure 1.1 whether you have labelled each correct bone. Now let your partner have a go!

case study
1.1

Osteoporosis

A key concept for sports development is to encourage people to follow an active lifestyle. A sports development officer ran a weekly session to increase participation in exercise for the elderly. Publicity material explained how exercise can help maintain health and fitness. It emphasised that exercise may also help combat osteoporosis in the elderly. People who attended the session said that they felt better and that they had become more mobile in their joints, although they were not sure why.

activity
INDIVIDUAL WORK

1. What are the main effects of osteoporosis?
2. How can regular exercise help combat osteoporosis?
3. What sort of activities suitable for the elderly would you include to ensure the positive effects of exercise on the skeletal system?

Flexion decreases the angle around a joint.
Extension increases the angle.
Abduction is away from the midline and adduction is towards the midline.
Plantarflexion means pointing the toes.
Dorsiflexion means pulling your toes upward.

Hyaline cartilage also thickens with exercise, which helps to cushion the joint, therefore preventing damage to the bone. **Tendons** thicken and the ligaments have a greater stretch potential, helping to protect the body from injury.

The bones of people that participate in regular exercise contain significantly higher amounts of calcium and phosphate than the bones of people who do not exercise regularly, and this applies to people of all ages. It is a compelling reason for regular exercise, even for the elderly.

 Link

For more information see Unit 2, page 53.

National Osteoporosis Society
www.nos.org.uk

Progress Check

1. Give four main functions of the skeleton.
2. What are the main classifications of joints?
3. What are the main effects of exercise on the skeletal system?
4. Identify the main types of muscle tissue.
5. Briefly describe how a muscle contracts.
6. Draw a diagram showing the main structures and blood vessels of the heart.
7. What is the vascular shunt?
8. What is the difference between tidal volume and minute ventilation?
9. Give the short-term responses of the respiratory system to exercise.
10. What is ATP?

Activities

are designed to help you understand the topics through answering questions or undertaking research, and are either *Group* or *Individual* work. They are linked to the Grading Criteria by application of the D, P, and M categories.

Case Studies

provide real life examples that relate to what is being discussed within the text. It provides an opportunity to demonstrate theory in practice.

An **Activity** that is linked to a Case Study helps you to apply your knowledge of the subject to real life situations.

Keywords

of specific importance are highlighted within the text in blue, and then defined in a feature box to the side.

Remember boxes

contain helpful hints, tips or advice.

Links

direct you to other parts of the book that relate to the subject currently being covered.

Information bars

point you towards resources for further reading and research (e.g. websites).

Progress Checks

provide a list of quick questions at the end of each Unit, designed to ensure that you have understood the most important aspects of each subject area.

Acknowledgements

I would like to thank my wife, Rebecca, and my daughters, Emmi and Jodie, for being so supportive and patient with me while writing this book.

The author and publisher would like to thank the following organisations for permission to reproduce material:

The Health and Safety Executive for Figure 2.6 (p. 62) (ISBN 978 0 7176 6195 4 available from HSE Books, PO Box 1999, Sudbury, Suffolk, CO10 2WA) and Tables 2.1 (p. 52), 2.4 (p. 69), 2.5 (p. 75), the Royal Society for the Prevention of Accidents for Table 2.2, the British Canoe Union for Table 2.3, Top End Sports for Table 6.1.

Figures 7.6 and 7.10 are modified from Wikipedia – Copyright © 2007 Nelson Thornes Ltd, Permission is granted to copy, distribute and/or modify this modified version under the terms of the GNU Free Documentation License, Version 1.2 or any later version published by the Free Software Foundation; with no Invariant Sections, no Front-Cover Texts, and no Back-Cover Texts. A copy of the license is included in the section entitled 'GNU Free Documentation License'.

Photo credits
Alamy Figures 1.6 (p. 7) (Nucleus Medical Art), 1.13 (p. 11), 1.30 (p. 22) (Popperfoto), 2.3 (p. 61) (Jack Sullivan), 2.4 (p. 61) (Photofusion), 2.7 (p. 63) (David Crausby), 2.11 (p. 71) Nordicphotos), 2.13 (p. 73) (Gianni Muratore), 3.9 (p. 100) (Jim West), 3.2 (p. 81) (Popperfoto), 3.5 (p. 84) (Associated Sports), 3.10 (p. 101) David Hoffman, 3.12 (p. 103) (Kolvenbach), 3.17 (p. 110), 4.1 (p. 114), 4.7 (p. 122) (Trevor Smith), 4.8 (p. 125) (Les Gibbon), 4.14 (p. 133) © Index Stock, 4.18 (p. 143), 5.3 (p. 149), 5.6 (p. 153) (Enigma), 5.7 (p. 153), 5.8 (p. 154), 5.9 (p. 155) (Imagebroker), 5.17 (p. 168) (Popperfoto), 6.2 (p. 189) (Profimedia), 7.9 (p. 231) (Popperfoto), 7.15 (p. 244) (Blickwinkel), 11.18 (p. 277) (George de Blonksy).

Allsport Figures 1.45 (p. 37), 1.49 (p. 42), 2.9 (p. 66), 2.12 (p.72), 3.7 (p. 90), 4.15 (p. 135), 5.5 (p. 151), 5.10 (p. 156), 5.12 (p. 159), 5.18 (p. 169), 5.20 (p. 172), 7.7 (p. 228), 11.15 (p. 269), 16.5 (p. 290), 16.16 (p. 302).

Corbis Figures 4.10 (p. 126) (Ariel Skelley), 5.4 (p. 150) (Mika/Zefa), 5.24 (p.181), 6.15 (p. 216) (Frank Bodenmueller/Zefa), 7.8 (p. 230) (B. Echavarri/epa), 16.12 (p. 299) (Wade Jackson).

Empics Figures 2.8 (p. 63) (Sean Dempsey/PA), 3.6 (p. 86) (Tony Feder), 3.8 (p. 92) (Ty Russell/PA), 3.14 (p. 104) (Martin Rickett/PA), 4.4 (p. 119) (Anna Gowthorpe/PA), 4.5 (p. 121) (Peter Byrne/PA), 4.11 (p. 128) (Barry Coombs/PA), 5.23 (p. 180) (Sergio Dionisio/PA), 6.6 (p. 195) (Jon Buckle/PA), 6.7 (p. 197) (Panoramic/PA), 11.5 (p. 254) (Martin Rickett/PA), 11.8 (p. 258), 11.11 (p. 264) (Gareth Copley/PA), 11.13 (p. 267) (Nick Blotts/PA), 16.2 (p. 286) (Mark Lees/PA), 16.14 (p. 300) (Nick Potts/PA), 16.17 (p. 303) (Matt Dunham/PA), 16.18 (p. 305) (Mark Baker), 16.19 (p. 307) (Rui Vieira/PA).

Getty Images Figures 1.3 (p. 5), 1.5 (p. 6), 1.12 (p. 10), 1.16 (p. 15), 1.36 (p. 27), 1.38 (p. 28), 1.46 (p. 38), 1.47 (p. 40), 3.1 (p. 80), 3.3 (p. 82), 3.4 (p. 83), 3.11 (p. 102), 4.2 (p. 115), 4.3 (p. 116) (Marc Douet), 5.11 (p. 157), 5.14 (p. 163), 6.3 (p. 191), 6.4 (p. 192), 6.5 (p. 193), 7.11 (p. 237), 7.16 (p. 245), 11.10 (p. 263), 16.3 (p. 287), 16.21 (p. 310), 7.12 (p. 240).

Mary Evans Picture Library Figure 11.1 (p. 249).

NT Figures 1.29 (p. 20) Ingram Sp (NT), 1.33 (p. 25) Digital Vision SC (NT), 1.34 (p. 26) Karl Weatherly/Photodisc 51 (NT), 1.35 (p. 26) Photodisc 18 (NT), 1.39 (p. 30) Photodisc 10 (NT), 1.40 (p. 31) Corel 205 (NT), 2.1 (p. 46) Peter Adams/Digital Vision BP (NT), 2.2 (p. 59) Rubberball (NT), 2.5 (p. 62) Instant Art (NT), 2.10 (p. 67) Photodisc 10 (NT), 3.13 (p. 104) Mike Watson RF (NT), 3.15 (p. 105) Jeff Maloney/Photodisc 51 (NT), 3.16 (p. 106) Ryan McVay/Photodisc 67 (NT), 4.6 (p. 122) Corel 423 (NT), 4.9 (p. 125) Digital Vision XA (NT), 4.12 (p. 129) Thinkstock/Alamy RF (NT), 4.17 (p. 140) Bananastock/ Alamy RF (NT), 4.13 (p. 132) Radius Images/Alamy RF (NT), 5.1 (p. 148) Ingram Sp (NT), 5.13 (p. 161) Corel 205 (NT), 5.15 (p. 166) Image 100 EE (NT), 5.16 (p. 168) Corel 745 (NT), 5.19 (p. 170) Corel 734 (NT), 6.8 (p. 198) Corel 772 (NT), 6.9 (p. 199) Ryan McVay/Photodisc 67 (NT), 6.12 (p. 207) Duncan Smith/Photodisc 67 (NT), 6.13 (p. 208) Keith Brofsky/Photodisc 59 (NT), 6.14 (p. 213) Keith Brofsky/Photodisc 40 (NT), 7.1 (p.220) Ingram S V2 CD6 (NT), 7.2 (p. 221) Corel 776 (NT), 7.3 (p. 223) Photodisc 27 (NT), 7.4 (p. 224) Digital Vision 11 (NT), 7.5 (p. 225) Ingram R V1 CD2 (NT), 7.13 (p. 242) Ingram S V2 CD6 (NT), 11.2 (p. 250) Corel 449 (NT), 11.3 (p. 252) Corel 530 (NT), 11.6 (p. 256) Digital Vision 12 (NT), 11.7 (p.257) Corel 205 (NT), 11.9 (p. 261) (Thinkstock) RF (NT), 11.12 (p. 266) Digital Vision 12 (NT), 11.14 (p. 268) Photodisc 10 (NT), 11.16 (p. 273) Ryan McVay/Photodisc 67 (NT), 11.17 (p. 276) Corel 739 (NT), 16.4 (p. 288) Photodisc 51 (NT), 16.6 (p. 291) Photodisc 10 (NT), 16.7 (p. 291) Photodisc 10 (NT), 16.9 (p. 296) Digital Vision XA (NT), 16.10 (p. 297) Lawrence Sawyer/Photodisc 51 (NT), 16.20 (p. 309) Corel 423 (NT), 16.22 (p. 313) Corel 174 (NT).

Science Photo Library Figure 1.44 (p. 35) (Mauro Fermariello).

The Body in Action

This unit covers:

- The structure and function of the skeletal system and how it responds to exercise
- The structure and function of the muscular system and how it responds to exercise
- The structure and function of the cardiovascular system and how it responds to exercise
- The structure and function of the respiratory system and how it responds to exercise
- The different energy systems and their use in sport and exercise

It explains how our bodies have adapted to cope with more exercise stress. Our skeletal systems change and help our muscles work more efficiently when training or participating in sport. It gives a detailed exploration of how our hearts, blood vessels and lungs also change as a result of exercise. We use a great deal of energy during exercise and it considers the different ways in which our bodies create and use energy.

grading criteria

To achieve a **Pass** grade the evidence must show that the learner is able to:	To achieve a **Merit** grade the evidence must show that the learner is able to:	To achieve a **Distinction** grade the evidence must show that the learner is able to:
P1 describe the structure and function of the axial and appendicular skeleton, including all the major bones, and the different classifications of joints and the range of movements at each Pg 5	**M1** explain why different classifications of joints allow different ranges of movement Pg 7	**D1** analyse how the skeletal system responds to exercise Pg 12
P2 describe how the skeletal system responds to exercise Pg 12	**M2** explain how the skeletal system responds to exercise Pg 12	**D2** analyse how the muscular system responds to exercise Pg 21
P3 describe the muscular system, including all the major muscles, and how muscles move Pg 17	**M3** explain how the muscular system responds to exercise Pg 21	**D3** analyse how the cardiovascular system responds to exercise Pg 30
P4 describe how the muscular system responds to exercise Pg 21	**M4** explain the function of the cardiovascular system and how it responds to exercise Pg 30	**D4** analyse how the respiratory system responds to exercise Pg 37

grading criteria

To achieve a **Pass** grade the evidence must show that the learner is able to:	To achieve a **Merit** grade the evidence must show that the learner is able to:	To achieve a **Distinction** grade the evidence must show that the learner is able to:
P5 describe the structure and function of the cardiovascular system Pg 28	**M5** explain the function of the respiratory system, including the mechanisms of breathing, and how it responds to exercise Pg 35	
P6 describe how the cardiovascular system responds to exercise Pg 30	**M6** explain the different energy systems and their use in sport and exercise activities Pg 41	
P7 describe the structure and function of the respiratory system, the mechanisms of breathing, respiratory volumes, and how the respiratory system responds to exercise Pg 35		
P8 describe the different energy systems and their use in sport and exercise activities Pg 41		

Understand the structure and function of the skeletal system and how it responds to exercise

This section explains the structure and function of the skeletal system and how it responds to exercise. It will help you understand what happens to the body during and after exercise.

Skeleton

Functions

There are five major functions of the skeleton:

- **To give shape and support to the body** – giving posture.

- **To allow movement of the body** – the skeleton provides sites for muscle attachment, to provide a system of levers. These levers are movable through the attachment of the muscles. The muscles pull on these levers to produce movement in different parts of the body.

- **To give protection to the internal organs** – such as heart, lungs, spinal cord and brain. The cranium protects the brain; the ribs and sternum protect the heart and lungs.

- **To produce red and white blood cells** – these cells are produced by the bone marrow of many bones in the skeleton.

- **To store minerals** – bones store calcium and phosphorus, for example. They are used by the body when the diet is inadequate.

The axial skeleton is the main source of support and is the central part of the skeleton. It includes the cranium, the vertebral column and the rib cage and the sternum. The rib cage has 12 pairs of ribs. The appendicular skeleton consists of the remaining bones and the girdles that join them to the axial skeleton.

Bones

The bones of the skeleton have designs related to their function:

- **Long bones**, e.g. the tibia – they consist of a hollow shaft of **compact bone**. The shaft is enlarged at each end and consists of spongy bone, or **cancellous bone**.

- **Short bones**, e.g. the carpals – they are shaped like cubes and consist mainly of cancellous bone covered by a thin layer of compact bone.

- **Flat bones**, e.g. the sternum – they protect the internal organs of the body and provide sites for muscle attachment.

Figure 1.1 Human skeleton showing the major bones

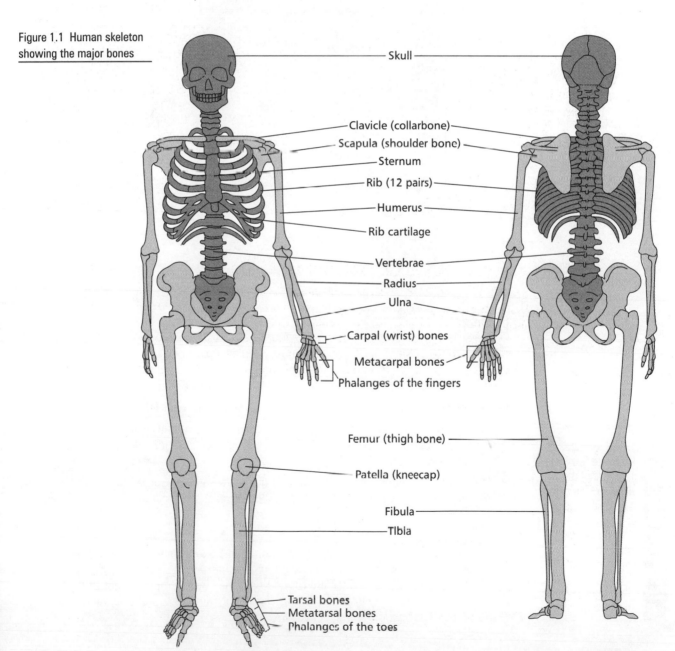

Skull

Clavicle (collarbone)
Scapula (shoulder bone)
Sternum
Rib (12 pairs)
Humerus
Rib cartilage
Vertebrae
Radius
Ulna
Carpal (wrist) bones
Metacarpal bones
Phalanges of the fingers

Femur (thigh bone)

Patella (kneecap)

Fibula
Tibia

Tarsal bones
Metatarsal bones
Phalanges of the toes

- Irregular bones, e.g. the vertebrae – they have a variety of shapes with projections. They have a variety of functions, such as protection.

- Sesamoid bones, e.g. the patella – they are small and very specialised bones that help with joint movements. They are covered with articular **cartilage**.

Figure 1.2 Structure of a long bone

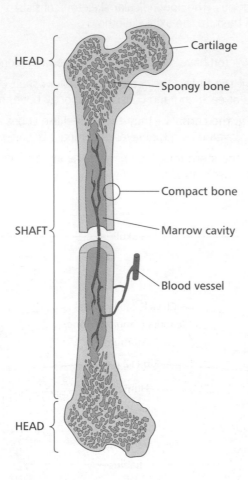

HEAD

Cartilage

Spongy bone

Compact bone

SHAFT

Marrow cavity

Blood vessel

HEAD

Cartilage

Cartilage is soft connective tissue. A newborn baby has a skeleton made of cartilage. As the baby get older, this cartilage is mostly replaced by bone in a process called *ossification*. Cartilage has no blood supply and receives nutrition by diffusion from the surrounding capillary network. There are three basic types of cartilage:

- Yellow elastic cartilage – flexible tissue, e.g. part of the ear lobe.

- Hyaline or blue articular cartilage – found on the articulating surfaces of bones, it protects them and helps them to move with minimal friction. Hyaline cartilage thickens with exercise.

- White fibrocartilage – tough tissue that acts as a shock absorber. It is found in parts of the body that experience large amounts of stress, such as the semilunar cartilage in the knee joint.

Bone formation

Bone is formed by a process called ossification. Flat bones, such as the flat bones of the skull, form in membranes; this is called *intramembranous ossification* or *direct ossification*. Short and flat bones are formed gradually by the replacement of hyaline cartilage. This takes place from the foetal stage right through to maturity; it is called *endochondral ossification* or *indirect ossification*.

remember

There are five main functions of the skeleton. There are two main parts of the skeleton: axial and appendicular. Cartilage is an important shock absorber that can guard against injury in sports activities.

activity
GROUP WORK
1.1

P1

Write the following major bones on separate Post-its: cranium, clavicle, ribs, sternum, humerus, radius, ulna, scapula, ilium, pubis, ischium, carpals, metacarpals, phalanges, femur, patella, tibia, fibula, tarsals, metatarsals, vertebral column, cervical vertebrae, thoracic vertebrae, lumbar vertebrae, sacrum, coccyx.

In pairs take turns to stick the Post-its on an appropriate area of your partner to indicate the position of each bone and tell your partner what type of bone it is (e.g. long bone). Check with Figure 1.1 to see whether you have labelled each bone correctly. Now let your partner have a go.

There are five main functions of the skeleton. There are two main parts of the skeleton: axial and appendicular. Cartilage is an important shock absorber that can guard against injury in sports activities.

Joints

The human body has many types of joint, including some that allow no movement or very little movement. Joints are important in the wide variety of movements used in sport.

Figure 1.3 Gymnast
performing a rings routine

There are three main types of joint:

- **Fibrous or fixed** – this does not allow any movement. Tough, fibrous tissue sits between the ends of the bones. The sutures of the cranium are an example.

- **Cartilaginous or slightly movable** – this allows some movement. The ends of the bones have tough fibrous cartilage, which allows shock absorption but also gives stability. The intervertebral discs in the spine are an example.

- **Synovial or freely movable** – this is the most common type of joint. It allows for a wide range of movement, so it is very important for sportspeople. It consists of a joint capsule lined with a *synovial membrane*. The synovial membrane secretes *synovial fluid*, which lubricates the joint. An example is the knee joint.

Figure 1.4 Synovial joint

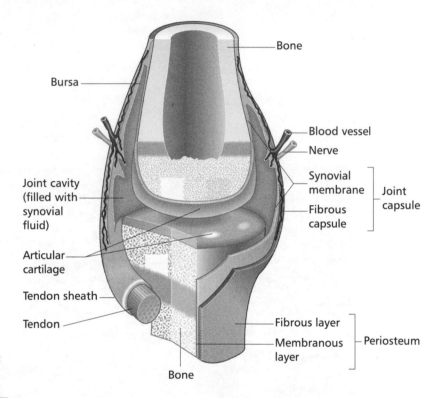

Figure 1.5 The shoulder joint provides a wide range of movement

Types or classification of synovial joints

- **Hinge joint** – this allows movement in one plane only; it is uniaxial. An example is the. knee joint.

- **Pivot joint** – this allows rotation only and is therefore uniaxial. An example is the axis and atlas of the cervical vertebrae.

- **Ellipsoid joint** – this allows movement in two planes; it is biaxial. An example is the radiocarpal joint of the wrist.

- **Gliding joint** – this is where two flat surfaces glide over one another and can permit movement in most directions, although gliding joints are mainly biaxial. An example is the carpal bones in the wrist.

- **Saddle joint** – this is where a concave surface meets a convex surface; it is biaxial. An example is the carpal–metacarpal joint of the thumb.

- **Ball and socket** – this is where a round head of bone fits into a cup-shaped depression; it allows a wide range of movement. An example is the shoulder joint.

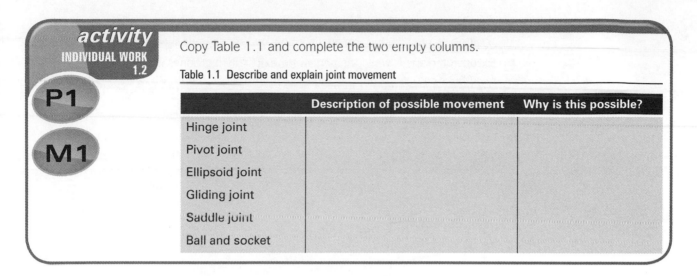

activity
INDIVIDUAL WORK
1.2

P1

M1

Copy Table 1.1 and complete the two empty columns.

Table 1.1 Describe and explain joint movement

	Description of possible movement	Why is this possible?
Hinge joint		
Pivot joint		
Ellipsoid joint		
Gliding joint		
Saddle joint		
Ball and socket		

Types of movement

The movements that occur around synovial joints are classified according to their actions or movement patterns. Movements are often described relative to **anatomical position**. Anatomical position is the position of a person's body standing upright, facing forwards, arms downward, with the palms of the hand facing forward.

Figure 1.6 Movements are often described in relation to anatomical position

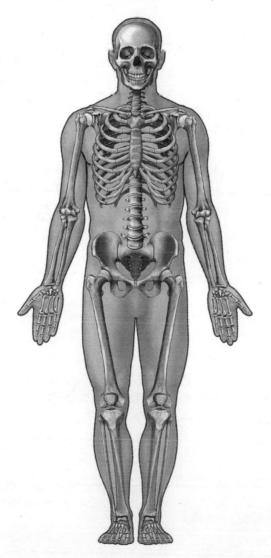

- **Flexion** – this is a decrease in the angle around a joint, e.g. from the anatomical position you bend your arm at the elbow and touch your shoulder with your hand.
- **Extension** – this is when the angle of the articulating bones is increased. For example, when you start in a squat position then stand up, the angle between your femur and tibia increases.
- **Hyperextension** – this is when the angle between the articulating bones goes beyond 180°.

Figure 1.7 Flexion and extension

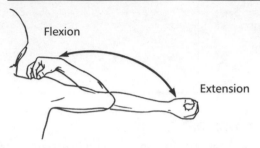

- **Abduction** – this is movement of the body away from the midline of the body, e.g. lying on your left side and lifting your right leg straight up, away from the midline.

Figure 1.8 Abduction and adduction

Figure 1.9 Circumduction

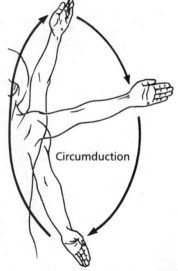

- **Adduction** – this is the opposite of abduction; it is movement towards the midline, e.g. lowering a leg you have lifted by an abduction.
- **Circumduction** – this is when the lower end of a bone moves in the shape of a circle. It is really a combination of flexion, extension, abduction and adduction. The only true circumduction occurs at the shoulders and hips, where there are ball and socket joints.
- **Rotation** – this is when the bone turns about its longitudinal axis within the joint. Rotation towards the body is called internal or *medial rotation*; rotation away from the body is called external or *lateral rotation*.

Figure 1.10 Medial and lateral rotation

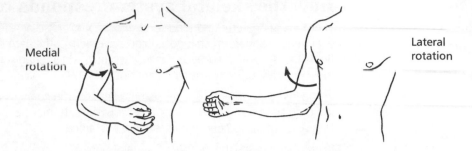

Medial rotation

Lateral rotation

■ **Pronation** – this occurs at the elbow and involves internal rotation between the radius and the humerus. Hold out the palm of your hand so it faces upwards, now move your arm to make the palm face downwards; that is a pronation.

Figure 1.11 Pronation and supination

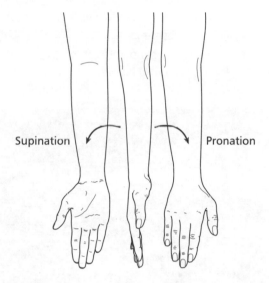

Supination

Pronation

Flexion decreases the angle around a joint. Extension increases the angle. Abduction is away from the midline and adduction is towards the midline. Plantarflexion means pointing the toes. Dorsiflexion means pulling your toes upwards.

remember

■ **Supination** – this is the opposite of pronation. Hold out the palm of your hand so it faces downwards, now move your arm to make the palm face upwards; that is a supination.

■ **Plantarflexion** – this is movement at the ankle joint and occurs when you point your toes.

■ **Dorsiflexion** – this is also movement at the ankle and occurs when you bend your foot up towards your tibia.

■ **Inversion** – this is movement at the ankle and occurs when you turn the sole of your foot inwards towards the midline of your body.

■ **Eversion** – this is the opposite of inversion and occurs when the sole of the foot is turned outwards.

■ **Elevation** – this occurs at the shoulder joint when the shoulders move upwards.

■ **Depression** – this occurs at the shoulder joint when the shoulders move downwards.

activity

INDIVIDUAL WORK 1.3

P1

Refer to Table 1.1, which you created in Activity 1.2. Draw an extra column on the right-hand side and write in the types of movement that each joint allows; use the descriptions above.

How the skeletal system responds to exercise

There are short-term and long-term effects of exercise on the skeleton. The joints experience short-term changes. Joint movements stimulate the secretion of synovial fluid. The synovial fluid becomes less viscous, which enables a greater range of movement; in other words, the joint appears to get looser.

In the longer term and with persistent exercise, the connective tissue around the skeleton becomes more flexible. Over a period of time the short-term improvement in the range of movement becomes more sustained.

Exercise increases the density of skeletal bone. This makes the bones stronger and can help to offset the effects of bone disease such as **osteoporosis**.

Osteoporosis

Osteoporosis is a disease that makes bones become fragile and more likely to break. If it is left untreated, osteoporosis can progress painlessly until a bone breaks. These broken bones, also known as fractures, occur typically in the hip, spine and wrist.

Osteoporosis occurs when the body fails to form enough new bone, when too much old bone is reabsorbed, or when both happen together. Two essential minerals for normal bone formation are calcium and phosphate.

Figure 1.12 Synovial fluid becomes less viscous, which enables a greater range of movement

The leading cause of osteoporosis is a lack of some hormones, particularly oestrogen in women. Women, especially women over age 60, are frequently diagnosed with osteoporosis. Other factors that contribute to bone loss in the over-60s are inadequate intake of calcium and vitamin D and a lack of weight-bearing exercise.

National Osteoporosis Society
www.nos.org.uk

Hyaline cartilage also thickens with exercise, which helps to cushion the joint, preventing damage to the bone. **Tendons** thicken and the ligaments have a greater stretch potential, helping to protect the body from injury.

The bones of people that participate in regular exercise contain significantly higher amounts of calcium and phosphate than the bones of people who do not exercise regularly, and this applies to people of all ages. It is a compelling reason for regular exercise, even for the elderly.

case study 1.1

Osteoporosis

A key concept for sports development is to encourage people to follow an active lifestyle. A sports development officer ran a weekly session to increase participation in exercise for the elderly. Publicity material explained how exercise can help maintain health and fitness. It emphasised that exercise may also help combat osteoporosis in the elderly. People who attended the session said that they felt better and that they had become more mobile in their joints, although they were not sure why.

activity
INDIVIDUAL WORK

1. What are the main effects of osteoporosis?
2. How can regular exercise help combat osteoporosis?
3. What activities suitable for the elderly would you include to ensure the positive effects of exercise on the skeletal system?

Figure 1.13 Exercise can help combat bone disease such as osteoporosis

activity
INDIVIDUAL WORK
1.4

P2

M2

1. Give an overview of how the skeletal system responds to exercise.
2. Give reasons for the effects of exercise on the skeletal system.

activity
INDIVIDUAL WORK
1.5

D1

What are the skeletal system's responses to exercise? Link its adaptations with becoming more flexible and with fighting bone disease.

Sports Coach fitness training – develops athletic performance and coaching expertise

www.brianmac.demon.co.uk

Understand the structure and function of the muscular system and how it responds to exercise

Muscular system

Muscles are crucial for doing sports. There are three types of muscle:

- **Smooth or involuntary muscle** – this is found in the body's internal organs. It is involuntary because it is not under our conscious control.

- **Cardiac muscle** – this is only found in the heart and it is also involuntary.

- **Skeletal or voluntary muscle** – this is under our conscious control and is used primarily for movement.

For sporting movements, our primary focus is skeletal muscle, so let us look at its structure in more detail. Skeletal muscle can lengthen when contracting; in other words, it has extensibility. Skeletal muscle is also very elastic and can return to its normal resting length after stretching. Skeletal muscle can also contract or shorten forcibly after being stimulated by the nervous or hormonal systems.

There are three important functions of the skeletal muscle:

- Movement
- Support and posture
- Heat production.

> **remember**
>
> There are three types of muscle and three important functions of muscle. The effective contraction of skeletal muscle is most important when analysing movements in sport.

Figure 1.14 Muscles of the body – anterior view

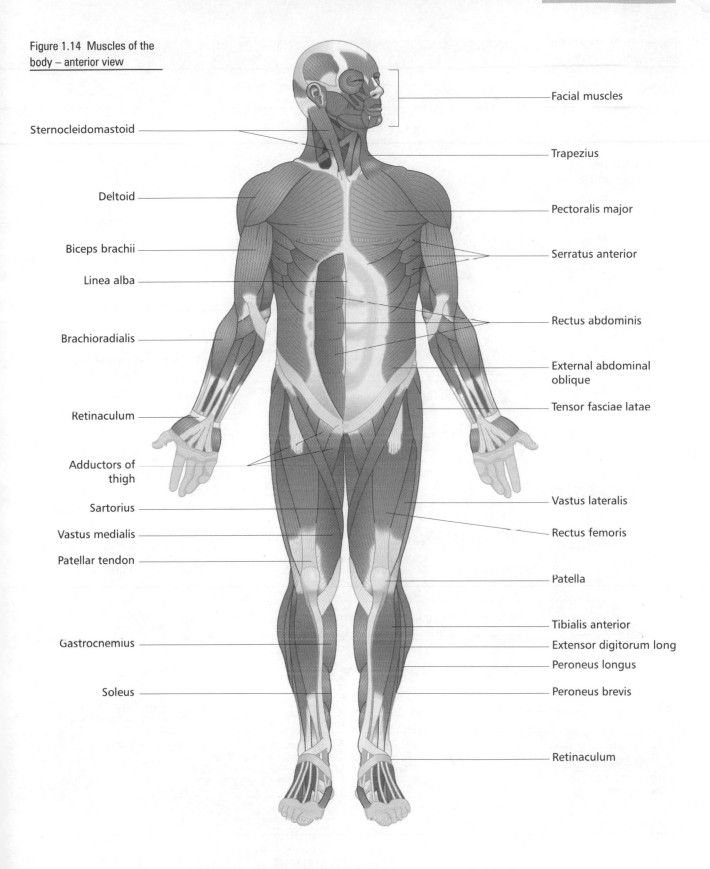

Facial muscles

Sternocleidomastoid

Trapezius

Deltoid

Pectoralis major

Biceps brachii

Serratus anterior

Linea alba

Rectus abdominis

Brachioradialis

External abdominal oblique

Retinaculum

Tensor fasciae latae

Adductors of thigh

Vastus lateralis

Sartorius

Rectus femoris

Vastus medialis

Patellar tendon

Patella

Tibialis anterior

Gastrocnemius

Extensor digitorum long

Peroneus longus

Soleus

Peroneus brevis

Retinaculum

Figure 1.15 Muscles of the body – posterior view

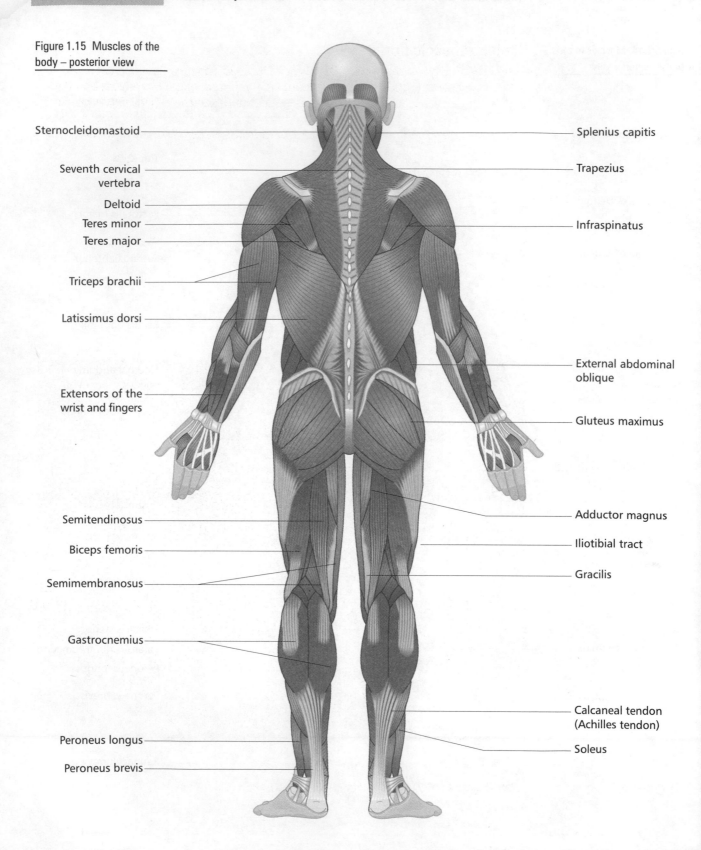

Sternocleidomastoid

Seventh cervical vertebra

Deltoid

Teres minor

Teres major

Triceps brachii

Latissimus dorsi

Extensors of the wrist and fingers

Semitendinosus

Biceps femoris

Semimembranosus

Gastrocnemius

Peroneus longus

Peroneus brevis

Splenius capitis

Trapezius

Infraspinatus

External abdominal oblique

Gluteus maximus

Adductor magnus

Iliotibial tract

Gracilis

Calcaneal tendon (Achilles tendon)

Soleus

Skeletal muscle fibres

There are three types of muscle fibre – *type 1*, *type 2a* and *type 2b* – and each type has its own characteristics. A person is born with a mixture of the three types and the mixture can vary from one person to another; it is something we inherit. Some people seem to be naturally fast runners, because they have slightly more type 2 muscle fibres, whereas others seem to be natural long-distance runners, perhaps they have more type 1 muscle fibres.

Type 1: slow oxidative fibre (slow twitch)

- Red colour
- Contracts slower than type 2 – thinner myelin sheath
- Exerts less force
- Aerobic – mainly endurance
- Can contract repeatedly.

Some suited sports: long-distance running such as the marathon (e.g. in calf muscle, gastrocnemius), triathletes (e.g. in leg muscles, vastus lateralis), canoeists (e.g. in shoulder muscles, deltoid).

Figure 1.16 Canoeists need muscular endurance in the shoulders

Type 2a: fast oxidative glycolytic fibre (fast twitch)

- White colour
- Contracts quicker than type 1 – thicker myelin sheath
- Exerts more force – more muscle fibres in each motor unit
- Aerobic and anaerobic but much more anaerobic – releases energy quickly
- Fatigues quickly.

Type 2b: fast glycolytic fibre (fast twitch)

- White colour

- Contracts quickly

- Exerts large amount of force – large motor neurone

- Mostly anaerobic – less aerobic than type 2a

- Fatigues extremely quickly.

Some suited sports: sprinter (e.g. in calf muscle, gastrocnemius), shot-putter (e.g. in shoulder, deltoid), powerlifter (e.g. in thigh muscle, vastus lateralis).

Muscle structure

When viewed under a microscope, the 'belly' of the muscle appears to be surrounded by a layer of thick connective tissue called the epimysium. The muscle is composed of bundles of fibres called *fasiculi*. Every fibre in the fasiculus is composed of many smaller fibres called *myofibrils*, which are long, tubular structures. Myofibrils have dark lines and light bands; the area between neighbouring dark lines is a sarcomere.

Figure 1.17 Structure of a muscle

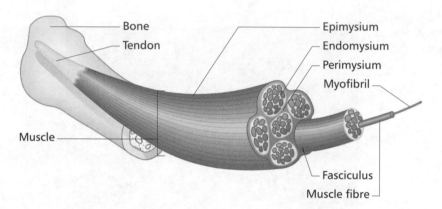

Sarcomeres are the contractile units of the muscle. In each sarcomere there are two protein filaments, a thick filament of *myosin* and a thinner filament of *actin*.

Figure 1.18 Microstructure of a muscle

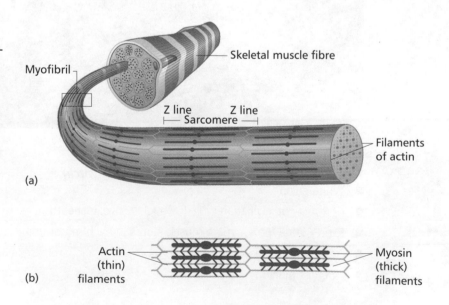

The sarcomere is indicated between the two Z lines. The I band contains only thin filaments of actin. The H zone contains only myosin filaments and the A band contains both actin and myosin filaments.

The sliding filament theory is used to explain the interaction between actin and myosin during muscle contraction.

Sliding filament theory

In 1969 Huxley proposed sliding filament theory to explain how a muscle alters its length. According to this theory, the I band shortens, the A band remains the same length, and the H band disappears. The myosin pulls the actin across so that the two filaments slide closer together, but the filaments do not actually get any shorter.

See Honeybourne *et al*. (2000: 311–332) for more information on sliding filament theory

activity
INDIVIDUAL WORK 1.6

P3

Make a copy of Figures 1.14 and 1.15 but blank out the labels. Now try to label each major muscle.

Muscle movement

Summary of muscular contraction

Muscular contraction involves the interaction of muscles with the nervous system. Here is a summary of the process:

- An electrical impulse is sent from the brain to muscles via the spinal cord and by cells called *motor neurones*.

- One motor neurone stimulates a number of fibres within the muscle. The neurone and the fibres that have been stimulated are called a *motor unit*.

- The number of fibres that are activated (or innervated) by a single motor unit depends on how finely controlled the movement has to be.

- The fibres in any given motor unit will usually be slow twitch or fast twitch, so the units that are triggered depend on what type of movement is about to happen.

- Once the motor unit is stimulated, all the fibres within the unit will contract; this is called the all-or-none law.

All-or-none law

The motor units do not necessarily work together. If the stimulus is strong enough to activate at least one motor unit, then all fibres within that unit will contract simultaneously and maximally. Neurones and muscle fibres either respond completely – *all* – or not at all – *none*.

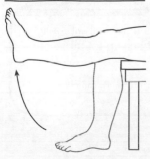

Figure 1.19 Concentric and eccentric muscle contraction

Muscle contraction

The human body can make a vast range of movements. When muscles contract to produce these movements, they shorten, lengthen or remain the same length. Here are the types of muscular contraction:

- Isotonic or concentric contraction – this is when a muscle shortens and creates movement around a joint.

- Eccentric contraction – this is when the muscle lengthens during contraction; it acts to control movement.

- **Isometric contraction** – this is when a muscle contracts but does not lengthen or shorten. During contraction there is no movement around the joint, which is important when the muscle is acting as a fixator.

Figure 1.20 Isometric muscle contraction

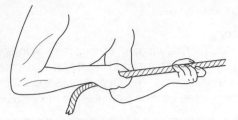

- **Isokinetic contraction** – this is when the muscle shortens and increases in tension while working at a constant speed against a variable resistance (Honeybourne 2000).

Agonist and antagonist, fixator and synergist

- **Agonist** – the agonist is the muscle that produces the desired joint movement; it is also known as the *prime mover*. For example, the biceps brachii is the agonist that produces flexion at the elbow.

Figure 1.21 Here the agonist is the biceps

- **Antagonist** – the muscle that opposes the agonist. Muscles work in pairs to coordinate movement and maintain control. At the elbow, shortening of the biceps is opposed by lengthening of the triceps. The biceps is the agonist and the triceps is the antagonist.
- **Fixator** – this stabilises the **origin** of the agonist; for example, the trapezius fixator contracts to stabilise the origin of the biceps agonist.
- **Synergist** – a muscle that actively helps the agonist to produce the desired movement; it is sometimes called a *neutraliser* because it prevents any undesired movements. Sometimes the fixator and the synergist are the same muscle. For example, the brachialis acts as a synergist when the elbow is bent and the forearm moves upwards.

remember

The all-or-none law for neurones and muscle fibres says that they all respond or none respond.

activity
GROUP WORK
1.7

P3

Take it in turns with a partner to perform a biceps curl. Pick up a dumbbell with a light weight and bend your arm steadily at the elbow. Bring the dumbbell up towards your shoulder. Describe each stage to your partner.

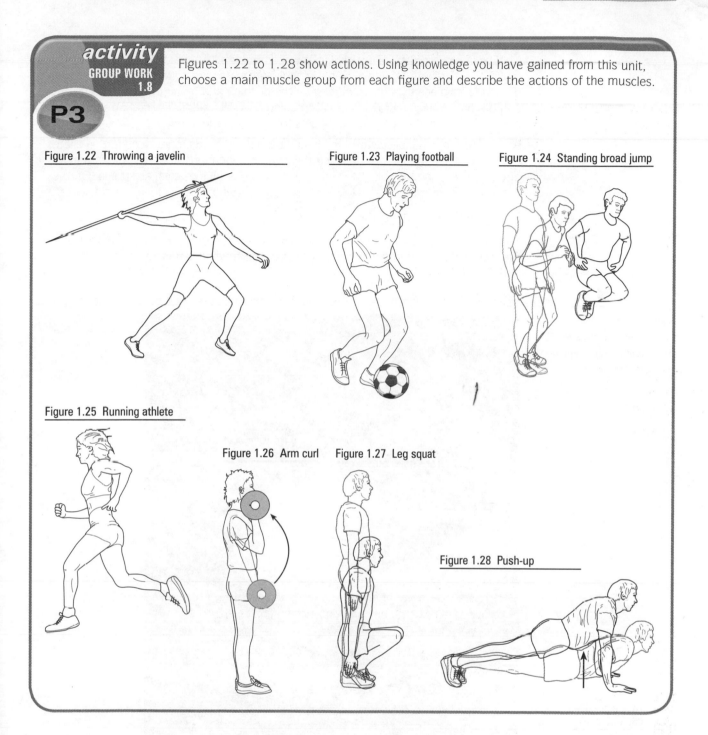

activity
GROUP WORK
1.8

P3

Figures 1.22 to 1.28 show actions. Using knowledge you have gained from this unit, choose a main muscle group from each figure and describe the actions of the muscles.

Figure 1.22 Throwing a javelin

Figure 1.23 Playing football

Figure 1.24 Standing broad jump

Figure 1.25 Running athlete

Figure 1.26 Arm curl

Figure 1.27 Leg squat

Figure 1.28 Push-up

Response of the muscular system to exercise

Short-term responses to exercise

The immediate effects of exercise on the muscular system involve an increase in temperature and **metabolic activity**.

Metabolism

Metabolic processes are the body's many chemical processes that are essential for living, moving and growing. The two main metabolic processes are *catabolism* – the breakdown of food to give energy – and *anabolism* – the building and repair of muscle tissue. The number of kilojoules the body burns is regulated by the *metabolic rate*. Strength training can offset the effects of ageing and helps to retain muscle mass.

An increase in metabolic activity means that the body needs more oxygen; this dilates the capillaries in the muscles, making them wider. When muscle fibres get warmer, they often become more flexible, hence less likely to suffer injuries such as strains. On the other hand, a short-term effect of exercise can be to induce muscle injury, causing pain.

Long-term responses to exercise

Long-term responses to exercise depend on the amount of exercise and the intensity of the exercise. A programme of weight or resistance training can increase muscle strength and muscle size.

Figure 1.29 Muscular strength and muscle size can increase with weight or resistance training

Following resistance training, there is an increase in the thickness of the muscle fibres due to an increase in muscle protein. This will increase the strength of muscles and tendons.

Following flexibility training, there is often an increase in the range of movement possible around a joint.

 Link See page 92 in Unit 3 for more information on flexibility training

Following endurance training, there is an increase in muscular endurance. The slow-twitch muscle fibres will become up to about 20% larger. This means there is a greater potential for energy production. Endurance training will also increase the body's capacity to carry oxygen and the athlete will become aerobically fitter.

Following high-intensity training, often called *anaerobic training*, the fast-twitch fibres will increase in size; this is called *hypertrophy*. Muscles will also be able to work for longer and the athlete's muscle fatigue will be delayed.

 Link See page 87 in Unit 3 for more information on different types of training
See page 38 in this unit for more information on energy production

activity
INDIVIDUAL WORK
1.9

P4

M3

1. Using the information from this unit, briefly list the short-term and long-term effects of exercise on the muscular system.
2. Now give reasons for why these responses or adaptations have taken place.

activity
INDIVIDUAL WORK
1.10

D2

Use the unit links suggested in this unit and make up a diagram for each of the major adaptations:

1. Show the positive long-term effects of training on the muscular system.
2. Show the causes of these effects.
3. Show the types of training required to make these positive effects more likely.

 Special Olympics – dedicated to helping those with intellectual disabilities through sports training and competition
www.specialolympics.org
Coachwise – sports coaching tools
www.1st4sport.com

case study 1.2

Football coach

A coach of a football striker was concerned that the player was not jumping high enough in the air to win the high ball against defenders. Although skilful on the ground, the player kept losing out on corners and high crosses. The coach constructed a training regime to improve his leg strength. Having followed a six-week pre-season programme, his performance improved and he is now more able to compete effectively for the high ball against defenders. The player also worked on his flexibility and reported improvement in the range of movement around his hips and greater toning in his leg muscles.

activity
INDIVIDUAL WORK

1. What are the possible reasons why the training improved the jumping ability of the player?
2. Why has the player experienced improved flexibility and muscle toning?
3. What activities would you have included in the leg strength training?

Figure 1.30 Leg strength training helps with jumping high

Understand the structure and function of the cardiovascular system and how it responds to exercise

Structure and function of the cardiovascular system

The **cardiovascular** system transports oxygen around the body. It is a very important system for maximising performance and needs to be well understood by athletes and coaches. The cardiovascular system includes the heart, the network of blood vessels and the blood that transports vital materials around the body.

Heart

The heart is part of the cardiovascular system. It is about the size of a closed fist, consists of four chambers and is made almost entirely of cardiac muscle. The heart can be seen as two separate pumps that pump blood around the body. The pump on the right sends *deoxygenated blood* to the lungs and the pump on the left sends *oxygenated blood* to the muscles. The septum is a muscular wall that separates these two pump systems. The muscular wall of the heart is called the *myocardium* and is found between the inner *endocardium* and its outer membrane, the *pericardium*.

The heart's upper two chambers, or superior chambers, are called atria. The heart's lower two chambers, or inferior chambers, are called ventricles.

Figure 1.31 Internal structure of the heart

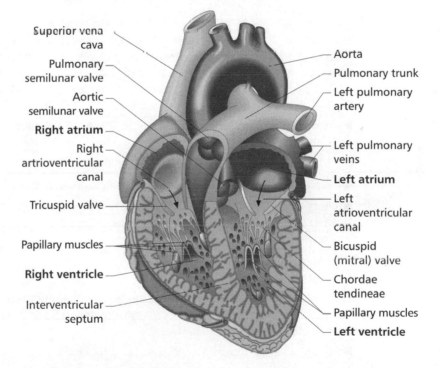

Superior vena cava
Pulmonary semilunar valve
Aortic semilunar valve
Right atrium
Right artrioventricular canal
Tricuspid valve
Papillary muscles
Right ventricle
Interventricular septum

Aorta
Pulmonary trunk
Left pulmonary artery
Left pulmonary veins
Left atrium
Left atrioventricular canal
Bicuspid (mitral) valve
Chordae tendineae
Papillary muscles
Left ventricle

Blood vessels enter and leave the heart. The inferior and superior venae cavae bring deoxygenated blood from the body to the right atrium. The *pulmonary* veins bring oxygenated blood from the lungs to the left atrium. The *pulmonary artery* takes deoxygenated blood from the right ventricle to the lungs. The *aorta* takes oxygenated blood from the left ventricle to the rest of the body.

Like other muscles, the heart requires its own blood supply. The *coronary artery* supplies oxygenated blood to the heart, delivered to cells via capillaries. The coronary sinus takes deoxygenated blood away from the heart and into the right atrium.

Figure 1.32 External structure of the heart

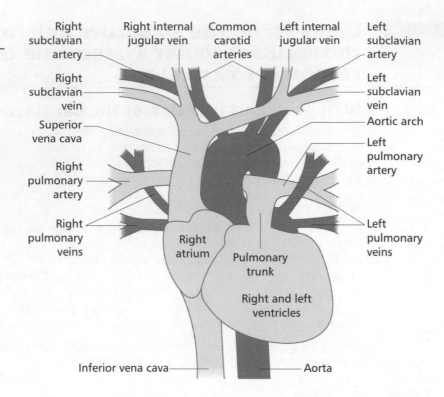

Right subclavian artery

Right internal jugular vein

Common carotid arteries

Left internal jugular vein

Left subclavian artery

Right subclavian vein

Superior vena cava

Right pulmonary artery

Right pulmonary veins

Right atrium

Pulmonary trunk

Right and left ventricles

Left subclavian vein

Aortic arch

Left pulmonary artery

Left pulmonary veins

Inferior vena cava

Aorta

> **remember**
>
> The right-hand pump sends deoxygenated blood to the lungs and the left-hand pump sends oxygenated blood to the body's muscles.

The heart has four valves that ensure the blood flows in one direction only. Two valves separate the atria from the ventricles, and two valves sit in the arteries that carry blood from the ventricles. The valves are one-way valves that stop the blood from flowing backwards, against the normal direction of flow. As blood flows from the atria to the ventricles, it pushes the valves open; the valves are then closed by connective tissue called *chordae tendineae*. Here are some names that are used to describe heart valves:

- **Atrioventricular valves** – a collective term for all the valves between atria and ventricles.
- **Tricuspid valve** – the valve between the right atrium and the right ventricle.
- **Bicuspid valve** – the valve between the left atrium and the left ventricle.
- **Aortic valve** – the valve between the left ventricle and the aorta.
- **Pulmonary valve** – the valve between the right ventricle and the pulmonary artery.
- **Semilunar valves** – a collective term for aortic and pulmonary valves.

Cardiac cycle

The cardiac cycle is a series of heart contractions that pump the blood around the body. Each cycle is one heartbeat; it takes approximately 0.8 s and is repeated about 72 times per minute. Here are the four stages:

- **Stage 1: atrial diastole** – the atria fill with blood.
- **Stage 2: ventricular diastole** – the ventricles now fill via the atrioventricular valves.
- **Stage 3: atrial systole** – the atria contract and all blood is now ejected into the ventricles; the atrioventricular valves close.
- **Stage 4: ventricular systole** – the semilunar valves open, the ventricles contract. Blood is forced from the right ventricle into the pulmonary artery and blood from the left ventricle is forced into the aorta. The semilunar valves close to complete the cycle.

Other definitions

Heart rate

Heart rate (HR) is the rate at which the heart contracts and relaxes. The heart contracts and relaxes in a rhythm, which produces a heartbeat. The rhythm is controlled by an electrical impulse from the sinoatrial (SA) node, the heart's natural pacemaker.

Beats per minute

Heart rate is measured in beats per minute (bpm). The average resting HR is 75 bpm. A decrease in resting heart rate is a good indicator of fitness. A trained athlete's resting heart rate falls below 60 bpm.

Figure 1.33 A low resting heart rate is a good indicator of fitness

Stroke volume

Stroke volume (SV) is the volume of blood pumped out of the heart by each ventricle during one contraction. It is measured in millilitres per beat (ml/beat) It depends on:

- the amount of blood returning to the heart (venous return)
- the elasticity of the ventricles
- the contractility of the ventricles
- the blood pressure in the arteries leading from the heart.

Cardiac output

Cardiac output Q is the volume of blood ejected from the left ventricle in 1 min. It is measured in litres per minute (dm^3/min). The cardiac output is equal to the stroke volume multiplied by the heart rate:

$$Q = SV \times HR$$

If an athlete's resting heart rate falls below 60 bpm, to produce the same cardiac output, the stroke volume has to increase to compensate for drop in heart rate. The higher the cardiac output, the more oxygen can be delivered to the muscles and the longer and harder the athlete can work.

Figure 1.34 A long-distance athlete

Blood pressure

Blood pressure (BP) is the pressure needed to pump the blood around the body. It is measured in millimetres of mercury (mm Hg) and is calculated as the product of the blood flow and the resistance to that blood flow:

$$\text{Blood pressure} = \text{blood flow} \times \text{resistance to that flow}$$

Systolic BP is measured when the heart forcibly ejects blood. Diastolic BP is measured when the heart relaxes. An average value for an adult is 120/80 (systolic/diastolic) in mm Hg. Regular exercise can reduce resting BP. Blood pressure is often measured using a sphygmomanometer. Other factors that affect BP are age, stress and diet.

Figure 1.35 A sphygmomanometer is used to take blood pressure

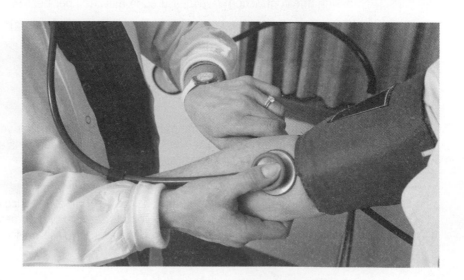

Figure 1.36 An endurance athlete needs a high cardiac output

Function of the cardiovascular system

Blood and blood vessels

Blood vessels are an integral part of the cardiovascular system and are essential for transporting materials around the body. During exercise, most of the blood goes to the working muscles so it can deliver oxygen and remove carbon dioxide.

Blood consists of cells and is surrounded by a liquid called *plasma*. The average total blood volume in a male is 5–6 litres and the average total blood volume in a female is 4–5 litres. *Erythrocytes* are red cells containing **haemoglobin**, *leucocytes* are white blood cells that combat infection, and *thrombocytes (platelets)* are important for blood clotting.

The blood vessels are called arteries, arterioles, capillaries, veins and venules.

Arteries and arterioles

Arteries and arterioles are blood vessels that carry blood at high pressure from the heart to the body tissues. The largest artery, called the aorta, leaves the heart and subdivides into smaller-diameter vessels called arterioles. The muscle tissue in the walls of the arteries causes them to increase in diameter, **vasodilation**, or decrease in diameter, **vasoconstriction**, changing the pressure of the blood; this is especially important during exercise.

Veins and venules

Veins and venules carry blood at low pressure and return it to the heart. Their walls are less muscular, but gradually increase in thickness as they approach the heart. The two largest veins, the inferior vena cava and the superior vena cava, enter the heart through the right atrium. The smallest veins are called venules, which transport the blood from the capillaries. Veins contain pocket valves that prevent the backflow of blood.

Capillaries

The walls of capillaries consist of a single layer of cells. This makes them thin enough for red blood cells to pass through them. There are many capillaries around the muscles to enable effective gas exchange.

Figure 1.37 Human blood vessels

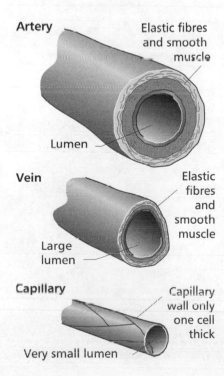

Artery   Elastic fibres and smooth muscle

Lumen

Vein   Elastic fibres and smooth muscle

Large lumen

Capillary   Capillary wall only one cell thick

Very small lumen

Summary of cardiovascular functions

- Delivery of oxygen and nutrients around the body and to the working muscles
- Removal of waste products
- Regulation of temperature (thermoregulation)
- Defence against disease and infection.

activity
INDIVIDUAL WORK
1.11

P5

1. Draw a diagram of the heart and label each of the main areas. Draw and label each type of blood vessel.
2. Write an account of the journey of blood from the heart and back to the heart. Describe what happens along this journey.

How the cardiovascular system responds to exercise

Exercise leads to short-term and long-term responses or adaptations in the cardiovascular system. In the *short term*, the heart rate is raised just before exercise and will increase during exercise so it can supply enough oxygen to the working muscles and remove waste products such as carbon dioxide. This rise in heart rate before exercise is called an **anticipatory rise**.

When exercise begins, the heart rate will rise rapidly. As exercise continues, the heart muscle also becomes warmer. When exercise ceases, the heart rate falls rapidly and adrenaline levels fall, along with a drop in heart temperature. The heart rate then returns to something close to its pre-exercise rate.

During exercise, the working skeletal muscles require more and more oxygen. Higher stroke volume and heart rate enable more oxygen to be delivered but still not enough, so the body has a mechanism called a *vascular shunt*.

Figure 1.38 A sprinter in the blocks experiences an anticipatory rise in heart rate

Vascular shunt

Two processes occur during a vascular shunt:

- *Vasodilation* of arterioles increases the blood flow to muscles that require more blood, and *vasoconstriction* of arterioles decreases the blood flow to organs that require less blood, such as the liver.

- *Precapillary sphincters* open in the capillaries that supply the skeletal muscles, increasing their blood flow. Precapillary sphincters close in the capillaries that supply other organs, decreasing their blood flow.

These two processes significantly increase the supply of oxygen to the working muscles during exercise.

The long-term effects of training depend on its duration and intensity, but most training programmes will make the heart bigger and stronger. This increase in size is known as *cardiac hypertrophy*; it occurs particularly with endurance training and endurance exercises. The wall of the left ventricle becomes thicker, increasing the strength of the heart contractions so that each contraction delivers more blood to the working muscles.

More blood is pumped from the heart per heartbeat, so the *stroke volume* will increase and the cardiac output will increase during high levels of exercise. Blood vessels increase in size and number, which enables more blood, hence more oxygen, to be delivered to the working muscles. The resting heart rate will also fall as a long-term consequence of exercise and training. This reduces how hard the heart needs to work, and the heart returns to normal more quickly following exercise. When the resting heart rate falls below 60 bpm it is known as *bradycardia*.

> **remember**
>
> During exercise, the working skeletal muscles require more and more oxygen. Higher stroke volume and heart rate enable more oxygen to be delivered but still not enough, so the body uses a vascular shunt.

case study 1.3 — Tour de France

The Tour de France cyclist Miguel Indurain is known to have a resting pulse rate of 30 beats per minute.

activity
INDIVIDUAL WORK

1. What has caused bradycardia in this cyclist?
2. How does the cyclist's cardiovascular system adapt in the short term just before and just after the race has begun?
3. Besides bradycardia, name one other effect of exercise on the cardiovascular system of such a cyclist.

Here are some other long-term effects of exercise on the cardiovascular system:

- Increased *capillarisation* of muscles means that new capillaries develop in the muscles. This enables more blood to flow, hence more oxygen to reach the muscle tissues. Existing capillaries become more efficient at delivering oxygen.

- Blood vessels become more efficient with the vascular shunt mechanism.

- *Blood pressure* decreases at rest, because the cardiovascular system has become more efficient.

- Increase in red blood cell volume, so the *haemoglobin* content is higher.

- Decrease in blood viscosity.

Figure 1.39 Long-distance cyclists uses endurance training to lower their resting heart rate

activity
INDIVIDUAL WORK
1.12

P6

M4

1. Using a treadmill or an exercise bike, cycle with moderate effort for 20 min. Record how you feel after 20 min is up.
2. Describe what has happened to the cardiovascular system during your ride.
3. Explain these effects. For example, say why your heart rate increased just before exercise.

activity
GROUP WORK
1.13

D3

Discuss the possible long-term effects of exercise on the cardiovascular system if you continued with the training in Activity 1.12 three times a week, increasing the effort over a period of 8 weeks.

i   Ultimate Exercise – personal weight training
www.ultimate-exercise.com
BBC Sport Academy
www.bbc.co.uk/sportacademy

Understand the structure and function of the respiratory system and how it responds to exercise

The respiratory system and the cardiovascular system work closely together to maintain a supply of oxygen to the working muscles, so crucial in sport. The *external respiratory system* exchanges gases between the lungs and the blood. The *internal respiratory system* exchanges gases between the blood and the cells. *Cellular respiration* is a process that produces adenosine triphosphate, or **ATP**.

Figure 1.40 A sprinter's respiratory and cardiovascular systems work together to supply enough oxygen

Structures

Nasal passages

Air is drawn into the body through the nose. A cartilaginous septum divides the nasal cavity into nasal passages. Inside the nasal passages, mucous membranes warm and moisten the air, and hairs filter and trap dust.

Pharynx and larynx

The pharynx is a cavity behind the nose and mouth that connects them to the oesophagus. The larynx is an air passage in the throat that leads to the trachea and ultimately the lungs; it contains the vocal chords. Air passes over the vocal chords of the larynx and into the *trachea*. Swallowing draws the larynx upwards against the epiglottis and prevents food from entering. Any food is sent down the oesophagus.

Trachea

The trachea is sometimes called the windpipe. It has 18 rings of cartilage lined with a mucous membrane and ciliated cells that trap dust. The trachea goes from the larynx to the primary bronchi.

Bronchi and bronchioles

The trachea divides into two bronchi. The right bronchus goes into the right lung and the left bronchus goes into the left lung. The bronchi divide into smaller bronchioles, and the bronchioles divide into alveoli.

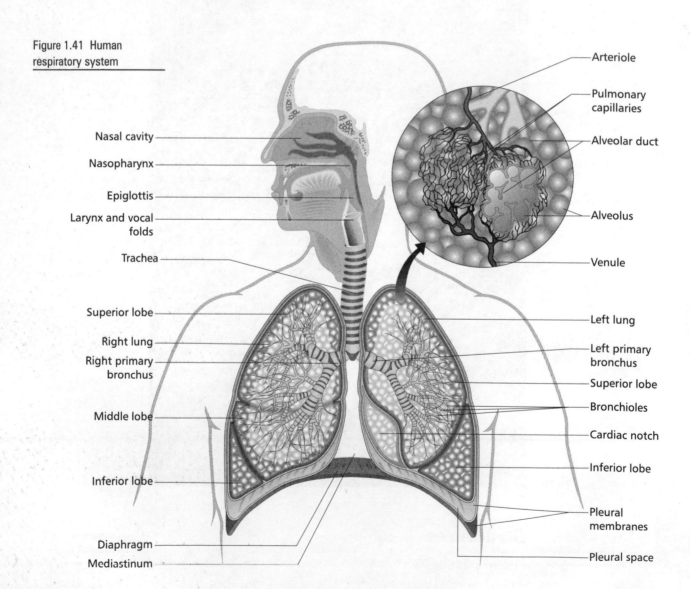

Figure 1.41 Human respiratory system

Nasal cavity
Nasopharynx
Epiglottis
Larynx and vocal folds
Trachea
Superior lobe
Right lung
Right primary bronchus
Middle lobe
Inferior lobe
Diaphragm
Mediastinum

Arteriole
Pulmonary capillaries
Alveolar duct
Alveolus
Venule
Left lung
Left primary bronchus
Superior lobe
Bronchioles
Cardiac notch
Inferior lobe
Pleural membranes
Pleural space

Alveoli

Alveoli are tiny air-filled sacs where gases can *diffuse* from the air into the blood and from the blood into the air. Each lung contains millions of alveoli, creating an enormous surface area – some estimates say it's the size of a tennis court. The walls of the alveoli are extremely thin and lined with a film of water, which dissolves oxygen from the inspired air (Figure 1.42).

Figure 1.42 Gas exchange between alveolus and capillary bed

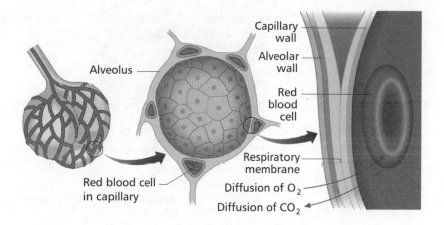

Lungs

The lungs are situated in the pleural cavity, a fluid-filled space between two membranes called the outer and inner pleurae. The *pleural fluid* between the membranes lubricates the cavity and reduces friction. The pleural cavity is part of the thoracic cavity, a protected area surrounded by the ribs and the diaphragm. The *diaphragm* borders the bottom of the lungs and is a sheet of skeletal muscle. The central compartment of the thoracic cavity, called the *mediastinum*, contains the heart.

Breathing

Inspiration

Inspiration, or breathing in, causes contraction of the respiratory muscles, which include the external intercostal muscles and the diaphragm. The *external intercostal muscles* are attached to the ribs, and when they contract, the ribs move upwards and outwards. The diaphragm contracts downwards, so the area of the thoracic cavity increases. The lungs are pulled outwards through surface tension, along with the chest walls, which increases the space within the lungs. The pressure within the lungs falls below the pressure outside the body. Gases move from areas of high pressure into areas of low pressure, so air is breathed into the lungs.

During exercise the *sternocleidomastoid* lifts the sternum; the *scalenes* and the *pectoralis minor* both elevate the ribs. These actions help to increase the size of the thoracic cavity.

Expiration

Expiration, or breathing out, is more passive than inspiration and is caused by the relaxation of the respiratory muscles. When the external intercostal muscles relax, the ribs are lowered and the diaphragm relaxes. The area of the lungs decreases and the pressure in the lungs rises above the pressure outside the body, so air is forced out of the lungs to equalise the pressure.

> *remember*
> The respiratory muscles include the external intercostal muscles and the diaphragm.

Figure 1.43 Muscles involved in respiration

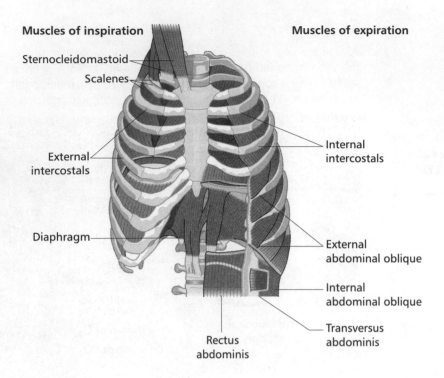

Muscles of inspiration   **Muscles of expiration**

Sternocleidomastoid

Scalenes

Internal intercostals

External intercostals

Diaphragm

External abdominal oblique

Internal abdominal oblique

Transversus abdominis

Rectus abdominis

Gas exchange

The concept behind gas exchange is *partial pressure*, the pressure exerted by an individual gas in a mixture of gases. The partial pressure of a gas is proportional to its concentration in the mixture. The sum of the partial pressures of the gases in the mixture equals the total pressure of the gas mixture. Partial pressure explains the movement of gases from one part of the body to another, such as gas exchange between alveoli and blood, and between blood and muscle tissue.

At the lungs

Gases move across the *respiratory membrane* because the concentration on one side of the membrane is not the same as the concentration on the other side. Oxygen moves from the alveoli into the blood and carbon dioxide diffuses from the blood into the alveoli. Endurance athletes have a greater ability to diffuse oxygen because they have a higher cardiac output and a higher surface area of alveoli.

At the muscles

The high partial pressure of oxygen in the blood enables oxygen to pass through the capillary wall and into the muscle cytoplasm. Carbon dioxide moves in the opposite direction. When oxygen is in the muscle, it attaches itself to myoglobin, which takes the oxygen to the mitochondria for glycolysis.

Respiratory volumes

The volume of air breathed in and out per breath is called the *tidal volume* (TV). The volume of air breathed in and out in 1 min is called the *minute ventilation*.

Minute ventilation

Minute ventilation ($\dot{V}_E$) in litres per minute (dm^3/min) is calculated by multiplying the tidal volume (TV) in litres per breath by the number of breaths per minute (*f*):

$$\dot{V}_E = TV \times f$$

The lungs can never get rid of all the air inside them and approximately 1.2 litres remain in the alveoli. This is called the *reserve volume*.

The external respiratory system exchanges gases between the lungs and the blood. The internal respiratory system exchanges gases between the blood and the cells.

Figure 1.44 Measuring an athlete's vital capacity using an exercise bike

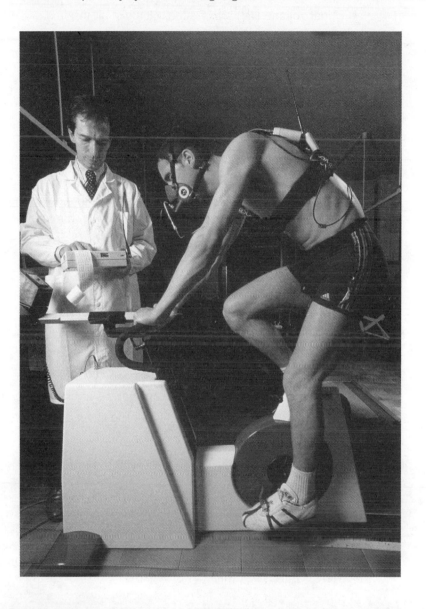

activity
GROUP WORK
1.14

P7

M5

1. Draw a diagram of the human lungs and label the main features. Construct a guide to breathing and describe the mechanisms of breathing. Make a list of the respiratory volumes.

2. Write a short presentation entitled 'Why keeping my lungs healthy is important'. It should explain the function of the respiratory system, including the mechanisms of breathing.

How the respiratory system responds to exercise

Short-term responses

- **Breathing rate** – rises due to demands for more oxygen.
- **Tidal volume (TV)** – this is the volume of air inspired or expired per breath; it *increases* during exercise.
- **Inspiratory reserve volume (IRV)** – this is the maximum volume inspired in addition to the tidal volume; it *decreases* during exercise.
- **Expiratory reserve volume (ERV)** – this is the maximum volume expired in addition to the tidal volume; it *decreases slightly* during exercise.
- **Residual volume (RV)** – this is the amount of air left in the lungs after maximal expiration; it *increases slightly* during exercise.
- **Total lung capacity (TLC)** – the vital capacity plus the residual volume, this is the volume at the end of maximum inspiration; it *decreases slightly* during exercise.
- **Vital capacity (VC)** – this is the maximum amount of air that can be forcibly exhaled after maximum inspiration; it *decreases slightly* during exercise.

Long-term responses

- Increase in *capillary density* and capillary efficiency
- Slight increase in *vital capacity*
- Slight increase in *tidal volume*
- Increase in strength of *intercostal muscles*
- Reduction in *resting respiratory rate*
- Reduction in breathing rate
- Increase in efficiency of gas exchange at the alveoli (*pulmonary diffusion*)
- Increase in surface area of the alveoli and increase in *capillarisation*.

case study 1.4 — Hockey training

A student who recently joined a hockey club has started to train twice a week. Training involves stamina or endurance running. The student's breathing is very rapid immediately after the training session. After about 8 weeks, the student is less out of breath after training, and on match days he seems able to keep running for longer without getting out of breath.

activity
INDIVIDUAL WORK

1. Why does the student get out of breath immediately after training?
2. What other short-term effects might be related to the respiratory system?
3. After 8 weeks, why is the student less out of breath during a hockey match?

Teach PE.com – free sports resources
www.teachpe.com

Figure 1.45 Hockey players use training to produce long-term adaptations of their respiratory system

activity
INDIVIDUAL WORK 1.15

P7

M5

Copy and complete Table 1.2.

Table 1.2 Say how the respiratory system adapts to exercise

	Adaptations
Short-term effects of exercise on the respiratory system	
Long-term effects of exercise on the respiratory system	

activity
INDIVIDUAL WORK 1.16

D4

Add a column to the right of the table in Activity 1.15 and head it 'Effects of these adaptations on the body' then write some relevant effects in the empty table cells.

Understand the different energy systems and their use in sport and exercise

Muscles need energy to move efficiently – very important in sports performance – and muscle cells get their energy from adenosine triphosphate (ATP). Each skeletal muscle cell has a limited amount of ATP; this limits its available energy and the numbers of times it can contract. The body *resynthesises* ATP so it has a constant supply of energy.

There are three energy systems, sometimes called *energy pathways*, that help to resynthesise ATP. The choice of system depends on how soon the energy is needed, the intensity of the activity and whether oxygen is present.

Energy systems

The three energy systems are:

- the alactic or ATP–PC system
- the lactic acid system
- the aerobic system.

Oxygen is not present in the ATP–PC system and the lactic acid system; their processes are *anaerobic*. Oxygen is present in the aerobic system; its processes are *aerobic*.

ATP–PC system

Oxygen is not used directly in the ATP–PC system. ATP is rapidly regenerated through **phosphocreatine** (PC), another energy compound in the muscles. Phosphocreatine is also called *creatine phosphate*.

This system is used during the start of very intensive activity such as sprinting or throwing in athletics. Just as with ATP, muscles contain limited amounts of PC. As PC is used to replenish ATP, its level falls dramatically and reaches a minimum 8–10 s after the onset of maximum effort.

Figure 1.46 Shot-putters rely on the PC system to provide an intense burst of energy

Resynthesis of PC requires energy, so PC cannot be resynthesised unless there is enough energy again, usually obtained through the aerobic pathway. If exercise continues beyond 8–10 s, then other energy sources have to be used.

An **enzyme** called creatine kinase breaks down the phosphocreatine **compound** to phosphate and creatine, which releases energy:

$$\text{Phosphocreatine} \rightarrow \text{phosphate} + \text{creatine} + \text{energy}$$

Creatine kinase acts when there is an increase in the level of adenosine diphosphate (ADP) in the muscle.

Adenosine diphosphate

Adenosine diphosphate (ADP) is a compound containing high-energy phosphate. When ATP gets resynthesised, ADP combines with another phosphate group to form ATP. For every molecule of PC broken down, there is enough energy to produce one molecule of ATP. The *coupled reaction*, or two-stage chemical reaction, produces energy in the first stage then uses it to resynthesise ATP in the second stage:

$$\text{Phosphocreatine} \rightarrow \text{phosphate} + \text{creatine} + \text{energy}$$
$$\text{Energy} + \text{ADP} + \text{phosphate} \rightarrow \text{ATP}$$

This system is the only one that can produce ATP quickly enough when performing very intense, short-duration actions in sport, such as the long jump. This process is quick because it does not rely on oxygen, plus PC is a simple compound to break down and is readily available in the muscle cells. There are no by-products that may lead to tiredness or fatigue in the performer.

Lactic acid system

When PC has been depleted in the muscle, ATP must be resynthesised from glycogen, a carbohydrate made of many glucose molecules that is stored in the muscles and the liver. The liver can store about 80 g of glycogen and muscles can store about 15 g per kilogram of muscle tissue. Glycogen is the preferred fuel for fairly high-intensity activities, such as the 800 m race.

ATP is resynthesised from glucose in a process called glycolysis. The first step converts the glucose into glucose 6-phosphate using one molecule of ATP. The glucose 6-phosphate then isomerises into fructose 6-phosphate, which is phosphorylated into fructose 1,6-bisphosphate using a second molecule of ATP. Next *glycolytic enzymes* break down the fructose 1,6-bisphosphate into dihydroxyacetone phosphate and glyceraldehyde 3-phosphate.

The next steps convert the glyceraldehyde 3-phosphate into pyruvate. Some of these reactions generate ATP and there is a net gain of *2 molecules of ATP*. In the anaerobic conditions, the pyruvate is often converted to lactic acid. Here is a summary of the lactic acid system:

$$\text{Glucose} \xrightarrow{\text{glycolysis}} \text{pyruvate} \xrightarrow{\text{no oxygen}} \text{lactic acid}$$
$$+$$
$$2 \text{ ATP}$$

This system also releases energy quickly and will supply ATP during high-intensity activity or short-duration exercise such as the 400 m sprint. It is used from about 10 s up to about 3 min.

Aerobic system

Unlike the previous two systems, the aerobic system requires oxygen and it creates 18 times more energy. In the presence of oxygen, pyruvate is converted to *acetyl coenzyme A*. This is then converted to *oxaloacetic acid* and finally to *citric acid*. The process then enters the *Krebs cycle*. The glucose molecule is broken down in the *mitochondria* of the muscle cells. Slow-twitch muscle fibres contain more *mitochondria* than fast-twitch muscle fibres, so there is a steady supply of energy over a long period of time. This is particularly important for endurance athletes such as cyclists, swimmers and long-distance runners.

Krebs cycle

- Citric acid is *oxidised* and hydrogen is removed.

- Carbon and oxygen are left and combine to produce carbon dioxide, which is exhaled through the lungs.

- It produces enough energy to resynthesise *2 ATP molecules*.

- Hydrogen is taken to the *electron transport system*.

Figure 1.47 Endurance athletes need a steady supply of energy over a long period of time

Figure 1.48 Production of ATP by aerobic respiration

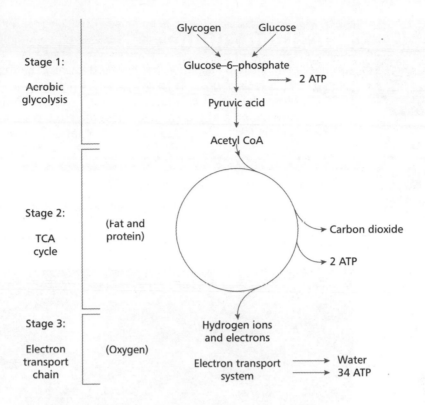

Electron transport system

Hydrogen produced in the Krebs cycle is carried into the electron transport system. The hydrogen ions (H⁺) combine with oxygen and become water. The hydrogen electrons (e⁻) provide the energy to resynthesise ATP. The electron transport chain leads to the resynthesis of *34* ATP molecules. The total number of ATP molecules is *38*:

- 2 produced by anaerobic glycolysis
- 2 produced by the Krebs cycle
- 34 produced by the electron transport chain.

Table 1.3 Energy systems and how much energy they contribute during sports activities

	Energy contribution (%) by energy system		
Sport	Phosphocreatine	Lactic acid	Aerobic
Distance cycling	10	20	70
Hockey	50	20	30
Tennis	70	20	10
Short sprints	90	10	0

> **remember**
>
> There are three energy systems: the ATP–PC or alactic system (anaerobic), the lactic acid system (anaerobic) and the aerobic system (aerobic = with oxygen).

Recovery

An *oxygen debt* occurs when exercise is entirely or partly anaerobic. The PC stores are depleted and there is a build-up of lactic acid in the muscles. There is now a need for oxygen to break down the lactic acid to pyruvic acid. Replacement of ATP and PC plus removal of lactic acid take place within about 20 min of completing an exercise. The higher the intensity of the exercise, the longer the body takes to recover. The fitter the performer, the less time their body takes to recover.

case study 1.5 Marathon runner

A runner in a marathon experienced 'hitting the wall', that extreme feeling of fatigue when it feels impossible to get your legs going again. He became sluggish and he reported later that his reactions seemed to slow down. He reported too that his coordination and then balance were affected, plus his concentration dwindled and he felt light-headed – all signs of fatigue setting in.

activity
GROUP WORK

1. What is the main cause of fatigue?
2. To combat the effects of fatigue, what should a marathon runner do before and during a race?

Figure 1.49 Hitting the wall – suffering fatigue in a marathon

remember

The cooldown is just as important as the warm-up as it helps rid the body of lactic acid, which helps to avoid injury.

Alactacid oxygen debt occurs when the exercise produces no lactic acid. The aerobic system replenishes the stores of PC and ATP. Approximately 50% of this replenishment occurs within the first 30 s and full recovery takes about 3 min. Lactacid oxygen debt takes longer to recover and the time depends on the intensity of the exercise. Oxygen is used to break down the lactic acid into pyruvate, which is then broken down into carbon dioxide and water.

case study 1.6 — Football match

After a football match, one of the players slowly jogs a few laps of the pitch and feels that this aids his recovery. Here are some effects of this steady cooldown:

- It rids the body of lactic acid more rapidly.
- It keeps the heart rate and breathing rate high.
- It increases the supply of oxygen to the working muscles.
- Oxygen helps to rid the body of lactic acid.

activity
INDIVIDUAL WORK

1. Why is it important to rid the body of lactic acid?
2. How does the body rid itself of lactic acid?

Sports Fitness Advisor – sports training tips
www.sport-fitness-advisor.com
Lactate.com – information on portable lactate analysers
www.lactate.com
Coaches Education – shares practical and theoretical information among coaches and other sports science professionals
www.coacheseducation.com

activity
GROUP WORK
1.17

P8

M6

Watch a video of an outfield team player in a sport of your choice for the first 15 min of the game.

1. Write down when each energy system might be used, such as a short sprint to get the ball or a longer run to find space.
2. Explain why each energy system is used.
3. Identify suitable training exercises that might help each energy system.

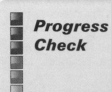

Progress Check

1. Give four main functions of the skeleton.

2. What are the main classifications of joints?

3. What are the main effects of exercise on the skeletal system?

4. Identify the main types of muscle tissue.

5. Briefly describe how a muscle contracts.

6. Draw a diagram showing the main structures and blood vessels of the heart.

7. What is the vascular shunt?

8. What is the difference between tidal volume and minute ventilation?

9. Give the short-term responses of the respiratory system to exercise.

10. What is ATP?

11. How many molecules of ATP are produced by each energy system?

Health and Safety

This unit covers:

- The key factors that influence health and safety in sport
- Carrying out risk assessments
- Maintaining the safety of participants and colleagues in a sports environment
- Planning a safe sporting activity

Health and safety matters are relevant in all sports settings. Sports leaders, coaches and instructors working in the sports industry must be aware of their own health and safety and the health and safety of all participants.

The unit applies health and safety to the sports working environment in order to promote an effective culture of health and safety. It covers the legislation, regulations and legal responsibilities and their impact on staff, clients and sports participants. It will help you to plan for a safe sporting activity and to complete risk assessments in a range of sports activities.

grading criteria

To achieve a **Pass** grade the evidence must show that the learner is able to:	To achieve a **Merit** grade the evidence must show that the learner is able to:	To achieve a **Distinction** grade the evidence must show that the learner is able to:
P1 describe four legislative factors that influence health and safety in sport Pg 57	**M1** compare and contrast the influences of legislation, legal factors and regulatory bodies on health and safety in sport Pg 63	**D1** review the risk assessment controls and evaluate their effectiveness Pg 69
P2 describe the legal factors and regulatory bodies that influence health and safety in sport Pg 60	**M2** carry out risk assessments for two different sports activities Pg 69	**D2** analyse three procedures used to promote and maintain a healthy and safe sporting environment Pg 71
P3 carry out risk assessments for two different sports activities, with support Pg 69	**M3** explain three procedures used to promote and maintain a healthy and safe sporting environment Pg 70	**D3** identify strengths and areas for improvement in the plan, suggest how it could be improved Pg 78
P4 describe three procedures used to promote and maintain a healthy and safe sporting environment Pg 70	**M4** explain the plan for the safe delivery of a selected sports activity and review the plan Pg 78	

To achieve a **Pass** grade the evidence must show that the learner is able to:	To achieve a **Merit** grade the evidence must show that the learner is able to:	To achieve a **Distinction** grade the evidence must show that the learner is able to:
P5 produce a plan for the safe delivery of a selected sports activity and review the plan Pg 73		

Know the key factors that influence health and safety in sport

Legislative factors

The key factors that influence health and safety in sport include health and safety laws, or *legislation*, other legal factors and their possible pitfalls, and the *regulatory bodies* that are appropriate to sports activities.

The following Acts and regulations are relevant. You should be able to name them and explain their impact on sport. For a merit or distinction, you need to compare and contrast the influences of legislation, legal factors and regulatory bodies related to health and safety in sport.

Health and Safety at Work Act 1974

The Health and Safety at Work Act 1974 (HSWA) was included in European legislation called the Management of Health and Safety at Work Regulations 1992, which became the Management of Health and Safety at Work Regulations 1999. The HSWA led to big improvements in the quality of premises and equipment. It also led to better working conditions for staff. Staff training has had to be radically overhauled to meet the requirements of the Act. Employers and employees have all become much more aware of health and safety as a result of this Act. The HSWA is an enabling Act as it allows for further regulations without full legislation via Parliament, such as the introduction of the Activity Centre (Young Persons' Safety) Act 1995 after the Lyme Bay tragedy.

Figure 2.1 Acts of Parliament have a big influence on health and safety in sport

The Act covers:

- securing the health, safety and welfare of persons at work and for protecting others against risks to health or safety;
- controlling the keeping and use of dangerous substances;
- controlling emissions into the atmosphere.

Responsibility of employers under the HSWA

All employers have a duty under the HSWA to safeguard the health, safety and welfare of employees and others who may be on the employer's premises. Here are some of the main duties of employers under the Act:

- To make sure that the workplace is safe and without **risks** to health.
- To ensure plant (equipment) and machinery are safe and that safe systems of work are set and followed.
- To ensure that articles and substances are moved, stored and used safely.
- To provide adequate welfare facilities.
- To give the information, instruction, training and supervision necessary for health and safety.
- To assess the risks to employees' health and safety.
- To make arrangements for implementing the health and safety measures identified as being necessary by the **risk assessment**.
- If there are five or more employees, to record the significant findings of the risk assessment and the arrangements for health and safety measures.
- If there are five or more employees, to draw up a health and safety policy statement, including the health and safety organisation and arrangements in force, and bring it to the attention of employees.
- To appoint someone competent to assist with health and safety responsibilities, and consult employees about this appointment.
- To cooperate on health and safety with other employers sharing the same workplace.
- To set up emergency procedures.
- To provide adequate first-aid facilities.
- To make sure that the workplace satisfies health, safety and welfare requirements, e.g. for ventilation, temperature, lighting, sanitary and washing facilities, and rest facilities.
- To make sure that work equipment is suitable for its intended use and that it is properly maintained and used.
- To prevent or adequately control exposure to substances which may damage health.
- To take precautions against danger from flammable or explosive **hazards**, electrical equipment, noise and radiation.
- To avoid hazardous manual-handling operations, and where they cannot be avoided, to reduce the risk of injury.
- To provide health surveillance as appropriate.
- To provide free any protective clothing or equipment whenever risks are not adequately controlled by other means.
- To ensure that appropriate safety signs are provided and maintained.
- To report certain injuries, diseases and dangerous occurrences to the appropriate health and safety authority.

Here are some of the main duties of employees under the Act:

- To take reasonable care for your own health and safety and that of others who may be affected by what you do or do not do.
- To cooperate with employers on health and safety.
- To correctly use work items provided by your employer, including personal protective equipment, in accordance with training or instructions.
- To not interfere with or misuse anything provided for health, safety or welfare.
- Attend health and safety training, normally as part of the induction process.

What to do if you think there is a health and safety problem in your workplace

- First discuss it with your employer, supervisor or manager.
- You may also wish to discuss it with your safety representative, if you have one. You, your employer or your safety representative can get information on health and safety in confidence by contacting the Health and Safety Executive (HSE).
- If you think your employer is exposing you to risks or is not carrying out legal duties, and you have pointed this out but received no satisfactory answer, you can contact the enforcing authority for health and safety in your workplace.
- Report the problem in the appropriate logbook.

Health and safety inspectors can give advice on how to comply with the law. They also have powers to enforce it.

Health and Safety Executive – information about health and safety at work
www.hse.gov.uk

> **remember**
>
> Employers, employees and participants in sports-related activities all have a role in ensuring a safe working environment.

Activity Centre (Young Persons' Safety) Act 1995 and the AALA

The Adventure Activities Licensing Authority (AALA) is an independent licensing authority for outdoor activity centres in Great Britain under the guidance of the HSE. The HSE is a government body charged with overseeing health and safety in all workplaces,. The AALA inspects and issue licences to providers of adventure activities. These licences give an assurance that, so far as is reasonably practical, participants and employees can be safe.

The AALA was created by the Activity Centres (Young Persons' Safety) Act in January 1995, following the *Lyme Bay* tragedy of March 1993, when four pupils drowned during a canoeing activity from an outdoor activity centre. The Act only applies to centres, companies or individuals that make a charge for providing adventure activities for people under age 18. This is only one sector of provision within Great Britain. The Act does not apply to voluntary organisations as long as they are only providing activities to their own members, schools providing for their own pupils, or Her Majesty's forces when on duty. Despite these exemptions, the standards are widely regarded as applying to any organisation providing outdoor activities and could be used as benchmark standards in any court case that might be brought related to negligence.

In 1995 a private member's bill was accepted and supported by the government; it gained Royal Assent in June 1995 as the Activity Centres (Young Persons Safety) Act 1995. The Health and Safety Commission (HSC) is charged with drawing up the proposals for regulations and guidance to implement the safety provisions of the Act. A consultative document was issued in autumn 1995 setting out proposals for a statutory scheme for the licensing of adventure activities for young people under 18. The paper also contained proposals for a non-statutory scheme to complement the statutory scheme.

case study 2.1

Lyme Bay canoeing tragedy

Four teenagers died in the Lyme Bay canoeing tragedy in March 1993. This terrible event will be remembered by many people, not least their families and friends. The canoeing tragedy was the result of a series of errors and circumstances. The report by Devon County Council says that it should never have happened. It says there was failure by the outdoor centre to organise and supervise the canoeing activity and to employ appropriate staff. The centre also failed to prepare and operate planned procedures when difficulties arose. The findings of the inquiry led to a successful prosecution.

The canoeing party set out from the Cob in Lyme Regis one morning in March 1993. The party of eight pupils and their teacher were accompanied by two instructors from the outdoor education centre. The plan was to cross to Charmouth and return to Lyme Regis by mid-morning. The teacher in the party almost immediately experienced difficulties. The pupils were rafted together while one of the instructors helped the teacher, but the raft quickly drifted away from the teacher and instructor.

The pupils wore life jackets and the instructors wore buoyancy aids. No flares were carried and the pupils did not have spray decks. As the raft of kayaks drifted away from the coast, the wave height increased, and one by one the kayaks were swamped until all nine individuals were in the water. Although the group had been due back for lunch at 1200 hours, the emergency services were not asked to help until 1530. The teacher and one instructor had remained in their kayaks and were rescued by the inshore lifeboat at 1731. The rest of the group were picked up by rescue helicopter between 1740 and 1840.

activity
INDIVIDUAL WORK

1. Following this tragedy, why did many people want new legislation to license outdoor education centres?
2. What does the Activity Centre (Young Persons' Safety) Act 1995 insist on and what are the exemptions?

Report of Injuries, Diseases and Dangerous Occurrences Regulations

The Report of Injuries, Diseases and Dangerous Occurrences Regulations (RIDDOR) are an addition to the HSWA and came into force in 1996. If you are an employer, self-employed or in control of work premises, you will have duties under RIDDOR. These regulations require employers to report work-related accidents, diseases and dangerous occurrences. They apply to all work activities. Reporting accidents and ill health at work is a legal requirement. If there is an accident connected with work and an employee or a self-employed person working on the premises is killed or suffers a major injury (including as a result of physical violence), or if a member of the public is killed or taken to hospital, then this is what must happen:

■ The employer must notify the HSE without delay.

■ Within 10 days this must be followed up with a completed accident report form.

■ If there is an accident connected with work (including an act of physical violence) and the employee, or a self-employed person working on the employer's premises, suffers an over-three-day injury, then the employer must have completed an accident report form to the enforcing authority within 10 days.

- An over-three-day injury is an injury that is not major but results in the injured person being away from work or unable to do the full range of their normal duties for more than three days (including any days they wouldn't normally be expected to work, such as weekends, rest days and holidays) not counting the day of the injury itself.

- If a doctor notifies you that your employee suffers from a reportable work-related disease, the employer must send a completed disease report form.

- If something happens which does not result in a reportable injury, but which clearly could have done, it may be a dangerous occurrence that must be reported immediately (e.g. by telephone) to the enforcing authority.

- Employers must keep a record of any reportable injury, disease or dangerous occurrence for three years after the date when it happened. An example is if the football nets or goalposts fall down due to incorrect assembly.

Here are the reportable major injuries under the Act:

- Fracture other than to fingers, thumbs or toes

- Amputation

- Dislocation of the shoulder, hip, knee or spine

- Loss of sight, temporary or permanent

- Chemical or hot-metal burn to the eye or any penetrating injury to the eye

- Injury resulting from an electric shock or electrical burn leading to unconsciousness or requiring resuscitation or admittance to hospital for more than 24 h

- Any other injury leading to hypothermia, heat-induced illness or unconsciousness, or requiring resuscitation, or requiring admittance to hospital for more than 24 h

- Unconsciousness caused by asphyxia or exposure to a harmful substance or biological agent

- Acute illness requiring medical treatment, or loss of consciousness arising from absorption of any substance by inhalation, ingestion or through the skin

- Acute illness requiring medical treatment where there is reason to believe that this resulted from exposure to a biological agent or its toxins or infected material.

Here are the reportable dangerous occurrences:

- Collapse, overturning or failure of load-bearing parts of lifts and lifting equipment

- Explosion, collapse or bursting of any closed vessel or associated pipework

- Failure of any freight container in any of its load-bearing parts

- Plant or equipment coming into contact with overhead power lines

- Electrical short circuit or overload causing fire or explosion

- Any unintentional explosion, misfire, failure of demolition to cause the intended collapse, projection of material beyond a site boundary, injury caused by an explosion

- Accidental release of a biological agent likely to cause severe human illness

- Failure of industrial radiography or irradiation equipment to de-energise or return to its safe position after the intended exposure period

- Malfunction of breathing apparatus while in use or during testing immediately before use

- Failure or endangering of diving equipment, the trapping of a diver, an explosion near a diver, or an uncontrolled ascent

- Collapse or partial collapse of a scaffold over 5 m high, or erected near water where there could be a risk of drowning after a fall

- Unintended collision of a train with any vehicle
- Dangerous occurrence at a well other than a water well
- Dangerous occurrence at a pipeline
- Failure of any load-bearing fairground equipment, or derailment or unintended collision of cars or trains
- A road tanker carrying a dangerous substance overturns, suffers serious damage, catches fire or the substance is released
- A dangerous substance being conveyed by road is involved in a fire or released.

Here are some reportable diseases under the Act:

- Some poisonings
- Some skin diseases such as occupational dermatitis, skin cancer, chrome ulcer, oil folliculitis or acne
- Lung diseases including occupational asthma, farmer's lung, pneumoconiosis, asbestosis, mesothelioma
- Infections such as leptospirosis, hepatitis, tuberculosis, anthrax, legionellosis and tetanus
- Other conditions such as occupational cancer, certain musculoskeletal disorders, decompression illness and hand–arm vibration syndrome.

Incident Contact Centre – further information about RIDDOR
www.riddor.gov.uk
Office of Public Sector Information
www.opsi.gov.uk

EU regulations

In 1992 the European Union passed six sets of regulations that relate to health and safety. Some of them have been updated since then.

Management of Health and Safety at Work Regulations 1992
The Management of Health and Safety at Work Regulations (MHSW) govern how employers and employees manage their facilities so there are adequate health and safety procedures.

Personal Protective Equipment at Work Regulations 1992
The Personal Protective Equipment at Work Regulations (PPE) govern the wearing of appropriate safety equipment such as goggles and ear defenders. PPE includes all equipment – including clothing that protects against the weather – intended to be worn or held by a person at work and which protects the person against one or more risks to their health or safety, e.g. safety helmets, gloves, eye protection, high-visibility clothing, safety footwear and safety harnesses.

Hearing protection and respiratory protective equipment provided for most work situations are not covered by PPE, because other regulations apply to them, but they do need to be compatible with any other protective equipment provided. Cycle helmets or crash helmets worn by employees on the roads are not covered by PPE. Motorcycle helmets are legally required for motorcyclists under road traffic legislation.

PPE's main requirement is that personal protective equipment is to be supplied and used at work wherever there are risks to health and safety that cannot be adequately controlled in other ways.

Table 2.1 Physical protection – hazards and protection options

Area to be protected	Hazards	Protective options
Eyes	Chemical or metal splash, dust, projectiles, gas and vapour, radiation	Safety spectacles, goggles, face shields, visors
Head	Impact from falling or flying objects, risk of head bumping, hair entanglement	A range of helmets and bump caps
Breathing	Dust, vapour, gas, oxygen-deficient atmospheres	Disposable filtering face piece or respirator, half- or full-face respirators, air-fed helmets, breathing apparatus
Body	Temperature extremes, adverse weather, chemical or metal splash, spray from pressure leaks or spray guns, impact or penetration, contaminated dust, excessive wear or entanglement of own clothing	Conventional or disposable overalls, boiler suits, specialist protective clothing, e.g. chain-mail aprons, high-visibility clothing
Hands and arms	Abrasion, temperature extremes, cuts and punctures, impact, chemicals, electric shock, skin infection, disease or contamination	Gloves, gauntlets, mitts, wristcuffs, armlets
Feet and legs	Wet, electrostatic build-up, slipping, cuts and punctures, falling objects, metal and chemical splash, abrasion	Safety boots and shoes with protective toecaps and penetration-resistant mid-sole, gaiters, leggings, spats

Manual Handling Operations Regulations 1992

The Manual Handling Operations Regulations (MHO) require employers and employees to find ways that make manual handling less hazardous.

Health and Safety (Display Screen Equipment) Regulations 1992

Workers are often in front of a computer display screen for many hours each day. The Health and Safety (Display Screen Equipment) Regulations (DSE) are designed to protect workers by ensuring adequate training, work breaks and a suitable working environment.

Workplace (Health and Safety and Welfare) Regulations 1992

The Workplace (Health and Safety and Welfare) Regulations (HSW) regulate the working environment. They have replaced the Factories Act. Most leisure situations, other than outdoor education, are covered by HSW. The regulations state that employers must provide a good working environment, appropriate facilities, such as toilets and rest areas, safety of pedestrians and vehicles, and safety of facilities including doors, windows, escalators, etc.

Provision and Use of Work Equipment Regulations 1992

The Provision and Use of Work Equipment Regulations (PUWER) require that equipment is suitable for the intended use and properly maintained and inspected, and that the people who use it have been properly trained.

Control of Substances Hazardous to Health Regulations 1994

The Control of Substances Hazardous to Health Regulations 1994 (COSHH) govern the storage and use of hazardous substances. A hazardous substance is a substance that is toxic, harmful, corrosive or an irritant. Common examples in the leisure and recreation industry are chemicals used for cleaning, hygiene and disinfecting, such as chlorine and ozone added to water in swimming pools. Under COSHH, employers are required to:

- have a code of practice for the control of hazardous substances
- have a trained risk assessor
- inform all staff of regulations and published guidance
- make sure that only absolutely necessary hazardous substances are used
- train staff adequately in the use of personal protection and emergency procedures
- have a system to maintain control of these substances, such as how long they are stored and how they are stored (e.g. in a locked cabinet)
- monitor the handling of hazardous substances.

Working Time Regulations 1998

The Working Time Regulations 1998 are to protect workers from exploitation and overwork. If staff work very long hours, it can create health and safety problems. Tired staff may lose concentration and are more likely to make mistakes, which could be very dangerous for themselves and others. In outdoor activities related to sport, group leaders may have responsibility 24 h a day for several days. The Working Time Regulations state that no worker is obliged to work more than an average of 48 h per week. If the employee wishes to work longer hours, they can sign an opt-out clause. Many people who work in the leisure industry are part-time; compared with full-time workers in other industries, they are not as greatly affected by the Working Time Regulations.

Health and Safety (First Aid) Regulations 1981

A workplace must have a procedure for treating injuries and that procedure must conform to the Health and Safety (First Aid) Regulations 1981. The leisure and recreation industry involves supervising and participating in activities that have risks. Sometimes supervisors or participants do not follow rules, sometimes they may suffer from a known or unknown existing medical condition, and there are many chance circumstances that may lead to injury.

Efficient record keeping is one of the most important elements of these regulations. Incidents must be properly recorded, giving their circumstances and possible causes. The records are used when risk assessments are reviewed and this helps to prevent future incidents. In the present climate of litigation, it is very important to keep records in case there are legal proceedings following an incident.

Some accidents or outbreaks of disease have to be reported to the appropriate authority, such as the local authority's environmental health department. Under *RIDDOR* (page 49) employers are required to report work-related accidents, diseases and dangerous occurrences.

Adventure First Aid – HSE-approved first-aid training
www.adventurefirstaid.co.uk

Children Act 1989 and 2004

The Children Act 1989 had a huge impact on the industry, especially playwork. It contributed significantly to a greater emphasis on care provision and child protection. The Children Act was aimed at children under age 8, but its interpretation has influenced the provision for all school-aged children. For instance, there has been a growing demand for trained and qualified playworkers because of the required ratios between number of fit persons and number of children. The required ratio is 8 children to one fit person for children under age 8. Playgroups must keep records of accidents, attendance and the names of all employees and volunteers.

There is increased awareness of child abuse and the sport and leisure industry has many situations where children are placed in positions of trust. The Children Act 1989 protects not only the children but also employees, as employers can be accused falsely or accidentally of abuse.

See page 118 in Unit 4 for more information

More information on the Children Act 2004
www.everychildmatters.gov.uk

The Children Act 2004 provides the legal basis for *Every Child Matters: Change for Children*, the programme aimed at transforming children's services and making them more formally mindful of the needs and safety of children. A series of documents have been published which provide guidance under the Act, to support local authorities and their partners in implementing new statutory duties. This guidance on the duty to cooperate (Section 10) shows the framework for children's trusts. The Act use the term 'well-being' to define the five Every Child Matters *outcomes*:

- Be healthy
- Stay safe
- Enjoy and achieve
- Make a positive contribution
- Achieve economic well-being.

See page 118 in Unit 4 for more information

case study 2.2

Examples of guidance

- Do not get into isolated situations with children.
- Physical contact must be minimal and involve only non-sensitive areas of the body, e.g. hands.
- Use physical restraint only in emergencies.
- Show appropriate role model behaviour, such as not swearing, not smoking and not drinking alcohol.
- All parents must give consent for pictures to be taken or for video cameras to be used.
- Check for past criminal convictions with the Criminal Records Bureau (CRB).

More information on CRB checks
www.crb.gov.uk

activity
GROUP WORK

1. If a child comes to you during a coaching session and requests a private word, what do you say?
2. If a child shows inappropriate behaviour in a coaching session, how might you deal with it?
3. What does being a good role model actually mean when delivering a sports coaching session to children?

Disability Discrimination Act 1995

The Disability Discrimination Act 1995 makes it illegal for any business to discriminate against people with disabilities, either for employment or for providing goods and services. It covers those who need support to carry out day-to-day activities. These disabilities include wheelchair use, sensory impairments and learning difficulties. The Act only applies to businesses with 20 or more employees. With suitable modifications to the equipment or the task, there are very few tasks that people with disabilities cannot do. It is an offence for any organisation to refuse to serve a person because that person has a disability, or to give them service of a lower standard than given to someone without a disability. Many outdoor activities can create problems for people with disabilities and the Act has exemptions to cater for this.

Safety at Sports Grounds Act 1975

The Safety at Sports Grounds Act 1975 is concerned with large sports stadiums that have at least 10 000 spectators. Stadium owners and managers are criminally liable if the Act is not implemented, so it is a powerful piece of legislation. Here are some of its requirements:

- A stadium can only be used after a safety certificate has been issued.
- This certificate is only for the activities applied for in the stadium.
- There is a stated number of spectators allowed in the stadium.
- There is a record of attendance.
- There are records of maintenance to the stadium.
- Stewards have to be suitably trained.

People in crowds can behave erratically. If there is panic, there may be crush injuries that lead to death. Very large football stadiums began to be built in the UK from the beginning of the twentieth century, but there was little control over the numbers of

---

case study

2.3

Hillsborough stadium disaster

Britain's worst sporting disaster happened in 1989, when 96 football supporters were crushed to death at Hillsborough stadium in Sheffield during the FA Cup semi-final between Nottingham Forest and Liverpool.

Police, fans and match officials attempted to help trapped individuals clamber over the safety barrier. At least 200 people were injured, about 20 seriously. Some fans have said bad ticket allocation contributed to the disaster. Liverpool has far more supporters than Nottingham Forest but were given 6000 fewer tickets and allocated the smaller Leppings Lane stand.

After a public inquiry, new safety measures were introduced at football grounds around Britain. Relatives of the victims pressed for police officers in charge of safety at the Hillsborough ground to be prosecuted. Finally, in 2002 the two most senior officers were put on trial. One was acquitted and charges against the other were dropped when the jury could not agree on a verdict.

The worst sporting disaster before Hillsborough was in 1971, when 66 fans were crushed to death during the Glasgow derby in Scotland. In 1985 a wall collapsed at the Heysel ground in Belgium and crushed to death 39 Italian fans.

---

activity
INDIVIDUAL WORK

1. How does the Safety at Sports Grounds Act 1975 help to maintain a safe environment?
2. What other pieces of legislation have helped maintain safety at sports events?

spectators let into each stadium and how they were looked after. Consequently, there were some dreadful disasters:

- There were injuries and loss of crowd control at the 1924 cup final.
- A public inquiry was prompted by disasters at Bolton Wanderers in 1946 and at Ibrox in 1971.
- There were 56 deaths in the Bradford fire disaster of 1986.
- There were 96 deaths in the Hillsborough disaster of 1989.

These disasters prompted more legislation to be enacted.

Fire Safety and Safety of Places of Sport Act 1987

The Fire Safety and Safety of Places of Sport Act 1987 applies to all sports grounds, including temporary stands and indoor sports venues. It expanded the scope of the Safety at Sports Grounds Act 1975. Here are some of its key provisions:

- Fire and safety certificates have to be issued by the fire authority.
- Grounds need to have facilities that prevent, control and allow escape from fire.
- Grounds that are deemed hazardous can be closed.

---

case study
2.4

The Taylor Report

The Taylor Report 1990 recommended that every Football League ground should be an all-seater ground and highlighted other safety issues. The Green Guide outlines the requirements of the Safety at Sports Ground Act 1975 and contains 76 recommendations for sports grounds; here are some examples:

- Defined maximum capacities for terraces
- Terraces should be stewarded and monitored
- Use of CCTV
- Gangways to be kept clear
- Fences and barriers less hazardous
- Planned police involvement
- One first-aider per 1000 spectators
- A doctor should attend if the crowd is over 2000.

activity
INDIVIDUAL WORK

1. Why is closed-circuit television (CCTV) used in football league grounds?
2. Why should football grounds be all-seater grounds?

Food Safety Act 1990 and Food Safety (General Food Regulations) Act 1995

In the sport and leisure industry, food is often prepared and sold. This act relates to limiting the likelihood of food poisoning. The Act has enabled other regulations concerning the preparation, handling, processing, manufacturing, storage and distribution of food. The Act and regulations demand that food premises are clean and well maintained and must have basic food hygiene. There must also be adequate training for employees.

Data Protection Act 1998

The Data Protection Act 1998 makes it illegal to use information about individuals for any purpose other than the purpose for which it was intended. Those that hold information must ensure its security and that it can only be accessed by authorised personnel. The sport and leisure industry often uses computer files that hold personal information about clients. The security of this information comes under the Data Protection Act. Data held on databases is protected by passwords known only to authorised personnel.

> **activity**
> **GROUP WORK**
> **2.1**
>
> **P1**
>
> Describe the following by giving a brief class presentation:
> - Health and Safety at Work Act 1974
> - RIDDOR
> - Fire Safety and Safety of Places of Sport Act 1987
> - Adventure Activities Licensing Authority.

Legal factors

Regulations applied to the sports industry arise from law. Law that arises from the government is called *statute law*. Law that arises from cases tried through judges is called *common law* or *case law*. Another type of law that is relevant to the industry is *civil law*, which involves an individual taking legal action against another individual or group.

Statute law

Statute law is instigated by the elected government and involves laws and regulations. There are many regulations that relate to sports development, coaching and fitness (see above). An Act of Parliament puts the laws into effect, such as the Health and Safety at Work Act. Laws are generally enforced by the police, and the courts impose penalties on those that break the law.

> **case study**
> **2.5**
>
> ## Statute law in swimming
>
> The Health and Safety at Work Act 1974 and the various Management of Health and Safety at Work Regulations create statutory duties to ensure the safe operation of swimming facilities. They cover all employers, employees and self-employed people and they are designed to protect members of the general public who may be affected by work activities.

> **activity**
> **INDIVIDUAL WORK**
>
> 1. Who are likely to be the employers and employees at a local authority swimming pool?
> 2. What is the meaning of 'statutory duty'?

General requirements

Here are some general requirements of the Health and Safety at Work Act:
- All equipment and plant are safe
- The workplace is safe
- There are safe systems of work

- There is provision of information, instruction and training
- There is supervision to ensure safety.

The Management of Health and Safety at Work Regulations 1992 ensures that the following areas are covered:

- Carry out risk assessment
- Implement procedures to reduce the risk
- Appoint competent persons to implement the procedures
- Establish emergency procedures
- Produce a written safety policy.

Legal consequences

Statute law takes precedence over common law. Prosecution for negligence under statute law is a criminal offence that may result in a fine or imprisonment. In addition, the victim may then pursue the case in the civil courts for compensation. In criminal and civil cases, it is for the court to decide whether the law has been broken. However, the degree to which safety recommendations have been observed is likely to have a strong influence on the outcome.

case study 2.6 — An act of omission

If a swimming teacher or coach fails to inform their pupils of any potential risks, then this is an act of omission. The teacher or coach must not assume that the pupils understand the risks; they must explain the risks and dangers.

activity — INDIVIDUAL WORK

1. Who is responsible for the safe operation of swimming facilities?
2. What aspects of safety would you expect to see at a safe swimming pool that follows the Management of Health and Safety at Work Regulations?
3. What are the legal consequences for negligence?

Common law

Common law includes all legal regulations that do not arise through government Acts. Judges in courts make their decisions based on the evidence before the court following a trial. All new cases take account of what has happened before. New judgements based on decisions made previously are called decisions embodied in precedent.

Civil law

Civil law involves legal action between two people or two groups of people. The person taking action is called the *plaintiff* and the person defending the action is called the *defendant*. The balance of probability is taken into account by the judge and financial compensation is often awarded.

Loco parentis

The Latin phrase in *loco parentis* 'in place of a parent' is used in a UK legal context to mean that a person is the equivalent of a parent and owes a duty of care to a child equal to the *duty of care* owed by a reasonable and careful parent. A careful parent will avoid activities and situations likely to harm their child. This duty means that coaches and teachers need to be thinking ahead and anticipating possible problems. There are important common law requirements for teachers and coaches who have children in their care and are acting in loco parentis.

If you are coaching children, are the parents required to stay and watch the session or do they leave the children and collect them at the end? If they leave their children, then you assume the duty of care. Schoolteachers accompanying children to the swimming pool, for example, cannot delegate their responsibility to the swimming teachers or coaches.

Duty of care

Under common law, you are negligent if you do not carry out the duty to take reasonable care to avoid acts of omission which you can reasonably foresee would be likely to injure your neighbour. This is known as a duty of care. It applies to teachers and coaches, their pupils and club administrators. The duty is to take reasonable care, which can be defined as what the reasonable person would have foreseen as being necessary. Some level of risk is acceptable and it is expected that safety measures will be applied as far as is reasonably practicable. The duty of care extends to the child's emotional well-being and takes into account the attitude of the teacher or coach, i.e. whether they are bullying. The teacher or coach must consider the duty of care when planning lessons and activities.

Negligence

If it can be shown that there was negligence by a teacher or coach which directly caused an injury to a pupil, this may result in a claim for damages by the parents or guardians against the employer of that teacher or coach. If damages are awarded against an employer or a governing body on account of the grossly negligent act or acts of a teacher or coach, they may counterclaim against the teacher or coach for a contribution towards the damages.

Figure 2.2 Everyone has a responsibility to maintain a safe environment

See page 116 in Unit 4 for more information

Here are same ways for teachers and coaches to avoid negligence:

■ Have an appropriate teaching or coaching qualification and attend regular refresher or update seminars or workshops.

■ Ensure there is appropriate safety equipment or, in the case of swimming, have lifesaving cover and/or hold an appropriate and current lifesaving award.

■ Perform a risk assessment (page 65) on the working environment and equipment, and take any appropriate steps to reduce risks.

■ Check that pupils have been taught safety rules and emergency procedures at an appropriate level for their age, intelligence and experience.

■ Ensure that pupils are appropriately prepared for the activities by having a warm-up period and using progressive practices.

■ Verify that the session conforms to accepted good practice.

■ For any competition events, training camps, residential visits or trips abroad, obtain prior agreement of an informed parent or guardian by having them sign a consent form.

activity
INDIVIDUAL WORK
2.2

P2

Describe the legal factors and regulatory factors that influence health and safety in a sport of your choice, e.g. swimming.

Figure 2.3 The coastguard is an enforcing authority

Regulatory bodies and the management and promotion of health and safety

Organisations related to sport and leisure include local authority sports centres, private health clubs, outdoor education centres and voluntary sports clubs.

The management of these organisations must consider the health and safety legislation highlighted in this unit. They will take account of safety clothing, provision of alarm systems and emergency action plans. There must be regular inspection of facilities and equipment to ensure safe use; this may include employing safety officers.

The enforcing authorities have a right to inspect premises and they have the power to close them down if necessary. *Inspectors* can suggest how improvements could be made and give a timescale for implementation.

Here are some enforcing authorities:

- Health and Safety Executive
- Police, e.g. crowd control
- Fire service
- Environmental health department, e.g. food preparation
- Coastguard.

Employers can carry out their own inspections, either formally or informally. Formal inspections will be scheduled; informal inspections may ask staff to keep an eye on possible hazards.

There are general health and safety inspectors and there are specific health and safety inspectors, such as fire safety inspectors. Employers should listen to the advice of inspectors and follow policies that will pass a future inspection.

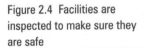

Figure 2.4 Facilities are inspected to make sure they are safe

Give staff and the public as much information as possible to help them recognise the risks of any activity and suggest ways to minimise them. Signs are a very good way to raise the safety awareness of the general public.

Training is very important to ensure a safe environment. Have training policies and a training programme that includes the updating of skills and safe practice, as well as ways of reporting and recording incidents and accidents.

Figure 2.5 Warning signs raise public awareness of health and safety

 See page 116 in Unit 4 for more information

Organisations should regularly review and update their health and safety documents; they should include rigorous monitoring and evaluation of procedures. Organisations should have promotional material related to health and safety, such as relevant posters and factsheets.

Figure 2.6 A typical health and safety poster

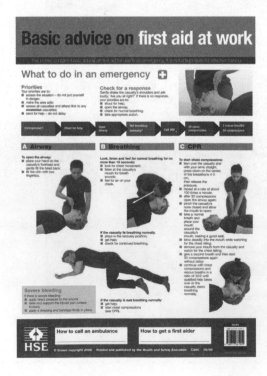

Figure 2.7 Sports facilities record people's movements on CCTV

Sound management strategies not only ensure a safe working environment, but will also:

- ensure efficient and cost-effective operations
- lower insurance premiums
- ensure the organisation retains a good reputation
- increase sales and client use
- ensure confident and secure staff.

Security

Security relates to the protection of facilities, equipment and people from attack and/or damage, including theft. It is increasingly important. Although attacks on staff are still rare, more are being reported in the public service sector. The main threat is theft, which is common in sport and leisure facilities.

Closed-circuit TV (CCTV) is increasingly being used as a deterrent for crime in public places. Proper monitoring of CCTV helps staff to deal with incidents promptly and effectively. CCTV produces a videotape record that may help to identify criminals. Bright lighting and removal of overgrown shrubbery also help to deter criminal activity.

Sports halls and leisure centres usually have secure lockers for staff and the general public. It is a good idea to mark equipment so it is easier to trace should it get stolen.

Private security is a growing industry. Many organisations hire private security staff to patrol premises and car parks. This can deter criminals and also gives peace of mind to employees and participants.

Figure 2.8 Stewards control crowds at a public football match

activity
GROUP WORK 2.3

M1

1. Make a list in separate columns of the legislative factors, legal factors and regulatory bodies and draw lines to show the links between them and how they influence each other.

2. Debate the types of law that might be involved when a football player is questioned by police following an allegation that during a match he thumped another player in the face while the player was not in possession of the ball.

3. Using examples, explain the differences between statute law and case law.

Be able to carry out risk assessments

An appropriate *risk assessment strategy* is required to minimise risks and offer safe practice in sports and leisure. Here are some facts about accidents in the sport and leisure industry:

- There were only 7 staff fatalities between 1991 and 1997.
- There were 21 deaths of participants between 1991 and 1997, including 4 deaths from horse-riding accidents.
- RoSPA has reported over 400 drownings per year, with 5% in swimming pools.
- RoSPA estimates that in 2002 over 693 000 accidents were associated with sport.
- The number of sport and leisure injuries is growing, many from slips and trips.

Table 2.2 Drownings in the UK during 2002

	Number of drownings	Fraction of total
Rivers, streams, etc.	167	39%
Coasts	87	20%
Lakes and reservoirs	50	12%
Home baths	42	9.8%
Canals	34	8%
Docks and harbours	18	4%
Swimming pools	15	4%
Garden ponds	13	3%
Other	1	0.2%
Total	**427**	

Royal Society for the Prevention of Accidents – more statistics on accidents and deaths related to sport and leisure

www.rospa.co.uk

HSE injury statistics

According to an HSE report, during the five-year period from 1994/95 to 1998/99 there were four fatal injuries in the sports and recreation industry.

Fatal injuries to members of the public

- A child was crushed by an unsecured mobile goalpost while playing on a football field. Children moved the posts from their usual secured storage place so that they could use them. The goalposts were very heavy and unstable, and needed secure fixing before use.

- A man died when his jet ski collided with a similar water craft piloted by a friend. The jet skis had been inspected and serviced by the proprietor of the jet ski centre. Observers said the two men were not observing sufficient caution while piloting the craft. The coroner reported a verdict of accidental death. No blame was attached to the proprietors. An engineer found the craft to be in perfect working order.

- A member of the public was killed when he crashed at a motor racing circuit. The man had been taking part in a motorcycle 'experience' activity. The rider died as a result of head injuries sustained in the accident. The investigation revealed that there was no obvious cause of the accident.

> **remember**
>
> Sports activities will always have some risks but we all have a duty to minimise them by looking ahead and planning to protect participants.

Here is a breakdown of the 999 major injuries:

- 349 (35%) resulted from a slip or trip (106 involved slipping on a slippery surface).

- 75 involved lost footing, 62 involved falling over an obstruction and 60 involved slipping while playing sports.

- 227 (23%) resulted from a fall from a height (97 involved a fall from an animal, 30 involved a fall down stairs and 25 resulted from a fall from another object).

- 95 (10%) resulted from being struck by a moving or falling object (17 involved being struck by an object falling from a shelf, table or stack, 15 were struck by a door or ramp, 11 involved being struck by a falling piece of structure and 11 involved being struck by flying chips or nails).

- 79 (8%) resulted from handling, lifting or carrying a load (of which 39 involved an awkward or sharp object and 24 involved a heavy object).

- 68 (7%) resulted from being injured by an animal.

Non-fatal injuries to members of the public

In the five-year period to 1998/99 there were 3675 non-fatal injuries to members of the public in the sports and recreation industry. Here is a breakdown of these 3675 non-fatal injuries:

- 1430 (39%) resulted from a slip or trip (762 involved slipping while playing sports).

- 228 involved slipping on a slippery surface, 148 involved lost footing and 122 involved falling over an obstruction.

- 1347 (37%) resulted from a fall from a height (640 involved falling from an animal, 297 involved falling while playing sport and 126 involved a fall from a motor vehicle).

- 319 (9%) resulted from striking a fixed object (216 involved walking into a fixed object, e.g. a wall, 43 involved walking into or striking another person, and 21 stepped on a nail or other similar object).

There are many examples of possible hazards in sport and leisure, from diving into a swimming pool to tripping over in a football crowd. Risk should be assessed so that accidents are prevented from happening.

British Safety Council – more on risk assessments and health and safety training
www.britishsafetycouncil.co.uk
British Safety Council Awards – qualifications to promote higher standards of health and safety in the workplace
www.bscawards.org
BBC Sport Academy – examples of how to keep safe in sports
www.bbc.co.uk/sportacademy

Risk assessment process

Identify hazards

The area of the activity must be examined and also other people's perceptions of the area. The facilities and equipment in use often carry warnings of possible injuries and these must be taken into account. For example, an AstroTurf all-weather surface is notorious for causing friction burns. There may be obvious risks associated with the activity, the equipment or the facilities. Remember that the risks in sports activities are part of what makes them popular and exciting, but the risks can still be minimised with sufficient care and attention to detail. Here are the main causes of accidents:

Figure 2.9 AstroTurf is notorious for causing friction burns

- Objects falling
- Trips and falls
- Electric shock
- Crowds
- Poisoning
- Being hit by something, e.g. a javelin
- Fire
- Explosion
- Asphyxiation.

Assess risks

Where the assessment identifies the need for preventative and protective measures, these measures should consider:

- avoiding risk altogether, e.g. doing the work in a different way
- evaluating the risks which cannot be avoided
- combating the risk at source
- adapting the work to the individual (consulting those who will be affected).

A risk assessment should:

- ensure all relevant hazards are addressed
- address what actually happens in the workplace or during the work activity
- ensure that all groups of employees and others who might be affected are considered
- identify groups of workers who may be particularly at risk
- take account of existing preventative or precautionary measures.

Identify who might be harmed

Make provision for those who may not be fully aware of obvious risks, such as children or those with learning difficulties. Once these people have been identified, assess how they might be harmed and introduce safety procedures to ensure the risks are minimised.

Evaluate whether existing safety measures are adequate

Assess the danger of a particular hazard then assess whether the risks associated with that hazard are high, moderate or low. If the hazard is particularly dangerous and the risks are high, then the situation is more serious than a fairly dangerous hazard with a low risk.

Here are three questions for hazard identification:

■ Is there a source of harm?

■ Who or what could be harmed?

■ How could harm occur?

To help with identification, hazards can be grouped under five headings:

■ **Physical hazards** – examples are moving parts of machinery, electricity, noise, vibration, manual handling, hand tools, pressure (including explosions), vehicles.

■ **Chemical hazards** – presented when using, maintaining or cleaning equipment or processes.

■ **Biological hazards** – presented by infection from contact with clients or through cuts and abrasions, etc., during manual work activities, e.g. tetanus, hepatitis, anthrax, leptospirosis, HIV.

■ **Ergonomic hazards** – examples are poor positioning of desks or workbenches, poorly designed equipment.

■ **Human behaviour hazards** – examples are assault from a client or other person while working in or out of the office.

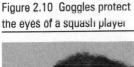

Figure 2.10 Goggles protect the eyes of a squash player

In many cases you may wish to remove the hazard altogether, such as a barrier erected in an unhelpful position or a broken swing on a children's playground. Sometimes the hazard needs to be modified to lower the risks. For example, glass can be replaced by non-breakable plastic. The risks from some hazards can be reduced by using protective equipment. For example, a squash player can wear protective goggles to reduce the risk of impact with the ball.

A hazard is often supervised so the risks are minimised. For example, a lifeguard supervises a swimming pool.

Make a record of your judgements

The assessment should be recorded. It is a legal requirement to record the assessment if the organisation has five or more employees.

Decide if risk is tolerable

An initial risk evaluation should be made using a risk assessment form (page 69). Each potential risk should be given a probability factor and an impact factor: 1 = very low, 2 = low, 3 = average, 4 = high, 5 = very high. Multiply the probability factor and the impact factor to obtain the priority. Then use the priority to rank the risk as low, medium or high.

Evaluate and revise the assessment regularly

Assessments are often out of date as soon as they have been completed, so review them regularly. Review procedures after any incident that may have caused injury or nearly caused injury. If any aspect of the risk assessment was not accurate or not realistic, redo the risk assessment, review procedures and change them if necessary.

Review

Risk assessments are not one-off activities. They need to be reviewed if developments cast doubt on their validity. Here are some situations when it may be wise to review a risk assessment:

■ Change in the nature of work

■ Increased appreciation of hazards and risks

■ After an incident, an accident or confirmation of occupationally induced disease.

case study
2.7

Canoeing risk assessment

OPERATOR	
ADDRESS	
TELEPHONE	
DATE OF ASSESSMENT	
DATE OF ASSESSMENT REVIEW	
SIGNED	
DATE	
Activity – flat water kayaking Introductory session (May to August) Location site: Safe practice lake	

Adapted from guidelines of the British Canoe Union

Table 2.3 Canoeing risk assessment

Hazard	Who might be harmed?	Is the risk adequately controlled?	What further action is necessary to control the risk?
Drowning (generic risk)	Staff Clients	Buoyancy aids (BAs) to be worn at all times on the water BAs comply with CEA standards BAs undergo flotation monitoring to standards laid out in British Canoeing Union (BCU) guidelines Kayaks are also monitored to this same BCU standard Staff are BCU-qualified for the type of water Ratio of 1 staff member to 8 students	All clients are given a pre-session briefing that includes what to do in a capsize BAs are sized and fitted Checks are made by staff
Hypothermia (generic risk)	Staff Clients	All staff and clients to wear warm clothing as appropriate Wetsuit long johns can be issued at the discretion of the instructor in charge of the session All staff and clients are issued with a waterproof kayak cag A head covering is always used	Staff judgement calls are to be upheld Established cut-offs for sessions: wind onshore force 3, offshore force 2 max (Beaufort scale) BCU defines Green Bay as a sheltered site with generally good landing points

activity
INDIVIDUAL WORK

1. What are the main safety precautions that should be taken to control the risk of drowning and hypothermia?

2. Identify two other possible hazards for canoeists. How might they be adequately controlled?

Table 2.4 How to record a risk assessment

Sports event							Reviewed		
RISK ASSESSMENT							**RISK CONTROL**		
Risk assesment	Risk	Risk identified[a]	Comments on identified risk	Probability factor[b]	Impact factor[c]	Priority[d]	Risk management[e]	Risk responsibility[f]	Risk monitoring[g]

[a]Describe the risk to be managed
[b]Use a factor of 1 to 5, where 5 is the most probable and 1 is the least probable
[c]Use a factor of 1 to 5, where 5 is the greatest impact and 1 is the smallest impact
[d]Priority = probability factor × impact factor: 0–8 is low, 9–17 is medium, 18–25 is high
[e]Describe how the risk will be managed
[f]Describe who will be responsible for seeing that the risk is managed
[g]Outline timescales, milestones and plans

activity

INDIVIDUAL WORK 2.4

P3

M2

Carry out a risk assessment for two different sports activities and rank the risks as low, medium or high.

activity

INDIVIDUAL WORK 2.5

D1

Review the risk assessment controls you introduced in Activity 2.4 and write a detailed evaluation of their effectiveness.

Know how to maintain the safety of participants and colleagues in a sports environment

Operating procedures and good practice

For an effective operating procedure, a long-term plan should be developed in a sports environment with specific goals for:

- reducing accidents and cases of work-related ill-health
- improving the health of the workforce
- compliance, as a minimum, with all relevant health, safety and environmental legislation
- development of a positive health and safety culture.

Here is what the sports organising body needs to do in order to have effective operating procedures:

- To define health and safety responsibilities of staff and volunteers. Say who should be doing what.
- To ensure that staff and volunteers understand and are competent to carry out their individual responsibilities with sufficient information, instruction and training. Ensure adequate training.
- To hold staff and volunteers accountable for meeting their individual responsibilities through a system of supervision, monitoring and review. If people in the organisation do not carry out their health and safety responsibilities, they will be held accountable and may get into trouble.
- To ensure that competent specialist advice on health and safety is available to all. Ensure your health and safety trainers are well qualified and suitably experienced.
- To maintain an effective and properly resourced health and safety management system. Health and safety should be managed effectively with enough money and equipment to do the job properly.
- To ensure effective communication and consultation with staff, volunteers and sports performers. Make expectations clear and communicate them effectively, verbally and in writing.
- To measure and review health and safety performance regularly with the aim of continuous improvement. Monitor and evaluate health and safety procedures. Are they working? If not, why not?

activity

INDIVIDUAL WORK
2.6

P4

M3

1. Using a sports activity of your choice, write a brief description of three procedures that can be used to promote a healthy and safe sporting environment.
2. Take the role of an organiser of a sports activity and, perhaps using posters or leaflets, explain to others how your procedures are used to promote and maintain a healthy and safe environment.

activity
INDIVIDUAL WORK
2.7

D2

Using the audience feedback you received in Activity 2.6, evaluate your procedures and write down how you would improve on them.

All employees are responsible for complying with the sports-related health and safety policy They should take reasonable care of their own health and safety and the health and safety of others that may be affected by their actions or inactions. They must carry out instructions as directed by managers and those in authority. They must use all equipment, materials and substances in accordance with the information, instruction and training given.

Figure 2.11 Sports equipment – follow the instructions on how to use it

Child and Youth Health – tips on safety in sport
www.cyh.com

Employees must not deliberately misuse equipment provided for the purposes of health, safety and welfare. Employees have a duty to report any health and safety problem they cannot deal with themselves, and a duty to report all accidents, injuries, risks, hazards and faults relating to health, safety and welfare.

case study 2.8 — Protective equipment

Children and young adults often do not wear protective equipment in sport because they consider it uncool. Some people have tried to make safety equipment more fashionable to encourage young people to keep safe.

activity
INDIVIDUAL WORK

1. What might be an uncool piece of safety equipment?
2. How could uncool equipment be made more attractive to a young sportsperson?

Figure 2.12 Safety equipment can seem uncool

remember

Most accidents recorded in all organisations are falls, cuts and bruises, often in corridors and offices that aren't normally considered dangerous. The numbers can be reduced by tidiness, general care, thoughtfulness and by reporting things that are obvious hazards, such as damaged flooring or steps or careless obstructions.

The Health and Safety at Work Act 1974 shows that employees have certain statutory duties: 'It shall be the duty of every employee while at work (a) to take reasonable care for the health and safety of himself and of other persons who may be affected by his acts or omissions at work; and (b) as regards any duty or requirement imposed on his employer or any other person by or under any of the relevant statutory provisions, to cooperate with him so far as is necessary to enable that duty or requirement to be performed or complied with.'

activity
GROUP WORK
2.8

P5

When planning a sports activity, what steps would you take to make it as safe as possible? Make a list of things you need to do.

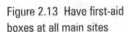
It may be necessary for the person finding an accident victim to remove the cause of the accident, such as switching off an electric current or moving a fallen object. The finder, if knowledgeable, may have to render first aid or artificial respiration. The victim's welfare is paramount but the helper must also look after their own safety. Do not move the victim unless it is essential to prevent further injury.

Management of health and safety

- Tools and equipment must be maintained in good condition and working order.
- Regular maintenance must be organised where appropriate and all faults and defects must be reported immediately they are observed.
- Only competent personnel may use equipment and machinery.
- Personnel not fully competent may be allowed to learn how to use a machine only under the continuous supervision of a competent person.
- Machinery and equipment should be left in a safe condition at all times.
- Floors and floor coverings must be free of dangerous defects.
- In general, take reasonable care for the health and safety of yourself and others around you who may be affected by your actions. Do not fool around – this is when accidents occur.

Fire

All employees must know the fire procedure. Fire notices must be displayed in each area. All employees have a responsibility to learn the correct procedure to follow during a fire evacuation.

First aid

There should be an adequate number of trained first-aiders. First-aid boxes should be available at all the main sites and maintained by the first-aiders. Accidents should be recorded in the accident books.

Figure 2.13 Have first-aid boxes at all main sites

Medical emergencies

There must be procedures for first-aid and emergency transport. There should be a way to make direct contact with a first-aider during an emergency.

What to do when someone has been injured

- A person who has sustained a minor injury must report to a first-aider.

- The injured person, or their representative, must fill in the accident book held by the first-aider.

- If you discover someone who has been injured or had an accident, summon immediate help from a first-aider, and if the injury is severe, alert the emergency services by dialling 999 or 112.

- A representative or the immediate manager of the injured person must fill in the accident book, and for reportable accidents they must inform the chief executive.

First-aiders

- First-aiders are employees who have been assessed as being suitable for training and appointment as a nominated first-aider.

- First-aiders are qualified and have received training and passed an examination in accordance with Health and Safety Executive requirements (Red Cross Award). This will incorporate refresher training at regular intervals and an examination to ensure their skills are maintained.

- Only specified first-aid supplies will be kept; no creams, lotions or drugs, however seemingly mild, will be kept in these boxes.

First aid at sport events

All events organised must have a nominated first-aider present. Where an accident results in a person being taken to hospital, or inability to continue to attend or subsequently becomes absent from work as a result of the accident, then reporting should take place under RIDDOR (page 49).

Managing health and safety

A good management system will help to identify problem areas, decide what to do, act on decisions made and check that the steps taken have been effective. Here are the ingredients of a good system:

- **Planning** – identify key areas of risk and set goals for improvement. Carry out a suitable risk assessment and identify equipment and work practices to prevent or contain slip and trip hazards. This helps to remove or minimise risks.

- **Organisation** – give staff appropriate training to help them reduce risks. Involve staff in risk reduction. Have the health and safety officer (HSO) arrange regular training and updates via staff meetings to consult with staff on any new or revised strategy for health and safety practices in the workplace.

- **Control** – have the HSO perform regular checks on working practices. Keep records of cleaning, maintenance work, etc., and encourage good health and safety.

- **Monitor and review** – regularly review incident and accident reports. Make recommendations for changes via the health and safety committee.

Fire prevention and evacuation

Fires can happen in any premises, such as a sports hall, through human carelessness or lack of reasonable precautions. Good housekeeping and sensible fire precautions will reduce the likelihood of a fire. Poor housekeeping will make a fire more likely and will allow it to spread more rapidly.

case study
2.9

Report form

Here is a report form for injury, ill health or dangerous occurrence, including near misses.

Table 2.5 Report for for injury, ill health or dangerous occurence, including near misses

Name and address of injured person	Age
	Male ☐
	Female ☐

Home telephone no.

Recording officer	Department or panel
Extension no.	Date

Date of incident	Time of incident	Date reported	Time reported	To whom reported

Exact location of incident

Brief description of incident
Continue on separate sheet if necessary

Name and address of any witness

Status of injured person – please complete one of the following:	
(a) Staff	Post held or staff no.
Department	
(b) Gymnast	Squad or competition member no.
Discipline	
(c) Visitor or member of public	
Reason for visit	
(d) Contractor	Nature of work
Contracting department	

Injury details	
First aid or medical attention	Administered by

activity
INDIVIDUAL WORK

1. Why would you use a form like this?
2. How would you use the information from this form to ensure more safety in the future?

FireSafety.gov – residential fire safety and fire prevention
www.firesafety.gov
Fire Kills, You Can Prevent It
www.firekills.gov.uk

Here are some common causes of fire:

1. Careless disposal of lighted cigarettes or matches
2. Accumulation of rubbish, paper or other materials that can easily catch fire
3. Electrical wiring, plugs and sockets in poor condition or overloaded
4. Electrical equipment left switched on when not in use
5. Flammable material left close to sources of heat
6. Obstructing the ventilation of heaters, machinery or office equipment
7. Inadequate clearing of work areas.

The most effective means of reducing the risk of fire is by adopting safe systems of work and good housekeeping. Here are some suggestions to reduce the risks from the seven causes above:

1. Avoid accumulation of rubbish, wastepaper or other materials which could catch fire in or adjacent to any building.
2. Do not store flammable materials unless you have to; store them in an appropriate place and in appropriate quantities.
3. Check that electrical wiring, plugs and sockets are sound, correctly fused and not overloaded.
4. Turn off electrical equipment when not in use.
5. Do not leave flammable material near to a source of heat.
6. Keep all machinery and equipment well ventilated; clean and maintain it regularly.
7. Clean all work areas regularly.

Also, keep escape routes clear at all times and observe any smoking policies.

Evacuation procedure

Have a prearranged plan for the evacuation of all buildings:

- Try to evacuate the premises in under 3 min.
- Familiarise occupants with normal and alternative escape routes.
- Have arrangements to summon the emergency services.
- Assemble in a designated area.
- Have a system to check that all occupants have been evacuated.

Be able to plan a safe sporting activity

Planning

Having covered the safety aspects of organising a sports activity, your planning needs to consider the following ideas.

> **remember**
>
> New laws in 2007 banned smoking in all pubs and private members clubs in England, Wales and Northern Ireland. Scotland has had a similar ban since 2006.

Roles and responsibilities of each helper

First-aid boxes should be checked regularly to ensure adequate stocks of first-aid equipment. Here are some questions to ask:

> **remember**
>
> Each organiser must be clear about their role and responsibilities. Produce a list or job description for each organiser. Here are some examples. What is expected of a qualified coach or sports leader. Are they responsible for the first-aid box? If not, who is? Where is the first-aid equipment and who is qualified to use it? Who is responsible for supplying, maintaining and checking the equipment? The leader or coach should check the equipment is safe but so should any other helpers.

- Is the equipment suitable for all participants? Is the equipment suitable for disabled performers?

- Does the equipment match the age and ability of the performers?

- Who is responsible for the site? If you are using a grass football pitch, who has checked for broken glass, obstacles or other potentially dangerous materials?

- Have you written guidelines for leaders, helpers and participants? Have you told them your guidelines? If not, how will they obtain these guidelines?

- Do you have insurance cover? Are your leaders, coaches and volunteers covered by the appropriate insurance? Have you sought advice on what would be the appropriate insurance?

See page 139 in Unit 4 for more information on planning a sports coaching activity

Review

> **remember**
>
> Try to identify all the hazards and risks to limit any possible unsafe situations in your planned sports activities.

After the event has taken place, review or evaluate your health and safety procedures. Record your evaluation and make any improvements you identify. An honest appraisal of what happened will help you to make future events safer for everyone and even more successful. Make notes on these items during your health and safety review:

- How good was your risk assessment? How effective was your risk management? Were there risks that you didn't foresee this time but will be able to consider next time?

- Were there any injuries? If so, how did you deal with them? How could you have prevented that injury? Perhaps you could not foresee the injury but were you able to help the injured person to recover or to get medical help?

- Did you record any near misses or dangerous occurrences? You may not be so lucky next time. Take action to avoid potential accidents and have help at hand to deal with accidents.

- Were the events suited to the age and ability levels of the participants?

- Were they too young or too old? Did they have too much ability or too little? Could this have led to any health and safety problems?

> **remember**
>
> Evaluate any activities you run and keep a record of your evaluations. If you identify ways to improve an activity, use those improvements next time you run the activity.

- Did you brief the organisers and participants effectively? Did they clearly understand their health and safety responsibilities? For example, in a sports hall, did they know what to do on hearing the fire alarm?

- Was the equipment suitable for the activity and the participants? If not, what would you do next time?

- If you had support from other agencies, such as St John Ambulance, what was it like? If you hired a sports hall, what did you think of its health and safety arrangements? Could you give useful feedback to help other agencies become more aware of health and safety matters?

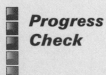

activity
GROUP WORK
2.9

M4

D3

1. Plan a sports event and include health and safety features. Present your plan to the rest of the group and highlight the health and safety features.

2. Put your plan into action.

3. Reflect on your sports event. Write down its strengths and any areas for improvement. Get someone who participated in your activity to give you some feedback. Now imagine that someone is going to plan a similar activity. What suggestions would you give them to improve health and safety?

Progress Check

1. Why is the Health and Safety at Work Act 1974 relevant to the sport and leisure industry?

2. Identify some substances that could be hazardous in a sports context.

3. What is RIDDOR ?

4. Using a football match as an example, explain the health and safety regulations that have to be adhered to.

5. What legislation was brought in after the Lyme Bay tragedy?

6. Give an example of an organisation associated with sports participation. Outline some health and safety strategies it may employ.

7. Why is it so important to record incidents related to health and safety?

8. What is a risk assessment and what are its main stages?

9. Outline one emergency procedure.

10. The manager of a leisure centre wants to improve the safety of the premises. What suggestions would you offer?

Training and Fitness for Sport

This unit covers:

- The fitness requirements of different sporting activities
- The different methods of physical fitness training
- Planning a fitness training programme
- Monitoring and evaluating a fitness training programme

Using the information in this unit, you should be able to construct a fitness training programme. You will be able to apply skills and knowledge gained through this unit to monitor and evaluate a fitness training programme.

It explains the fitness requirements for a range of sporting activities. It covers the principles of training, different methods of fitness training and the concept of periodisation. This will enable you to plan a fitness training programme that includes setting appropriate goals and will help you outline the structure of the training year with a detailed six-week plan.

The unit contains invaluable information on how to monitor and evaluate a fitness training programme. It shows how to keep a training diary, how to record training activities and how to log achievements.

grading criteria

To achieve a **Pass** grade the evidence must show that the learner is able to:	To achieve a **Merit** grade the evidence must show that the learner is able to:	To achieve a **Distinction** grade the evidence must show that the learner is able to:
P1 describe the physical fitness requirements and skill-related fitness requirements of three different sporting activities Pg 87	**M1** explain the physical fitness requirements and skill-related fitness requirements of three different sporting activities Pg 87	**D1** compare and contrast the physical fitness requirements and skill-related fitness requirements of three different fitness activities Pg 87
P2 describe one method of fitness training for six different components of physical fitness Pg 89	**M2** explain one method of fitness training for six different components of physical fitness Pg 80	**D2** evaluate a selected six-week fitness training programme providing recommendations for improvement and future activities Pg 111
P3 produce a safe and effective six-week fitness training programme for a selected individual that incorporates the principles of training and periodisation Pg 108	**M3** explain the strengths and areas for improvement following completion of a selected six-week fitness training programme Pg 111	

grading criteria

To achieve a **Pass** grade the evidence must show that the learner is able to:	To achieve a **Merit** grade the evidence must show that the learner is able to:	To achieve a **Distinction** grade the evidence must show that the learner is able to:
P4 produce a training diary for a selected individual　Pg 109		
P5 describe the strengths and areas for improvement following completion of a selected six-week fitness training programme　Pg 111		

Understand the fitness requirements of different sporting activities

Components of fitness

Often used as a catch-all term, 'fitness' may refer to aerobic endurance or stamina or any skills you might have. Fitness is complex and involves different elements or components that add up to give your overall fitness. Depending on the type of sport you do, you may be very fit in one component but not another. For example, **strength** and **power** are very important for throwing a javelin but less important for archery.

Figure 3.1　Javelin throwers need strength and power

Yet all sports activities require good general fitness in all components. For most team games, all components of fitness are equally important, but this may vary from one position to another. A rugby forward requires strength and power but a rugby winger requires more **speed** and **agility**. Here are the recognised main components of physical fitness.

See page 186 in Unit 6 for more information on testing fitness components

Aerobic endurance

Aerobic endurance is the ability to do continuous exercise without tiring. The more oxygen that can be transported around your body and the more your muscles can use this oxygen, the greater your level of aerobic endurance.

A person's level of endurance fitness is indicated by their $V_{O_2\ max}$, which is the maximum amount of oxygen an individual can take in and use in 1 min. The body adapts to endurance training and develops aerobic adaptations. A person can reach a higher $V_{O_2\ max}$ before they reach their anaerobic threshold. The greater their aerobic endurance, the more they can delay the onset of fatigue. High levels of *aerobic endurance* can allow the body to exercise whole muscle groups over an extended period of time at moderate intensity, using *aerobic energy*. The aerobic system uses oxygen to break down *carbohydrates* and convert them into energy that lasts.

Some activities that rely heavily on aerobic endurance are long-distance running in athletics, invasion games and outdoor activities.

Figure 3.2 Athletes need high levels of aerobic endurance

See page 27 in Unit 1 for more information on the function of the cardiovascular system and its response to exercise

Muscular endurance

Muscular endurance is the ability of a muscle or group of muscles to contract repeatedly without rest. It measures how well muscles can repeatedly generate force, and the amount of time they can maintain activity. It is the effective use of raw strength. Muscular endurance is crucial for many sports activities from weightlifting to intense aerobic activities such as middle-distance running. Muscular endurance combines *aerobic energy* and *anaerobic energy*.

Some activities that require high levels of **muscular endurance** are athletics, swimming and gymnastics.

See page 18 in Unit 1 for more information on the muscular system and its response to exercise

Strength

Strength is the ability of a muscle to exert force for a short period of time. The amount of force that can be exerted by a muscle depends on the size of the muscles and the number of muscles involved, as well as the type of muscle fibres used and the **coordination** of the muscle involved. Muscular strength is the capacity of your body's

Figure 3.3 Strength is the ability of a muscle to exert force for a short duration

muscles to apply force in a short period of time using *anaerobic energy*. Anaerobic energy produces short-term bursts of energy and does not require oxygen. Muscular strength training (page 88) often increases muscle and *connective tissue* size and density by enlarging cells. Larger muscles are less prone to accidents and help in weight control, because muscle tissue burns more calories than fat, even while resting.

Some activities that require high levels of strength are weightlifting, sprinting, gymnastics and combat sports.

Flexibility

Flexibility is the amount or range of movement that you can have around a joint. The structure of the joint restricts movement as well as the muscles, tendons and ligaments. Flexibility is the ability to stretch your muscles and the tendons and ligaments that connect them to your bones. You increase **flexibility** by stretching the elastic fibres beyond their normal limits and maintaining that stretch for a few moments (page 92). Increased flexibility decreases the risk of injury while exercising, and increases your exercise performance.

Some activities that require high levels of flexibility are gymnastics, dance and swimming.

Figure 3.4 Gymnasts require high levels of flexibility for balance and control

Sports Coach – to develop athletic ability
www.brianmac.demon.co.uk
British Gymnastics
www.british-gymnastics.org

Speed

Speed is the ability of the body to move quickly. It can be seen as the maximum rate that a person can move over a specific distance or the speed of specific body parts, such as the legs. Genetics influences how quick you are but training can improve your rate of movement. The amount of *fast-twitch muscle fibres* also influences speed. The movements may be for the whole body or parts of the body, such as arm speed in cricket bowling.

Figure 3.5 Speed is important for a fast bowler

 Link

See page 16 in Unit 1 for more information on muscle structure and function

Some activities that require speed are athletics, swimming and games.

Power

Power, often called fast strength, is a combination of strength and speed. It is the amount of work that can be carried out per unit time. Some activities that require power are combat sports, throwing events in athletics, and sprinting. Power can be improved by **plyometrics**.

 Link

See page 91 in this unit for more information on plyometrics

Body composition

Body composition refers to the percentage of muscle, fat, bone and internal organs in your body. These percentages provide an overall view of your health and fitness in relation to your weight, health and age. Weight and fat are often used together, but they are not the same. Being overweight does not mean being obese. Many physically fit people are classified as overweight because they have a high level of muscle gain. Having too much body fat poses health risks such as heart disease, high blood pressure and *diabetes*. It is difficult to assess your **body composition** accurately. Good estimates can be obtained by water displacement or skinfold measurement.

Our body shapes are classified into three *somatotypes*:

- Endomorphic – essentially pear-shaped body type
- Mesomorphic – a muscular build
- Ectomorphic – a linear, slim and lean build.

We are all a mixture of these types but will probably be more of one type than another. A more mesomorphic build is associated with many sports activities but particularly with power events such as sprinting. A more endomorphic person may well be more suited to sports that rely on the stability of the body, such as a prop forward in rugby. A person that is more ectomorphic may find their build more suitable when the centre of gravity needs to be higher, such as in the high jump, or when height is important, such as a striker in football or a centre in basketball.

Eat well, be well – information on healthy eating from the Food Standards Agency
www.eatwell.gov.uk

Food Standards Agency – protects public health and consumer interests in relation to food
www.food.gov.uk

UK Sport – works in partnership to lead sport in the UK to world-class success
www.uksport.gov.uk

See page 200 in Unit 6 for more information

case study 3.1 — Body composition

A healthy male's body should be approximately 12–18% fat, a healthy female's approximately 14–20%. Knowing your body composition can help you formulate a training programme and set sensible fitness goals.

activity
INDIVIDUAL WORK

1. What is your own body composition?
2. What types of sport require high levels of muscle?
3. Are there any activities that require high levels of fat?

Skill-related fitness components

Agility

Agility is how quickly you can change direction under control. For example, a netball centre can change direction quickly to receive a pass or a gymnast can change direction in a floor routine.

Figure 3.6 Agility is important for netballers

Coordination

Coordination is the ability to perform tasks accurately. Good coordination is when a performer makes a decision then puts it into action effectively. We often associate good coordination with the ability to move different limbs at different times or to do more than one task at a time, such as passing a rugby ball at the same time as running down the field.

Balance

Balance is the ability to keep your body mass or centre of mass over a base of support, such as a gymnast performing a handstand on a **balance** beam. Balance can be static (still) or dynamic (moving but in control).

Reaction time

Reaction time is the time it takes someone to decide to move. An example of **reaction time** is how long it takes a sprinter between hearing the starting gun and driving off the starting blocks.

> **remember**
>
> Reaction time is the time between the onset of the stimulus and the initiation of the response An example is hearing the gun in a sprint race and making the decision to drive off the blocks. Movement time is the time it takes to move (driving from the blocks to finishing the race). Response time is the time between the onset of the stimulus to the completion of the movement (from hearing the gun to finishing the race).

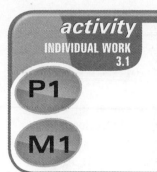

activity

INDIVIDUAL WORK 3.1

P1

M1

1. Draw up a table with four columns and put all the fitness components in the left-hand column. Choose three different sports activities and write them as headings for the other three columns. For each of your three sports activities, put a tick in the table cells for its most important fitness components. Make a presentation of your findings.

2. Using the table you have constructed, explain the physical fitness and skill-related fitness components to a novice performer in each of your chosen sports activities.

activity

INDIVIDUAL WORK 3.2

D1

Write a report that compares and contrasts six components for all three of the sports activities you researched in Activity 3.1. Make some of your six components physical components and some of them skill-related components.

Understand different methods of physical fitness training

Training for aerobic endurance

Continuous training activities such as jogging or swimming can be very beneficial for aerobic endurance. Cardiovascular adaptations can arise from endurance training. For example, the heart will get bigger and stronger and develop a higher *stroke volume*; it will not have to work as hard because each beat will force more blood around the body. *Continuous training* includes **Fartlek training**. Intermittent training methods include interval training. Interval training is related to rhythmic exercise that stresses the aerobic system. This should be carried out at a steady rate or with low intensity – for 20–30 min to 2 h to avoid building up lactate associated with anaerobic training.

See page 28 in Unit 1 for more information on cardiovascular adaptations

Interval training

Interval training is one of the most popular types of training for aerobic endurance. It is adaptable to individual needs and sports, and it can improve aerobic and anaerobic fitness. It is called interval training because there are intervals of work and intervals of rest.

■ For training the aerobic system – there should be intervals of slower work, which is suitable for sports such as athletics and swimming and for team games such as hockey and football.

■ For training the anaerobic system – there should be shorter intervals of more intense training.

Here are some factors to consider before designing a training session:

- **Duration of the work interval** – the work interval should be 3–10 s at high intensity for anaerobic exercise and 7–8 min for aerobic exercise.

- **Speed (intensity) of the work interval** – this should be 90–100% of maximum intensity for anaerobic and moderate for aerobic exercise.

- **Number of repetitions** – this depends on the length of the work period. If the work period is short, an appropriate number for anaerobic exercise is 50 repetitions. For aerobic exercise with a long work period, a more appropriate number is 3–4 repetitions.

- **Number of sets of repetitions** – repetitions can be divided into sets. For example, 50 repetitions could be divided into 10 sets of 5 repetitions.

- **Duration of the rest interval** – the rest period is the length of time that the heart rate falls to about 150 bpm. Aerobic training requires a shorter rest interval.

- **Type of activity during the rest interval** – aerobic exercise requires only light stretching, whereas anaerobic exercise may require some light jogging to help disperse *lactic acid*.

Fartlek training

Fartlek training is also known as speed play and is often used to maintain and improve aerobic endurance. The speed and intensity of exercise are varied throughout the training session. A one-hour session may include a walking activity (low intensity) and very fast sprinting (high intensity). Fartlek training is good for aerobic fitness because it is an endurance activity. It is good for anaerobic fitness because of the speed activities over a short period of time. Cross-country running with sprint activities every now and again is a reasonable, albeit simplistic, way to describe Fartlek training; it could also be incorporated into road running. Fartlek has the advantage of being a more varied and enjoyable way of endurance training. It helps to train the aerobic and anaerobic systems and is ideal for many team sports that include intermittent sprinting and long periods of moderate activity.

Physical fitness training for muscular endurance, strength and power

For strength and power training, the performer needs to work against *resistance*. The training is effective only if it is *specific* enough. In other words, the training needs to be targeted to the type of strength that needs to be developed, such as explosive strength or endurance strength.

case study
3.2   **Fartlek in action**

Fartlek sessions need to achieve two main aims:

- To provide a session that benefits a runner's development

- To provide an environment that is different from a runner's normal surroundings when doing a quality session determined by their effort.

Runners are known to do block Fartlek sessions where they run for 45–60 min with varying speeds. The recoveries are determined during the running. Rolling hill courses are popular routes for these sessions. They are also useful when weather or availability does not permit running on a track.

activity
GROUP WORK

1. Why do Fartlek sessions rather than track running?

2. What do you need to vary in Fartlek training sessions?

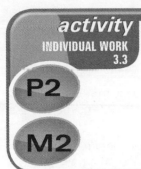

activity
INDIVIDUAL WORK
3.3

P2

M2

1. Describe the aerobic fitness training method through a presentation and handout.
2. Write a thorough explanation of the aerobic fitness training method.

Circuit training

Circuit training is a series of exercises arranged in a sequence of stations around a circuit. In one circuit, each exercise has its own number of repetitions, and a circuit can be repeated several times. Body weight is the principal resistance used in **circuit training** and each exercise in the circuit is designed to work on a particular muscle group.

For effective training, each station should work just a few muscle groups and consecutive stations should not work the same muscle groups. For instance, a station that works the main muscle groups in the arms should be followed by a station that works muscle groups in the legs. Circuit training uses exercises such as press-ups, star jumps, dips and squat thrusts.

Circuit training exercises can also incorporate skills. A circuit for footballers may include dribbling activities, throw-ins, shuttle runs and shooting activities.

The *duration* and *intensity* depend on the types of exercise, but a circuit could have one minute of exercise followed by one minute of rest. The whole circuit could then be repeated three times. The score at the end of the circuit may be related to time or

case study
3.3

Typical circuit exercises

- Running, skipping, bounding, step-ups
- Press-ups, triceps dips, burpees or squat thrusts, chin-ups
- Crunchies, trunk twists, dorsal raises
- Squats, standing jumps, leg raises, sprints.

activity
INDIVIDUAL WORK

1. For each group of exercises, state the main muscle groups they work on.
2. What other factors have to be considered before starting the circuit?

activity
INDIVIDUAL WORK
3.4

P2

M2

1. Describe the circuit training method by devising and drawing a circuit to improve muscular endurance. Present your findings.
2. Write a thorough explanation of how the circuit training method can improve muscular endurance.

Weight training is potentially dangerous, so never train alone, always train within your capabilities and rehydrate yourself. Poor technique can do lasting damage. Weights that are too heavy for you may cause you to have poor technique. It is better to use lighter weights and perform each lift correctly.

repetitions and is a good way of motivating people during training. It is also easy to see fitness progression as the weeks go by, because people can do more repetitions in the same time or complete the same activity in a shorter time.

Weight and resistance training methods

Circuit training uses body weight as the *resistance* to enable the body to work hard and to adapt physiologically to the training stresses. To develop strength, it is possible to use greater resistance in the form of weights or pulleys.

Weight training involves a number of repetitions and sets; the exact design depends on the type of strength to be developed. For throwing events in athletics, the training needs very high resistance and low repetition. For strength endurance in swimming or cycling, the training needs more repetitions with lower resistance or lighter weights.

- If maximum strength is required, such as for throwing events in athletics, use high resistance and low repetition, e.g. 3 sets of 5 reps at 80% maximum strength.

- If strength endurance is required, then use higher repetition and lower resistance, e.g. 3 sets of 20 reps at 55% maximum strength.

Figure 3.7 Weight training uses repetitions and sets to develop strength

Fit Map – information about weight training and foods
www.thefitmap.co.uk
BBC Sport Academy – safety information for a variety of sports
www.bbc.co.uk/sportacademy

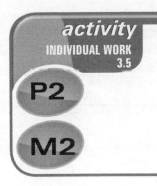

activity
INDIVIDUAL WORK
3.5

P2

M2

1. Describe the strength training method through a presentation and handout.
2. Write a thorough explanation of the weight training method; include brief guidance related to safe practice.

Plyometrics

Plyometrics is designed to improve *dynamic strength*. It improves muscles' speed of contraction and therefore affects power.

Link | See page 84 in this unit for more information on power

If muscles have previously been stretched, they tend to generate more force when contracted. Any sport that involves sprinting, throwing and jumping will benefit from this type of training, as will many team sports such as netball or rugby.

Plyometrics involves bounding, hopping and jumping, when muscles have to work *concentrically* (jumping up) and *eccentrically* (landing). One type of jumping it uses is *in-depth jumping*, which is when the athlete jumps onto boxes and then off. This type of training is very strenuous on the muscles and joints, so develop a reasonable degree of fitness before attempting it. As usual, warm and stretch the muscles before starting the training.

NetFit Online – information on fitness, gym exercises and healthy eating
www.netfit.co.uk

activity
INDIVIDUAL WORK
3.6

P2

M2

1. Describe the plyometric training method in a presentation and handout.
2. Write a thorough explanation of why this training method increases power in the performer.

Core stability training

The main aim of core training or core stability training is to exercise the trunk muscles but control your lumbar spine position during exercise. Core stability training involves performing exercises for your abdominals and lower back. These muscles play a big part in any sport, so it is very important to maintain and develop their strength.

Strengthening the abdomen and lower back should be part of all training programmes. It involves a variety of abdominal and lower back exercises performed three or four times a week. Weight or resistance machines will strengthen the muscles of the abdomen and lower back, as will exercises on mats and exercises using a Swiss ball, a large ball made of rubber.

case study 3.4

Core exercises

The plank

Hold a straight body position, supported on elbows and toes. Brace the abdominals and set the low back in the neutral position. Hold this position for an increasing length of time up to a maximum of one minute. Perform two to three sets.

The side plank

Lie on one side, ensuring the top hip is above the bottom hip. Push up until there is a straight bodyline through feet, hips and head. Keep the elbow under the shoulder. Lower under control and repeat on the opposite side. Hold this position for an increasing length of time up to a maximum of one minute. Perform two or three sets.

activity
INDIVIDUAL WORK

1. Why are the holds for an increasing amount of time?
2. What should you do before doing core exercise training?

 Physiotherapy.co.uk – supports relationships between physios and their clients
www.physiotherapy.co.uk

Flexibility training

Sometimes called mobility training, **flexibility training** involves exercises that stretch the muscles. It can help to improve performance and avoid injury.

Active stretching

In active stretching the performer holds a contraction for 30–60 s. When performed regularly, active stretching may cause a muscle to elongate if is relaxed at the limit of its stretching range. So the more you stretch, the more flexible you become. Keep the stretching under control and warm up your muscles before you begin stretching. One method of active stretching is **ballistic stretching**.

Figure 3.8 Ballistic stretching is useful for gymnasts

Ballistic stretching

In ballistic stretching, you use bouncing movements to give the limb enough momentum to carry it through a wider range. Ballistic stretching should be attempted only by people who are extremely flexible, such as gymnasts and some athletes, as it can easily damage muscle tissues.

Passive stretching

In passive stretching, another person pushes or pulls your limb to stretch the appropriate muscles. This is potentially dangerous, so you must be thoroughly warmed up and you should already have done some active stretching. Gymnasts often favour **passive stretching**. One type of passive stretching is called **proprioceptive neuromuscular facilitation** (PNF).

---

case study

3.5

Proprioceptive neuromuscular facilitation

Proprioceptive neuromuscular facilitation (PNF) tries to decrease the reflex shortening of the muscle being stretched, when the muscle is at its limit of stretch:

- The limb is moved to its limit by the subject.
- It is then taken to the passive limit by a partner.
- Just before the point of real discomfort, the muscle is contracted isometrically for a few seconds, then relaxed.
- The muscle can be moved a little more during the next stretch.

activity

INDIVIDUAL WORK

1. What happens to the muscle when it is moved beyond its limit?
2. What is the important preparation for PNF training?

---

activity

INDIVIDUAL WORK

3.7

1. Describe a flexibility method of training using a handout and diagrams.
2. Write an explanation of a flexibility training method and say why it will increase flexibility

---

Speed training

Interval training is a useful way of improving speed. There should be shorter intervals of more intense training to improve the anaerobic fitness needed for speed. Therefore the best way is to have short bursts of speed running with long recovery periods. *Resistance training* can build muscle essential for speed but use light weights with lots of repetitions. Another way to do **speed training** is to work on stride length and cadence, and that requires flexible hips.

case study
3.6

Sprinting techniques

Sprinting techniques must be practised at slow speeds then tried out at full speed. Effective warm-ups and flexibility training will affect stride length and frequency. Stride length can be improved by developing muscular strength, power, strength endurance and running technique.

To develop speed you should ensure that flexibility is regularly trained; strength is developed as a priority to increase speed; sprinting skills and sprinting techniques are properly learned and practised before trying them at high speed; speed training is performed at brief intervals.

activity
INDIVIDUAL WORK

1. Which other fitness components should be worked on to improve speed?
2. Besides sprinting techniques, what other techniques do you need to improve to move speedily in your sport?

activity
INDIVIDUAL WORK
3.8

P2

M2

1. Describe what fitness training method you would use to increase the speed of a performer.
2. Write a thorough explanation of a fitness training method that would improve the speed of a performer. Choose a method you have not explained before.

Be able to plan a fitness training programme

Although individual needs will differ widely, all training programmes should follow the same overall structure. Consider the *principles of training* (page 100) as well as the FITT method (page 105). Planning is crucial for an effective training programme and the first step is to collect information about yourself, your client or your player.

Collecting the information

Our lifestyle can significantly affect our overall fitness for sport. Increasing numbers of people are overweight or obese. Many of us now live more sedentary lives and time- and energy-saving technology is continually being developed. Here are some of the main lifestyle factors that affect our physical fitness and need to be considered when planning a fitness training programme.

Stress levels

Our hectic lives leave little room for relaxation and this is one reason why there has been an increase in stress-related ailments. Modern life is very competitive, so for many people, competitive sport is the last thing they want to do (Honeybourne 2006a, b). When constructing a fitness training programme, consider whether the performer is suffering from undue stress related to work, family commitments or sports competition. Time is often a stress-inducing factor; detailed discussion with the performer should help you to build up a picture of how they are feeling about the pressures around them. An effective fitness training programme must not put undue stress on the performer, otherwise they are likely give up or spiral into illness because their bodies become less immune to disease.

Alcohol, smoking and drugs

Alcohol consumption

Alcohol is a concentrated source of energy but cannot be available during exercise for our working muscles. Consequently, many elite sports performers do not drink alcohol and most drink very little. It is advisable to find out about the performer's drinking habits and advise them to drink moderately or abstain.

---

case study 3.7

Alcohol guidelines

Here are the Health Development Agency's recommendations on alcohol intake for adults, not necessarily sporting adults:

■ Males 3–4 units per day

■ Females 2–3 units per day.

Most advisers agree that binge drinking is particularly bad for you, but binge drinking is a growing habit among teenagers and young adults. It is better to spread your alcohol consumption across the week and to have some alcohol-free days.

activity
GROUP WORK

1. What advice about alcohol consumption would you give your client when planning a fitness training programme?

2. How does alcohol affect fitness in sport?

---

remember

Half a pint (284 ml) of an ordinary strength beer is 3.0–3.5% alcohol and contains 90 calories; it is approximately one unit of alcohol. A standard glass of wine is 11% alcohol and contains 90 calories. A single measure of spirits is 38% alcohol and contains 50 calories.

Smoking

Few serious sportspeople smoke. There is overwhelming evidence that smoking has an adverse effect on health and fitness, whatever your age. Cigarettes contain tar, nicotine, carbon monoxide and other irritants that cause coughing. Haemoglobin in the blood normally carries oxygen but if carbon monoxide is present in the body, it seems to prefer it to oxygen. Once haemoglobin has taken up carbon monoxide it is unable to take up oxygen again, so less oxygen is available for the body to work effectively. Up to 10% of the blood's oxygen-carrying capacity can be lost in this way (Honeybourne 2006a, b). A fitness training programme for smokers should include targets related to giving up. In the early stages of a smoker's training programme, remember that oxygen uptake may be seriously curtailed, so do not make them train for long period or do high-intensity exercises.

Smoking and sport

■ The time to complete exercise trials increases after smoking.

■ Endurance and capacity for exercise are reduced in proportion to the number of cigarettes smoked – the more you smoke, the less fit you will be.

■ Training has less effect on smokers, so you can train really hard but smoking can undo all the good work.

case study 3.8 — Fitness programme

You are developing a fitness programme for a client who has told you that they smoke regularly.

activity
INDIVIDUAL WORK

1. What information would you concentrate on giving your client about smoking and fitness?

2. Suppose a smoker is trying to follow a fitness training programme. How would you help them give up smoking or cut it down?

Drugs

Recreational drugs such as cannabis and performance-enhancing drugs such as anabolic steroids can seriously affect the health and well-being of a sports performer.

Even when drug use has serious consequences, a person will not always want to stop using their chosen drug, be it tobacco, alcohol, cannabis, heroin or a steroid. If and when they do decide to give up, they may find that it is harder than they thought (Honeybourne 2006a, b).

Some symptoms of addiction are anxiety, depression and lowered self-esteem. The exact nature of the symptoms will depend on the drug, the psychological make-up of the person taking it, and the circumstances in which they are taking the drug. Be aware of a performer's mental health when setting goals for them and motivating them in a physical fitness training programme.

Prohibited classes of substances

- Stimulants
- Narcotic analgesics
- Anabolic agents
- Anabolic androgenic steroids
- Other anabolic agents
- Diuretics
- Peptide hormones, mimetics and analogues
- Substances with anti-oestrogenic activity
- Masking agents.

Prohibited methods

- Enhancement of oxygen transfer
- Blood doping
- Administration of products that enhance the uptake, transport and delivery of oxygen
- Pharmacological, chemical and physical manipulation
- Gene doping.

Prohibited substances in certain circumstances

- Alcohol
- Cannabinoids
- Local anaesthetics
- Glucocorticosteroids
- Beta blockers.

case study 3.9

Prohibited substances in sport

Athletes are advised to check all medications and substances with their doctor or their governing body's medical officer. All substances should be checked carefully when travelling abroad as many products outside the UK contain different substances than products obtainable in the UK (Honeybourne 2006a, b). Here are a few prohibitions:

- **Performance-enhancing effects** – effects that contravene the ethics of sport and undermine the principles of fair participation.

- **Health and safety of the athlete** – some drug misuse may cause serious side effects, which can compromise an athlete's health. Using substances to mask pain or injury could make an injury worse or cause permanent damage. Some drug misuse may be harmful to other athletes participating in the sport.

- **Illegality** – it is forbidden by law to possess or supply some substances.

activity
INDIVIDUAL WORK

1. When planning a fitness training programme, what advice would you give a client about taking medication?

2. What would you look for if you were suspicious that your client may be misusing drugs?

Drug Information Database – information about the status in sport of licensed pharmaceutical and over-the-counter medicines
www.didglobal.com
100% Me – increases understanding of drug-free sport
www.100percentme.co.uk

Other lifestyle factors

There are other lifestyle factors that affect your fitness levels. For example, the amount of sleep you get can affect your sports performance as well as the way you feel. It is important to get enough sleep. Physical fitness is also affected by the type of job you have. Some people have sedentary jobs, which involve sitting at a desk all day. Others who have active jobs may be more physically fit even before training for sport. Ask the client to tell you their occupation and take it into account when planning their fitness training programme. Ask the client what their job involves and whether they are physically active on the journey to and from their workplace or whether they simply go by car. This will give you a lifestyle pattern on which to base their training targets or goals.

Medical support

All top-level sportspeople and many at the lower levels have medical support for their training and competitions. Professional footballers have in-house physiotherapists and masseurs and weekend footballers may well visit a physiotherapist because of an injury (Honeybourne 2006a, b).

Pressure and demands

There are many different pressures and demands on sportspeople, whatever their level of performance. Factors that can affect sports performance include family commitments and expectations. Training for sport can be a very selfish activity because you need to train mostly on your own in individual sports or with the rest of a team in team sports. Coaches and managers can also be very demanding and their demands may sometimes be unrealistic. Share your goals with your client so that you agree what is expected.

case study

3.10

Medical support

A wide range of medical support is now available for sportspeople: chartered physiotherapy, sports therapy, sports massage, osteopathy, chiropractors, doctors, surgeons, podiatry, chiropody and complementary therapy.

activity
GROUP WORK

1. When planning your fitness training programme, what types of checks on medical history would you make?
2. If there were still medical or injury problems, who should you refer the performer to in the first instance?

Goal setting

Effective goal-setting relies on collecting the right information as a starting point for the fitness training programme. Discuss and record the needs of your client so you will be better able to plan a programme that matches what they require. The most effective training programmes are tailored to motivate an individual performer towards greater fitness and performance levels. The setting of targets or goals ensures they gain confidence and can plan for the future. Goals can be short-term, medium-term or long-term.

By setting goals you can:

- achieve more
- improve performance
- improve training
- increase motivation
- increase pride and satisfaction.

Goal setting is a very powerful technique that can lead to high rewards and significantly higher motivation. It is a great help to a client if they have a clear understanding of what they want to achieve, what they need to concentrate on and perhaps what they need to ignore. For example, it may help a gymnast if they realise that they need to concentrate on attaining a certain level of flexibility and can put less emphasis on cardiovascular training.

Goal setting is an effective strategy that is widely used in sport for training and performance. It is a proven way of increasing *motivation* and confidence and controlling *anxiety* (Honeybourne 2006a, b). A performer or their coach can set goals without consulting the other person, but goals tend to be more effective if the coach and performer set them together.

Two types of goal are set for sportspeople:

- **Performance goals** – these goals are related directly to the performance or technique of the activity.
- **Outcome goals** – these goals are concerned with the end result, such as whether you win or lose.

Outcome goals tend to be medium- to long-term goals and performance goals tend to be short-term goals.

There are four possible ways in which goals can affect performance:

- They direct attention or concentration.
- They control the amount of effort put into an activity.
- They motivate or drive a performer until the goal is reached.
- They encourage a performer to develop a variety of success strategies or tactics.

Tennis training

A tennis player is trying to improve his speed of serve by improving his timing. Another tennis player is trying to win the grand slam by winning each open tournament.

activity
GROUP WORK

1. Which one is an outcome goal and which one is a performance goal?
2. What possible effects do these goals have on the motivation of the performer?

Effective goal setting must break down the overall goal into a series of smaller goals. For instance, to win the league, a team may have to concentrate on sustaining their efforts by improving their aerobic endurance. To do this, there may be short-term goals of maintaining stamina training over future weeks. It can be more motivating to split *long-term goals* into *medium-term goals* and *short-term goals* which are more specific and manageable over a short period of time.

Setting SMARTER targets

Effective goal setting is often called setting SMARTER targets. SMARTER targets are specific, measurable, agreed, realistic, timed, exciting and recorded:

- **Specific** – if goals are clear and unambiguous, they are more likely to be attained. Example. a hockey player to complete a fitness circuit 30 s faster.

- **Measurable** – this is important for monitoring and makes you accountable. Example: the flexibility in a netballer's hips can be measured using the sit and reach test.

 Link

See page 186 in Unit 6 for more information on fitness testing

- **Agreed** – shared goal setting, where the coach and performer agree goals together, give a sense of teamwork. Example: a sprinter agrees with their coach that they will aim to bench-press 10% more weight by the end of four weeks.

- **Realistic** – motivation will improve if goals can actually be reached. Example: a midfield footballer aims for a short-term speed increase measured in fractions of a second.

- **Timed** – split goals into short-term goals that are planned and progressive. Example. a swimmer will take four weeks to increase their shoulder flexibility by 5%.

- **Exciting** – the greater the stimulation, the greater the motivation. Example: a rugby player will use Fartlek training with a variety of activities for aerobic endurance.

- **Recorded** – records make it easier to monitor progress and are good for motivation. Once a goal has been achieved, the records can be deleted. Example: a dancer keeps a training diary with records of their fitness tests and milestones.

Goal evaluation

Goal evaluation is an essential part of making progress and improving performance. It requires measurable goals that have been clearly defined. This is easier with sports that involve objective measurements such as sprinting times. The measurements show how close the person is to their goal, which helps to motivate them and guides them in setting new goals.

Sports performers need to know how they are progressing. Most of them are highly motivated and need feedback to maintain their enthusiasm and commitment.

Figure 3.9 Sports performers need to know how they are progressing

case study 3.12

Fitness training programme

Goals for an elite athlete following a fitness training programme must consider these things:

- Any changes of coach and or clubs
- A second career, e.g. a career as a coach, teacher or sports centre assistant.
- Plans in case of injury or illness
- Their present level of fitness
- Dates of top competitions.

activity
GROUP WORK

1. What further goals would you include for a novice sportsperson?
2. How would you measure these further goals?

Principles of training

Any training programme should consider *individual differences*. An individual's goals must be understood: Does the performer want to get generally fit or fit for a particular sport? The individual's current activity level must be assessed and initial fitness testing may be appropriate.

See page 216 in Unit 6 for more information

Consider a person's age and skill level plus the available time and equipment then apply the following principles of training.

The principles of training, as well as individual differences, include specificity, overload, progression, reversibility and variance.

Figure 3.10 Many athletes have medical support during training

Specificity

Specificity indicates that the training should be specific and therefore relevant to the needs of the activity or the type of sport involved. For instance, a sprinter would do more anaerobic training because sprinting is mostly anaerobic. Besides energy systems, muscle groups and actions also have to be as specific as possible. Most experts agree that good general fitness is required before introducing a high degree of specificity.

Overload

In weight training the lifter will eventually attempt heavier weights or an increase in repetitions, which overloads the body.

Overload underpins the need to work the body harder than normal so there is some stress and discomfort. *Adaptation* and progress will follow overload because the body will respond by adapting to the stress experienced. For instance, in weight training the lifter will eventually attempt heavier weights or an increase in repetitions, which overloads the body. Overload can be achieved by a combination of increasing the *frequency*, the *intensity* and the *duration* of the activity.

Figure 3.11 Sprinters do
more anaerobic training

Progression

Overload should become progressively more difficult. Once adaptations have occurred,
then the performer should make even more demands on the body. For example,
progression might include running faster, training for longer or increasing the resistance
weights in strength training. Progression does not mean overdoing things. Training must
be sensibly progressive and realistic if it is to be effective, otherwise injury may occur
and there will be regression instead of progression.

Reversibility

Reversibility says that performance can regress or deteriorate if training stops or
decreases in intensity for any length of time. That is why this principle is often known
as regression. If training is stopped, the fitness gained will be largely lost. For instance
$V_{O_2 max}$ and muscle strength can decrease.

Figure 3.12 Progression
does not mean overdoing it

Variance

Variance says there should be a variety in training methods. If training is too predictable, performers can become demotivated and bored. Overuse injuries are also common when training is too repetitive with one muscle group or part of the body, so variance can also help prevent injury.

case study

3.13

Basketball training

A basketball player has moved and has not been able to train properly for seven weeks. He started at a new club and they ran some fitness tests on him. He found he had 25% less aerobic endurance and was weaker in his leg strength.

activity

INDIVIDUAL WORK

1. What other fitness components might be affected?
2. What should his training programme consider from now on?

Figure 3.13 Fitness gains largely disappear when you give up training

Training must always continue. Even out of season, performers should top up their fitness levels by remaining active, often known as *active rest*.

FITT method

The FITT method helps performers adhere to the principles of training. FITT stands for frequency, intensity, time and type:

- **Frequency of training** – this is the number of training sessions each week. It depends on the performer's fitness and ability. An elite athlete will train every day, whereas a lower-level club player may train only once a week. The type of training also dictates the frequency: aerobic training can be done 5 or 6 times per week, but strength training can be done only 3 or 4 times per week.

Figure 3.14 Variety in training motivates people and prevents boredom

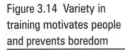How frequently you train depends on your ability and fitness level. Bear in mind the progression and overload principles. Too much training can be as harmful as not enough.

- **Intensity of the exercises** – consider the individual performer and the type of training. For aerobic training, a training zone is often created where the intensity is dictated by changes in heart rate. The training zone can be calculated using the Karvonen principle. This is a formula that identifies the correct training intensity:
  - maximum heart rate = 220 – age
  - maximum heart rate – resting heart rate = maximum heart rate reserve
  - training intensity should be based on 60–70% of the maximum heart rate reserve.

  The performer must remain within this range for training to be effective and to ensure aerobic gains.

- **Time to do the training** – aerobic training should last a minimum of about 20 min. Also consider the intensity of the training.

- **Type of training to fulfil specific needs** – training types were described earlier in this unit. The type of sport or your role in that sport will dictate what type of training you follow. A triathlete will train all areas of fitness but pay particular attention to aerobic and muscular endurance because of the nature of triathlon. Archery training might include aspects of muscular endurance to keep muscles steady for effective aiming.

Low-intensity exercise must last from 20 min to 2 h at 60–80% of maximum heart rate. A widely recognised training formula is the **Karvonen principle**. Anaerobic training involves high-intensity work that may be less frequent, although elite athletes will frequently train aerobically and anaerobically.

Figure 3.15 Continuous training can improve aerobic capacity

Warm-ups and cooldowns

Warm-ups and cooldowns are very important aspects of any training programme. A warm-up enables the body to prepare for the onset of exercise. It decreases the likelihood of injury and muscle soreness. It also releases adrenaline and this will begin to speed up the delivery of oxygen to the working muscles. An increase in muscle temperature will help ensure a ready supply of energy; it also makes the muscles more flexible, which helps prevent injury.

A cooldown is light exercise after training. It helps to flush oxygen through the muscle tissue, which oxidises lactic acid. It also prevents blood pooling in the veins and causing dizziness.

Periodisation

A fitness training programme should consider the cycle of seasons or periods of competition and training. Training should be specific to periods that are out of season, just before season or in season. Training in periods like this is called periodisation training.

- **Off-season or out-of-season training** – this usually involves steady general conditioning to recharge the batteries that have had heavy demands during the previous season.

- **Pre-season training** – this is training that leads up to the beginning of the competitive season. Training is normally associated with endurance and high intensity.

- **In-season training** – this maintains fitness levels and involves achieving *short-term goals* to reach peak performance at a particular time of the year, such as an athlete preparing for the Olympics.

Figure 3.16 All training sessions need a warm-up and a cooldown

These periods often focus on specific goals and may be subdivided into three time intervals that help to focus on those goals:

- Macrocycle – the number of weeks over the whole training period, e.g. 12 months.
- Mesocycle – a set number of weeks to attain short-term goals, e.g. 8 weeks.
- Microcycle – the short phase, usually 1 week, that is repeated up to the end of the mesocycle.

Here are the essential aspects of planning any training programme:

- Identify the individual's training goal.
- Identify the macro-, meso- and microcycles.
- Identify the fitness components to be improved.
- Establish the energy systems that will be used.
- Identify the muscle groups that will be used.
- Evaluate the fitness components involved.

> **remember**
>
> An effective training programme needs to use a training diary, it needs variety so it maintains the performer's motivation, it needs to include rest for recovery, and it needs to evaluate and reassess goals.

Table 3.1 Periodisation training for strength

Macrocycle	Mesocycle	Mesocycle	Mesocycle	Mesocycle	Mesocycle
Variable	Phase 1: hypertrophy	Phase 2: strength	Phase 3: power	Phase 4: peaking	Active rest
Sets	3–5	3–5	3–5	1–3	General activity or light resistance training
Repetitions	8–20	2–6	2–3	1–3	
Intensity	Low	High	High	Very high	
Duration	6 weeks	6 weeks	6 weeks	6 weeks	2 weeks

Adapted from Wilmore and Costill (2005)

Lets-tri.com – downloadable training diaries

www.lets-tri.com

case study 3.14 — Premiership footballer training

Here are two days of a week's training programme for a Premiership footballer.

Monday

Rehab work such as massage and physiotherapy

30 min – own programme of core exercises and warm-up

10 min – run at moderate pace followed by ballistic stretching

20 min – interval work with ladder training for quick footwork; 10 sprints followed by stretching.

10 min – keepball in small grids

10 min – further grid work, including 4v1 and 3v2

20 min – separate drills for defenders and attackers, e.g. forward-shooting drills

30 min – all involved in link-up play

10 min – warmdown and further rehab where necessary.

Tuesday

Rehab work and physiotherapy where required

30 min – own programme of core exercises and warm-up, including ballistic stretching and ending in short sprints

30 min – keepball and a 9v9 possession game with restrictions to improve quick passing and control

30 min – grid work from 1v1 through to 4v4

10 min – five-a-side with two touch restrictions

20 min – short running intervals with 100% intensity

20 min – circuit training

10 min – warmdown

60 min – rest

10 min – warm-up

60 min – weight training for strength and power

10 min – warmdown and further rehab if necessary.

activity
GROUP WORK

1. What fitness components are being trained for each session?

2. What type of rehabilitation might be necessary following a match?

activity
GROUP WORK
3.9

P3

Produce a safe and effective six-week fitness training programme for a selected individual, such as a friend, classmate or teammate. Incorporate the principles of training and periodisation.

Training diary

One way to record progress and set out goals is to have a training diary and complete it before, during and after the training programme. A well-planned training programme should monitor and record the programme and the work done during training. This helps to maintain progression and training intensity. It usually helps if the coach and the performer keep their own training records, but you should produce only one diary for this unit. A training diary can give an enormous amount of information about what has happened in the past and how training can be developed. This information is important when planning future training cycles.

Information to record in a training diary

Day-to-day information from training

■ Feeling of the performer and how healthy they are

■ Physiological data: body weight, resting heart rate, etc.

■ The fitness component that is trained: aerobic endurance, muscular endurance, speed, strength, flexibility and power

■ The training intensity: distance, sets and repetitions, etc.

■ The conditions: wet, windy, hot, etc.

■ The response to training: the work completed, heart rate recovery, tiredness, etc.

Information that measures fitness
- Speed – time trials
- Muscular endurance – chins, push-ups, dips
- Strength – single repetitions, maximum repetitions
- Flexibility – objective measurements of the range of movement.

Link

See page 210 in Unit 6 for more information on fitness testing

---

case study

3.15

Simple training diary

Here is an extract from a simple training diary.

Table 3.2 Sample training diary

Day	Activity	Intensity			Time or distance
		High	Medium	Low	

activity

INDIVIDUAL WORK

1. What other information is it important to record?
2. What type of goals would be recorded for an intermediate-level performer?

Outline diary

Here are some items you must put in your diary:

- Date and detail of each training session
- The targets or goals for each session, e.g. 3 circuits in 20 min
- The fitness components being developed and trained
- Fitness test results
- Competition results
- Coaching feedback and reviews.

activity

INDIVIDUAL WORK
3.10

P4

Produce a training diary for a selected individual, such as a friend, classmate or teammate.

Be able to monitor and evaluate a fitness training programme

Evaluation is the process of analysing the programme you have planned. This can help identify what went well and what could be improved. Effective evaluation is essential for progress. Good exercise trainers, coaches and sports development officers are always trying to improve what they do, so they evaluate their fitness sessions to identify strengths and weaknesses and learn lessons for the future.

Here are some items to monitor:

- Training diaries
- Test results (recorded in the diary)
- Feedback from coaches and instructors
- The performer's own views on progress.

When evaluating a fitness training programme, review the fitness progress, but also how the programme was planned. The key to really effective programming is to plan well.

Consider how the participants felt about the fitness training programme. Their views are important and probably more objective than your own views. You could obtain their views by asking them to write an evaluation in their diary.

Figure 3.17 Ask participants how they felt about the training programme

remember

Fitness training programmes are meaningless unless they are evaluated and the evaluations are then acted on. So record how you would modify the programme in light of progress made and feedback received.

Address issues that arise from poor evaluations and make them part of an action plan for improvement. Update personal action plans and revise goals accordingly.

activity
GROUP WORK
3.11

P5

M3

1. Make a presentation to feed back the strengths and areas for improvement following a six-week fitness training programme.
2. Give possible explanations of these strengths and areas for improvement.

activity
INDIVIDUAL WORK
3.12

D2

Take your recommendations from Activity 3.11 and present them as an action plan for a future fitness programme. Highlight any changes to frequency, intensity, time and type (FITT).

Progress Check

1. Name the main fitness components.
2. Relate each component to one example of a sports activity.
3. Describe one fitness training method designed to improve aerobic endurance.
4. What is plyometrics?
5. Describe two types of flexibility training methods.
6. What sorts of information do you need to collect before planning a fitness training programme?
7. Name the main principles of training.
8. What is the FITT principle?
9. Describe periodisation and give examples for each period of training.
10. Why are warm-ups and cooldowns so important?

Sports Coaching

This unit covers:

- The roles, responsibilities and skills of sports coaches
- The techniques used by coaches to improve performance of athletes
- Planning a sports coaching session
- Delivering a sports coaching session

The unit explores the many and varied roles of a sports coach, the skills they need and the responsibilities they take on. A central part of the unit are the techniques used by successful and recognised coaches; they will help you build on your successes as you develop your own techniques to improve the performance of athletes. The unit will also help you plan, deliver and evaluate your own coaching performance so you can make the most of future coaching opportunities.

grading criteria

To achieve a **Pass** grade the evidence must show that the learner is able to:	To achieve a **Merit** grade the evidence must show that the learner is able to:	To achieve a **Distinction** grade the evidence must show that the learner is able to:
P1 describe four roles and four responsibilities of sports coaches, using examples of coaches from different sports Pg 127	**M1** explain four roles and four responsibilities of sports coaches, using examples of coaches from different sports Pg 127	**D1** compare and contrast the roles, responsibilities and skills of successful coaches from different sports Pg 130
P2 describe three skills common to successful sports coaches, using examples of coaches from different sports Pg 128	**M2** explain three skills common to successful sports coaches, using examples of coaches from different sports Pg 130	**D2** evaluate three different techniques that are used by coaches to improve the performance of athletes Pg 139
P3 describe three different techniques that are used by coaches to improve the performance of athletes Pg 138	**M3** explain three different techniques that are used by coaches to improve the performance of athletes Pg 138	**D3** justify suggestions made in relation to development in identified areas for improvement Pg 145
P4 plan a sports coaching session Pg 141	**M4** deliver a sports coaching session Pg 142	

	To achieve a **Pass** grade the evidence must show that the learner is able to:	To achieve a **Merit** grade the evidence must show that the learner is able to:	To achieve a **Distinction** grade the evidence must show that the learner is able to:
grading criteria	**P5** deliver a sports coaching session, with support Pg 142	**M5** evaluate the planning and delivery of a sports coaching session, suggesting how improvements could be made in the identified areas Pg 145	
	P6 review the planning and delivery of a sports coaching session, identifying strengths and areas for improvement Pg 144		

Understand the roles, responsibilities and skills of sports coaches

The growth in sports coaching has mirrored the growth of competitive and professional sport. Most coaches are assessed largely by results, hence most are driven by a need for achievement. The majority of sports coaches in the UK are unpaid volunteers, so their employment status is low.

Roles

Innovator

A coach must often adopt the role of strategy-maker. New and creative strategies may help to innovate the performance of an individual or team.

---

case study 4.1

Hockey team coach

A newly appointed coach to a county hockey team adopted the role of an innovator by introducing a new playing strategy involving all players being both attackers and defenders when appropriate. The coach calls this 'complete hockey' and all players are required to recognise that there are periods in the game when they are either an attacker or a defender regardless of their named positions.

activity
GROUP WORK

1. What will help the coach to get their message across to the players?
2. What barriers might there be to the players adopting this strategy?

Friend

Coaching a person can lead to a close relationship with them, which can develop into friendship. This can make it harder for the coach to be objective and may also create ethical problems. Coaches must be careful to develop appropriate relationships.

Teachers and coaches sometimes discover that familiarity can breed contempt. Be aware of child protection issues and be particularly careful about using mobile telephones and the Internet, especially instant messaging and chat rooms.

Figure 4.1 Familiarity can breed contempt – keep coaching relationships professional

See page 53 in Unit 2 for more information on child protection

Manager

A coach needs to be a good manager. People management skills are important to get the most out of performers, but many coaches also have to manage money, equipment and facilities. Some coaches also have to book hotels and taxis and deal with lots of other things connected with sports performance and events.

case study 4.2

Netball club coach

The coach of a netball club that has reached the national finals manages the team as well as coaching it. The accommodation, travel arrangements, equipment and team kit all have to be organised before the date of the finals.

activity
INDIVIDUAL WORK

1. What personal skills should the coach have to be able to carry out their management role?
2. What other management responsibilities might this coach have in the lead-up to the national finals?

Trainer

A coach often has to be a physical fitness trainer or skills trainer. Then they must give accurate, well-informed instruction and devise training programmes based on solid scientific criteria. Coaches sometimes train other coaches; this is crucial if coach training is to be valid and relevant to the needs of performers.

Figure 4.2 Coaches often have to be physical fitness trainers

Educator

A coach is often an educator rather than just an instructor or trainer. They often have to explain why activities and fitness sessions are important to a performer. The educator role also includes educating performers about sportsmanship, appropriate behaviour and adopting the right attitude to training and competition.

See page 87 in Unit 3 for more information on training and fitness for sport

Coaches often have to give advice about nutrition and general lifestyle. A coach often has to educate performers about avoiding performance-enhancing drugs on the lists of banned substances. A coach must reinforce good practice and explain sport's ethical standards, morals and codes of behaviour.

Effective coaches are coaches who have a good level of knowledge about all aspects of sports preparation. It is a good idea to subscribe to your governing body journal to keep up with the latest training and coaching ideas. Refresh and improve your knowledge through regular coaching courses.

remember

All coaches in sport must have relevant qualifications to coach their activity.

To find out about courses, contact your governing body or Sports Coach UK
www.sportscoachuk.org

Role model

Coaches have a great responsibility, especially to young performers. They are looked up to because of their status and therefore they are often copied and emulated. A coach's behaviour must always meet the highest professional and sporting standards so that performers, other coaches and spectators can follow their lead. The coach should also wear the right clothes and equipment for the activity and strictly follow health and safety rules. The coach should adopt a healthy diet, have an appropriate sportsmanlike attitude and use appropriate language. Follow the maxim: Do as I say and do as I do! A coach's behaviour, demeanour and attitude all have an influence on the people they coach.

---

case study 4.3 — Football manager

A Premiership football manager has once again been sent to the stands during a match when his team are losing to close rivals. The press will interview this manager after the game and will ask him to comment on his behaviour.

activity
GROUP WORK

1. What sort of questions might the coach be asked about him being a role model for others?
2. What advice would you give this coach about him being an appropriate role model?

Responsibilities of the coach

A coach has many responsibilities and some of them are legal obligations.

 Link

See page 57 in Unit 2 for more information on the legal obligations of sports coaching and training

Figure 4.3 Every coach must work within the law

Equal Opportunities Commission – detailed guidance and codes of practice
www.eoc.org.uk
Disability Rights Commission – another useful source of information
www.drc-gb.org.uk
Commission for Racial Equality
www.cre.gov.uk

The main anti-discrimination laws in the UK

Race Relations (Amendment) Act 2001

The Race Relations (Amendment) Act 2001 makes it unlawful to discriminate directly or indirectly on the grounds of colour, race nationality, ethnic or national origin. Discrimination as a result of selection for sports on the basis of nationality, place of birth or length of residence is exempted.

Special Educational Needs and Disability Act 2001

- Discrimination against disabled students in the provision of education, training and other related services is unlawful.

- The new Act covers pre- and post-16 education.

- The new Act is an amendment to the existing Disability Discrimination Act 1995 (DDA).

- The definition of disability in the DDA is based on an individual's ability to carry out 'normal day-to-day' activities.

- This law gives responsibilities to all further and higher education institutions, schools with post-16 provision (although these are covered by the pre-16 sections of the Act, not the post-16 sections), and local authorities when these organisations provide further, adult or continuing education or training.

- This law affects all education and training provided by the above bodies, admissions to courses, exclusions, and the provision of other 'student services'.

- It is unlawful for institutions or other education providers to treat a disabled person 'less favourably' than they treat, or would treat non-disabled people for a reason which relates to the person's disability. For example, it would be unlawful for an institution to turn a disabled person away from a course or mark them down in an assessment because they had dyslexia or were deaf.

- Part of not discriminating is making 'adjustments'. If a disabled person is at a 'substantial disadvantage', the education provider is required to take such steps as are reasonable to prevent that disadvantage. This might include changes to policies and practices, changes to course requirements or work placements, changes to physical features of a building, the provision of interpreters or other support workers, the delivery of courses in alternative ways, or the provision of materials in other formats.

Sex Discrimination Act 1986

The Sex Discrimination Act 1986 makes it unlawful to discriminate directly or indirectly on the grounds of a person's sex or marital status.

Disability Discrimination Act 1995

The Disability Discrimination Act 1995 makes it unlawful for an employer of 15 or more staff to discriminate against current or prospective employees on the grounds of disability. Private sports clubs are exempted from the Act.

Other relevant Acts

- Special Educational Needs and Disability Act 2001

- Rehabilitation of Offenders Act 1974

- Employment Protection (Consolidation) Act 1978.

Parliament – the home page of the UK parliament
www.parliament.uk
Office of Public Sector Information
www.opsi.gov.uk

Principles and ethics for coaches in sports facilities

Staff in sports facilities may be managers, facility staff, coaches and trainers. Several principles underpin the ethical rules in these facilities. Here are some examples of the standards expected for good practice by coaches and trainers:

- Give the participants and other people appropriate time and attention.

- Help the participants and other people to feel welcome and at ease.

- Communicate with participants and other people using the most effective methods, providing them with the information they need.

- Encourage participants and other people to ask questions when they need to.

- Listen to what participants and other people have to say; take their opinions into account.

- Handle any disagreements with participants and other people in a way that will allow the session to continue and achieve its objectives.

- Make sure your relationships with participants are supportive and in line with accepted good practice and relevant codes of practice.

- Provide participants and other people involved in the session with clear information on the ground rules for behaviour and the reasons for these rules.

- Encourage and reinforce behaviour that helps participants work well together and achieve the session's goals.

- Identify and respond to any behaviour likely to cause emotional distress or disruption to the session, in a way that meets with accepted good practice.

- Manage the participants' behaviour effectively and fairly, in a way appropriate to their need.

The general principles and ethics that relate to staff employed in sports facilities involve the following factors: treating people with dignity; building respectful relationships; taking responsibility for your actions and acting responsibly; being committed to the aims and principles of the organisation; being cooperative with others and showing high standards of integrity, including appropriate confidentiality; not abusing any privileges; having high standards of personal behaviour; honouring the trust expected by clients, employers, colleagues and the general public; showing a high degree of sportsmanship where appropriate; having due regard to the law. Another very important principle is to have particular regard for health and safety issues. There is also the need to minimise any impact on the environment, e.g. litter.

Child protection

Every adult involved in sport – the coach, the referee, the adult helper and the club member – needs to be aware of child protection issues. To assist those working with children in sport, the National Society for the Prevention of Cruelty to Children (NSPCC) and Sport England have set up the Child Protection in Sport Unit, to help sports bodies implement child protection policies, helping to ensure that all sporting activity is safe.

remember

When similar legislation was introduced in Australia in 1993, 90% of the court cases related to learning and teaching. Cases related to discrimination in delivery of programmes, failure to make handouts and overhead projector (OHP) slides available in accessible formats, access to field trips and other practical activities, including sport and means of assessment. It is anticipated that any litigation in the UK will follow a similar pattern.

Figure 4.4 A professional coach can still celebrate success

Photographs and images of children

There have been concerns about the risks to children and young people through the use of photographs on sports websites and other publications. Photographs can be used as a means of identifying children when they are accompanied by captions like this: 'Child X is a member of Club Y and likes Beyoncé'. This information can make a child vulnerable to an individual who may wish to start to groom that child for abuse. Secondly, the content of the photo can be used or adapted for inappropriate use. There is evidence of this adapted material finding its way onto child pornography sites.

General rules

- If the athlete is named, avoid using their photograph. If a photograph is used, avoid naming the athlete.

- Ask for the athlete's permission to use their image. This ensures they are aware of how the image will be used to represent the sport. One way to ask is by using an athlete permission form.

- Ask for parental permission to use an image of a young person. This ensures that parents are aware of the way the image of their child is representing the sport. One way to ask is by using a parental permission form.

- Only use images of athletes in suitable dress to reduce the risk of inappropriate use. Given the wide diversity of sports, it is difficult to specify exactly what counts as suitable dress.

- There are some sports activities, such as swimming, gymnastics and athletics, where the risk of potential misuse is much greater than for other sports. With these sports the content of the photograph should focus on the activity not on a particular child and should avoid full face and body shots. For example, shots of children in a pool would be appropriate, ideally from waist up or from the shoulders.

- When coaching athletes one-to-one, it is advisable not to be alone with the athlete. Many sports organisations have clear guidelines to protect the athlete against abuse and to protect the coach against any misunderstandings.

Use of photographic filming equipment at sporting events

- Provide a clear brief about what is considered appropriate content and behaviour.

- Issue the photographer with identification which must be worn at all times.

- Inform athletes and parents that a photographer will attend an event, obtain their consent for films or photographs to be taken, and obtain their consent for any publication of films or photographs.

- Do not allow unsupervised access to athletes or one-to-one photo sessions at events.

- Do not approve or allow photo sessions outside the events or at an athlete's home.

- If parents or other spectators are intending to photograph or video at an event, they should also be made aware of your expectations.

- Spectators should be asked to register at an event if they wish to use photographic equipment.

- Athletes and parents should be informed that if they have concerns, they can report them to the organiser.

- Coaches should report any concerns about inappropriate or intrusive photography to the event organiser or official.

Child Protection in Sport Unit

www.thecpsu.org.uk

National Society for the Prevention of Cruelty to Children – help and advice for adults

www.nspcc.org.uk

---

case study 4.4 **Keeping Children Safe in Sport**

The National Society for the Prevention of Cruelty to Children (NSPCC) has designed Keeping Children Safe in Sport to help sports organisations deal appropriately with child protection issues. It will help clubs safeguard the children in their care by enabling staff and volunteers to recognise and understand their role in child protection.

Here are the key benefits outlined by the NSPCC:

- You will gain an understanding of child protection issues.

- You will be able to recognise signs that a child needs help.

- You will feel more confident to take that first vital step to get assistance.

- You can demonstrate to others that you have completed a formal programme on child protection awareness.

- You will be making an important contribution to preventing children suffering from child abuse.

- You will get a completion certificate from the NSPCC.

activity INDIVIDUAL WORK

1. Why should coaches be more aware of child protection issues?

2. When coaching your sport to a group of 10 year olds, what measures should you take to ensure the children under your guidance are appropriately protected?

Sports Coach UK offers a range of resources to support coaches working with children:

- Safe and Sound – introductory leaflet
- Good Practice and Child Protection – workshop for sports coaches
- Protecting Children – home study pack.

Sports Coach UK

www.sportscoachuk.org

Professional conduct

Sports coaches have a responsibility to show and reinforce professional conduct. They should follow the principles, values and ethics in this section.

Principles

One principle is that sport must be played fairly, without discrimination by officials or coaches. For example, the umpire in a hockey match is expected to make decisions about what has happened on the field of play, regardless of who the player is. This illustrates the principle of fair play in sport. A coach must select a side on the basis of ability, not by discriminating against individuals or groups.

In Premiership football teams it is often thought that international players and high-profile coaches get away with behaviour that is against the principle of fair play and that would be deemed unacceptable in other people.

Figure 4.5 Coaches should encourage fair play

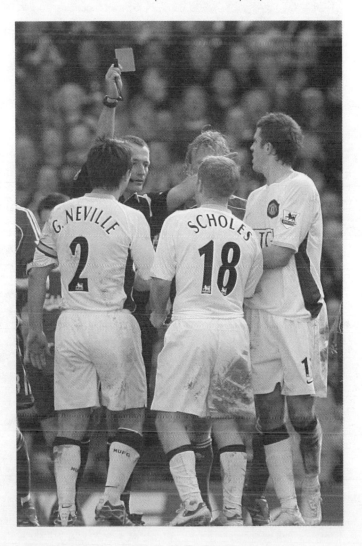

Values

One value is that a player endeavours to play well and a coach endeavours to coach fairly, for the team's sake and not for individual benefit. For example, a hockey goalkeeper would put themselves at risk by saving a hard-driven shot. This upholds the value of playing for the sake of others. A coach takes the blame for their side playing poorly and does not blame individuals.

In Premiership football a goalkeeper does not try very hard to save a shot and risk injury because he is due to gain as an individual in a forthcoming transfer deal. This would be deemed as not upholding the value of playing for others.

Figure 4.6 One value in sport is to play for the benefit of others

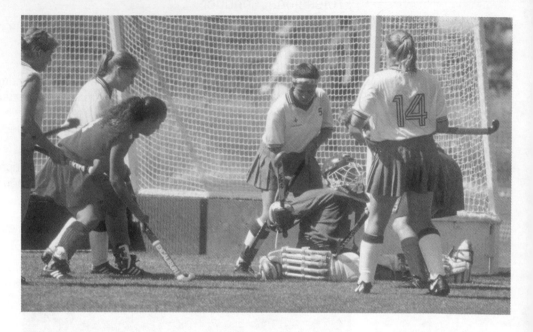

Ethics

In sport it is ethical to acknowledge that you have broken the rules of your game. For example, in snooker a player tells the referee when he has committed a foul, even if the referee has not noticed. A coach should promote ethical behaviour in the people they coach and should set a good example. A coach is behaving ethically if they decline to play a talented person who is ineligible because they are too old or too young.

Figure 4.7 Coaches should foster sporting ethics

A coach is behaving unethically if they encourage an athlete to take a performance-enhancing drug that breaks the rules of competition. Coaches should not encourage anyone to take drugs and should educate their performers against drug-taking. Sadly, some coaches have behaved unethically and pressurised performers to take drugs.

See page 96 in Unit 3 for more information on drug use to enhance performance

case study 4.5

Doping offences and sporting ethics

This case study is adapted from a report in the UK Sport newsletter. After six weeks of deliberation, the Court of Arbitration for Sport (CAS) in October 2002 decided to confirm the decision of the International Olympic Committee (IOC) to disqualify Alain Baxter from the men's alpine skiing slalom at the Winter Games in Salt Lake City.

Baxter finished third in the slalom and was awarded the bronze medal, but a subsequent doping test revealed traces of methamphetamine in his urine sample, a stimulant on the IOC's list of prohibited substances.

Though Baxter maintained that the US Vicks nasal inhaler he used prior to the slalom race contained L-methamphetamine – a non-performance-enhancing isomer of methamphetamine – the CAS ruled that the anti-doping code of the Olympic movement prohibits all forms of methamphetamine and the presence of any prohibited substance results in automatic disqualification, whether or not ingestion was intentional.

'The panel is not without sympathy for Mr Baxter, who appears to be a sincere and honest man who did not intend to obtain a competitive advantage in the race,' the tribunal concluded.

'I'm gutted not to be getting my medal back but there's a lot of positive things to come out of this,' said Baxter. 'I also feel it's not just my loss. I'm getting things back as normal and in future maybe the policies will change a little bit.'

Baxter now falls under the British Olympic Association (BOA) doping by-law, which states that any athlete found guilty of a doping offence is ineligible to represent Great Britain at any future Olympic Games. An athlete can appeal against the by-law on the basis that there were significant mitigating circumstances and/or the offence was minor.

'Alain has paid a most severe penalty for a modest mistake and it is clear that the principle of strict liability underscored this decision,' added Simon Clegg, chief executive of the BOA.

'I know that I can continue to look Alain in the eye with confidence that he did not knowingly take the US Vick's inhaler to enhance his performance.'

activity
INDIVIDUAL WORK

1. What are the principles, values and ethics involved in the above account?
2. What measures might you take to ensure that anyone you are coaching is aware of the drug-taking issue?

The National Training Organisation (NTO) has four targets for every individual in the sports and recreation field, paid or unpaid:

■ Aim to be competent in your role – measured against national standards.

■ Be able to become qualified for recognition of competence.

- Have access to appropriate training.
- Have a professional development programme to maintain competence.

And the government's coaching review produced this vision: 'By 2012 the practise of coaching in the UK will be elevated to a profession acknowledged as central to the development of sport and the fulfilment of individual potential.'

case study 4.6

Sportsability

Four teaching staff were given training on the Sportsability programme of the Youth Sport Trust (YST). In addition, a full-time sport development officer for disability – a double amputee and member of the GB sled hockey team – was employed at the school as a coach. See page 172 in Unit 5 for more information on the role of a sports development officer.

Outside providers were employed to help deliver specific activities during a six-week series of activities. There was an improvement in the school attendance of the students who took part. Also, their self-esteem and confidence rose. The club has competed at the County Youth Games and been featured on a video that was sent to MPs working on the new Children's Bill. Nine young disabled people have accessed the course for the Junior Sports Leaders Award (JSLA).

Boccia

Boccia, pronounced *bot-cha*, is similar to the French game of boules or petanque. It is played with 6 red balls, 6 blue balls and 1 white target ball and the aim is to get as many boccia balls as close as possible to the white target ball. The team with their ball closest to the white target ball scores one point. They also score a point for every one of their balls that is closer to the white ball than the opposing team's closest ball.

There are no limitations on how to propel your boccia ball. You can roll, push, kick or throw it. You can use a ramp, called an assistive device, or a head aid if that is more suitable. This makes the game open to people of all ages and abilities, regardless of impairment. The game is played at a local level in schools and clubs right up to international competitions, such as the Paralympics.

activity
GROUP WORK

1. How could the game of boccia be promoted in a school? Use the description of the Sportsability programme to help you answer this.

2. What aspects of discrimination need to be overcome by a coach wanting to promote a sport for disabled people?

Coaching sport to disabled people

To realise the government's vision, coaching must have:

- professional and ethical values and inclusive and equitable practice
- agreed national standards of competence
- a regulated and licensed profession
- appropriate funding
- a culture of professional development.

Figure 4.8 Coaches and performers need good listening skills

A coach should have professional and ethical values. The NTO and other organisations related to sport and recreation recognise the importance of suitable ethical standards that include equality of opportunity and inclusiveness; in other words, no one is discriminated against within the industry.

Level 2 of the National Occupational Standards

Four key assumptions underpin the coaching process and will help coaching to have its intended impact on the participants:

- The participant must be at the centre of the process; when coaching, the coach should support, coordinate and manage the process effectively, always starting with the identification and recognition of the participant's needs, and should aim to address those needs via their coaching.

- Coaches should empower participants, supporting their right to make choices, discover their own solutions, and enable them to participate and develop at their own pace and in their own way.

- Coaches should provide opportunities and an environment that motivates, controls risk, and engenders challenge, enjoyment and above all achievement.

Figure 4.9 Safe challenges are a fun way to reach achievements

■ Coaches should aim to grow a participant's confidence and self-esteem. Coaching is fundamentally about providing a safe and ethical environment where a participant is able to maximise their potential within a sport or activity.

Figure 4.10 Maximise potential within a sport or activity

For participants to achieve their maximum potential, they must learn in an environment that is safe, supportive and free from distractions. This will be achieved by the coach providing the right equipment, having good working relationships with all those involved, maintaining their health, safety and welfare, and controlling the behaviour of participants and other people involved in the session.

Insurance for sports coaches

A coach needs to have appropriate insurance cover to protect themselves and the people they coach. Seek advice from your sports governing body. A coach has a big responsibility to ensure that they are properly qualified for the activity they are coaching. Here are some ingredients of an appropriate code of conduct for sports coaches:

■ Provide participants and other people involved in the session with clear information on the ground rules for behaviour and the reasons for these rules.

■ Encourage and reinforce behaviour that helps participants work well together and achieve the session's goals.

■ Identify and respond to any behaviour likely to cause emotional distress or disruption to the session, in a way that is in line with accepted codes of conduct.

A coach has these responsibilities:

■ Assess and minimise likely risks during the coaching session.

- Identify and take account of existing risk assessments for the activities you are planning and the resources you will be using.

- Check your plans and the environment in which the session will take place.

- Check the implications of any participant's special needs or medical conditions that may endanger the participant or others.

- Identify the likely hazards involved in the session and assess the risks of these hazards causing harm.

- Get advice from a competent person if there are hazards or risks you are not competent to identify and assess yourself.

- Plan how to minimise these risks so they satisfy national guidelines.

- Have information about the emergency procedures for the place where the session will be held.

Top 10 tips for good coaching

1. **Know yourself** – why do you want to coach and what do you want to achieve?

2. **Know your sport** – the better you understand the techniques and skills of a sport, the better equipped you are to pass them on.

3. **Be positive** – patience and praise work a lot better than criticism and shouting.

4. **Variety is the key** – avoid games where kids have to sit out and don't make all your sessions competitive.

5. **Teach skills and demonstrate** – demonstrating a skill works much better than talking about it. If you can't do it, find someone who can.

6. **Involve everybody** – always make sure there's enough equipment or kit for all. Create small groups of children rather than one big group.

7. **Communicate well** – actions speak louder than words. Body language is important. Smiles and positive gestures work wonders.

8. **Mind and body** – have a good grasp of how the body responds to exercise and training; always adopt safe practices and prevent injury. Other important aspects are confidence building, goal setting, emotional control and concentration skills. Coaches work on the mind as well as the body.

9. **Be sensitive** – some children learn more slowly than others, so choose your style accordingly. To keep children motivated, be consistent, set achievable goals and give frequent feedback.

10. **Take it from the top** – lead by example and gain trust and respect. Coaches of children are role models and this carries responsibility. Your behaviour, your appearance and your attitudes all set an example. If you show consistently high standards, they will be copied by the people you coach.

Link

See page 64 in Unit 2 for more information on risk assessments

activity
GROUP WORK
4.1

P1

M1

1. Make a detailed poster presentation that describes four roles and four responsibilities of sports coaches from at least three different sports.

2. Write a set of guidelines explaining the roles and responsibilities you have identified.

Skills needed for coaching

A good coach needs many skills. A very important skill is *communicating* with performers, officials and other coaches to get the best out of everyone. Communication can be verbal and non-verbal. Effective communication includes listening, but many coaches are not very good at listening.

Figure 4.11 Good communication brings out good performances

Here are some ways to make your messages effective:

- **Be direct** – make your statements coherent and concise.
- **Be consistent** – avoid double meanings.
- **Separate fact from opinion** – be accurate in your analysis.
- **Focus on one thing at a time** – too much information causes information overload.
- **Repeat key points** – this reinforces your message and helps avoid misunderstandings.
- **Adapt to your audience** – adapt what you say and how you say it so it suits your audience.

An effective coach is *well organised*. Good organisation can relieve possible sources of stress and can ultimately help performance. A performer has more confidence in their coach if they think the coach is organised. You can increase your self-confidence as a coach by having good personal organisation.

Effective coaches need to be good at *analysing* and *problem solving*. Good strategies and successful tactics depend on sound analysis. If a coach is skilled at identifying the key things going right and the key things going wrong, they are more likely to solve any problems. These skills come with experience but can also be learned by watching other experienced and skilful coaches.

Figure 4.12 Effective strategies begin with sound analysis

activity
INDIVIDUAL WORK
4.2

P2

Identify and describe three skills common to successful sports coaches. Using coaching examples from at least three different sports, make a visual presentation showing these skills.

Coaches also need skills for educating the people they coach about nutrition, sports psychology, motivation and physiology:

- **Nutrition** – includes types of hydration, reasons for hydration, recommended hydration before, during and after exercise; energy production and the role of carbohydrates, fats, proteins, vitamins and minerals; nutritional recommendations during exercise.

- **Sports psychology** – includes basic goal setting such as SMART and SMARTER goals, type and definitions of goal setting; this is an important aspect following *evaluation* and for effective *time management*.

See page 98 in Unit 3 for more information on goal setting
See page 312 in Unit 16 for more information on sports psychology

- **Motivation** – what motivates people to exercise and the difference in motivating children and adults; principles of anxiety and arousal, including definitions of anxiety and arousal, signs of anxiety and arousal, anxiety and arousal management; differences between a novice, intermediate and advanced performer.

- **Physiology** – includes the principles of warm-ups and cooldowns; fitness components, strength, speed, flexibility, power, agility and muscular endurance; basic principles of strength, speed, power and endurance training; aerobic and anaerobic energy; flexibility for injury prevention and improved performance; principles of training, including overload, progression, specificity, adaptation, variability, reversibility, recovery and overtraining.

See page 38 in Unit 1 for more information on energy systems

activity

INDIVIDUAL WORK 4.3

M2

D1

1. Write a document that explains three skills common to successful sports coaches; use examples of coaches from different sports.

2. Research the roles, responsibilities and skills of coaches from three different sports. Present your findings by comparing and contrasting the roles, responsibilities and skills of these successful coaches from different sports.

Understand the techniques used by coaches to improve the performance of athletes

Coaching techniques

Depending on the situation, the coach should be able to incorporate some of the following practices that meet individual needs and are effective practice methods:

- **Whole, part, whole** – this is a coaching technique that teaches a whole skill, teaches its separate parts, then reteaches the whole skill.

- **Shaping** – this is a coaching technique where reward or praise is given when the performer's behaviour or technique is correct. It reinforces the right technique so it is more likely to be repeated. The coach shapes the behaviour of the performer. Shaping is sometimes called operant conditioning.

Massed and distributed practice methods

The structure of the practice session is important for effective coaching. Massed practice is a *continuous* practice period. Distributed practice involves relatively long rests between trials. The rest intervals could involve tasks that are unrelated to the main practice activity. Many coaches encourage performers to use the intervals between activities to practise *mental rehearsal*.

Research has shown that distributed practice is generally best, as **massed practice** can lead to poor performance and hinder the learning process because of fatigue and demotivation. Massed practice may help performers learn discrete skills that have a relatively short duration, but **distributed practice** is best for learning continuous skills

where the player rapidly becomes tired. With tasks that are potentially dangerous, distributed practice is also best because it ensures that physical and mental fatigue do not impair performance and put the performer in danger.

Reinforcement

■ **Positive** – positive reinforcement gives a stimulus to encourage a performer to repeat a behaviour, e.g. a badge for swimming.

■ **Negative** – negative reinforcement removes a stimulus to encourage a performer to repeat a behaviour, e.g. no verbal praise if the performer shows the wrong movement.

■ **Punishment** – this is a stimulus to prevent a behaviour occurring, e.g. dropping a performer from the squad for not trying hard in training.

Modelling

The technique of **modelling** involves using demonstrations or models of performance. The performer can readily see what is required then attempt to copy it.

Simulation in coaching

Coaches often use a simulation of a real game situation. It may simulate the environment or it may simulate some aspects of a game or competition. Simulation can prepare athletes for the physiological and psychological influences they may experience in real competition. Performers can then work on executing skills and tactics under the type of pressure normally experienced in competition. This allows performers and coaches to develop strategies to overcome anxiety and to focus or to use selective attention to aid concentration and to block out distractions. When athletes have to make decisions in the heat of competition, they may feel so much anxiety that they miss important cues in the environment or they react more slowly. Many coaches have used simulation to reconstruct scenarios so that athletes and coaches can develop strategies to overcome potential difficulties.

See page 297 in Unit 16 for more information on anxiety management techniques

case study 4.7 Women's football club

A local women's football club is preparing for a cup final in their area. A large crowd is expected to watch the match. The coach is concerned that the women are not used to being watched by large numbers of people and their performances on the pitch may suffer.

activity
INDIVIDUAL WORK

1. As their coach, what sort of simulation could you set up for these footballers?
2. What could be achieved by using simulation?

Demonstrations

Consider these points before using demonstrations as a type of visual guidance:

■ Demonstrations must be accurate and should hold the performer's attention.

■ Demonstrations must be repeated but should not be too time-consuming.

■ Videos can be useful, especially if they have a slow-motion facility, but the student must be able to copy the model presented.

■ Position the performer so they will gain maximum benefit. For example, it is best for a performer to view a swimming stroke from above on the poolside.

Teaching and coaching styles can be adapted to suit the situation, the performer and the coach:

- **Command coaching** – this is a technique where the coach makes all the decisions, directs the performer and is authoritarian.
- **Reciprocal coaching** – this is a technique that involves group work where performers learn from one another.
- **Discovery coaching** – this is when the coach takes a back seat and encourages the performer to discover solutions to problems. It is also called a *laissez-faire* style.
- **Democratic coaching** – this is when the performer participates in decision-making.

Learning styles are ways in which individual participants prefer to learn; some learn better through instructions and demonstrations, whereas others prefer discovery learning and problem-solving experiences. Some prefer to learn through visual means, some more *kinaesthetically*. The coach can adopt a variety of different *guidance* methods:

- Visual, e.g. demonstration

Figure 4.13 People learn a lot from a good demonstration

- Verbal, e.g. instructions about technique, sometimes known as technical instruction

case study 4.8   **Trampolinist**

A coach gives a trampolinist a large amount of technical instruction before, during and after each practice sequence. The trampolinist seems not to improve her techniques and becomes confused over the requirements of the sequence.

activity
INDIVIDUAL WORK

1. What factors may have led the trampoline performer to become confused?
2. How would you guard against such confusion reoccurring?

- Mechanical, e.g. a twisting belt in trampolining
- Manual, e.g. supporting a gymnast for a handspring.

Figure 4.14 Manual guidance gives a performer confidence

Feedback

Feedback can be given during the performance or after. Feedback is most effective if it is given close to the performance so the performance is fresh in the participant's mind. Feedback motivates, changes performance or actually reinforces learning. The more precise the feedback, the more beneficial it is. There are several forms of feedback.

Table 4.1 Types of feedback

Type of feedback	Definition
Continuous	Feedback during the performance in the form of kinaesthesia or proprioception
Terminal	Feedback after the response has been completed
Knowledge of results	Feedback that gives the performer information about the end result of the response
Knowledge of performance	Information about how well the movement is being executed rather than the end result
Internal or intrinsic	A type of continuous feedback that comes from the proprioceptors
External, extrinsic or augmented	Feedback that comes from external sources such as sound or vision
Positive	Information on a successful outcome that reinforces skill learning
Negative	Information on an unsuccessful outcome that helps build more successful strategies

Two types of feedback are more important than others in sports performance: knowledge of results and knowledge of performance.

■ **Knowledge of results** – this feedback is external, and can come from the performer seeing the result of their response or from another person, usually a coach or teacher. It is extremely important for the performer to know what the result of their action has been. There can be very little learning without this type of feedback, especially in the early stages of skill acquisition.

- **Knowledge of performance** – this is feedback about the pattern of movement that has taken place or is taking place. It is normally associated with external feedback but can be gained through kinaesthetic awareness, especially if the performer is highly skilled and knows what a good performance feels like.

Knowledge of results and knowledge of performance can help to motivate a performer, but if used incorrectly they can also demotivate. Reinforcement (page 131) is essential for effective skill learning, and feedback serves as a good reinforcer. If the movement or the result is good, the performer will feel satisfaction, and the *stimulus–response* (SR) bond is strengthened (learning). Knowing that the movement and results are good will help the performer form a picture of what is correct and associate future performance with that picture, image or model.

External feedback should be used with care because the performer may come to depend too heavily on it and will not develop internal feedback. The type of feedback that should be given depends on the ability of the performer, the type of activity and the personality of the performer – different performers respond differently to different types of feedback.

case study 4.9 — Feedback and setting goals

There is an important link between feedback, goal setting and future motivation and performance. In research carried out by Bandura and Cervone in 1983, 20 cyclists were given performance goals, 20 cyclists received performance feedback but were not set goals, 20 were set goals and received feedback, and a further 20 acted as a control group. The control group were given no feedback and were not set goals. The results of this experiment show clearly that goal setting enhances the effects of feedback.

activity
INDIVIDUAL WORK

1. Why is goal setting so motivating?
2. In your sport, what types of feedback would you give as a coach with a group of beginners for a five-week course on basic skills?

When performance is measured and is given to performers as feedback, their motivation can be enhanced and their performance improved. Negative feedback can be used effectively at times as a motivational tool and to encourage self-reflection. Sports performers often set themselves targets from their previous performances but teachers and coaches can help by constructing performance or goal charts that the performer updates as necessary. These charts serve as feedback on current performance and set clear and progressive targets.

Performance profiling and observation analysis

When you analyse a performer or a team's performance, you may wish to use some form of performance analysis. This includes observing a player's performers with a video recorder. Obtain permission from the performer to do this and fulfil the requirements of the Child Protection Act.

 Link

See page 53 in Unit 2 for more information on child protection

The analysis can be quite simple, such as highlighting the performer's main strengths and weaknesses, or it can be deeper, such as **notational analysis**. Often the greater the depth, the more reliable the analysis (Honeybourne 2006a, b).

Notational analysis

Notational analysis involves taking notes about the performance of a person or team during an activity. The notes provide important information for assessing what went well and what needs improvement.

Notational analysis may consider statistics related to the activity or game, such as how many shots on target or how many successful passes. Tennis coaches, for example, may record the numbers of aces, double faults and forehand winners. The results of these analyses can highlight areas of concern or may give important information that the coach can use can use to develop a player's tactics. For example, if you know your opponent hits all their successful shots on the forehand, you will try to avoid playing the ball to their forehand. A coach may use such analyses to will on strengthening a particular skill. A hockey coach, for example, finds through analysis that one of their players is failing to pass successfully. The coach can then work on passing skills to improve the player's game.

Analysis model

A successful analysis has these five stages:

1. Analyse
2. Evaluate
3. Plan
4. Perform
5. Observe.

Figure 4.15 Is your coaching effective? Observe then analyse

All analysis must lead to an evaluation of what is going wrong and what is going right, what needs to be praised and what needs to be developed. The next stage is to formulate a plan with realistic goals, such as to work on shooting techniques in basketball. Following the plan, there needs to be practice or performance – the player works on their shooting skills. The player's performance in the next match is observed then a new five-stage analysis is begun.

Reflective cycle

The Gibbs reflective cycle encourages a clear description of the situation, an analysis of your feelings, an evaluation of the experience, an analysis to make sense of the experience, a conclusion where other options are considered, and reflection on the experience (Gibbs 1988). All this helps you to examine what you would do if the situation should arise again. Try relating the Gibbs cycle to a recent experience in coaching your sport (Figure 4.16).

Figure 4.16 The Gibbs reflective cycle. Adapted from Gibbs (1988)

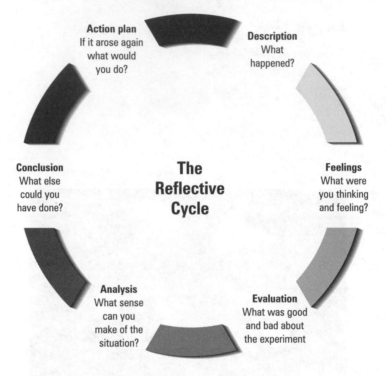

Performance profile

The performance profile involves gathering information about a performer to give a profile or picture of their strengths and weaknesses. Table 4.2 is an example of how you can assess performance. It includes what is expected, what is currently being seen and the difference between the two. The higher the number under area for improvement, the more work has to be done in that area. This is an excellent way to prioritise skill and tactical development.

Fitness assessments

Fitness assessments, if done properly, are a useful way to establish a performer's strengths and areas for development. They can also be a useful monitoring device to see how well the fitness programme is working and how hard the performer is working. The results can then be used to inform and update the next stage of the fitness programme. For example, it may be discovered that speed is an issue and the performer shows low scores on speed. The training programme would then be modified to incorporate much more speed work. Fitness assessments are often used as a screening device for selection to a particular team, because they may indicate a performer's potential.

> **remember**
> Encourage performers to view the tests as benchmarks for their own improvements instead of norms, which are notoriously invalid because they rarely take account of all the variables present.

Assessing a performer's fitness levels

■ Identify exactly what you want to assess and choose the fitness tests accordingly. For example, if you wish to test an athlete's flexibility in the hips, the sit and reach test would be appropriate.

■ If a specific type of fitness needs to be assessed, only use the tests that are required.

■ Make sure the athlete is medically fit to take a test. If you or they have any doubts, ask them to see a doctor. Get the athlete to complete a physical activity readiness questionnaire (PAR-Q); this is common practice in health clubs.

Sports Coach UK

www.sportscoachuk.org

Successful Coaching – links to fitness test information

www.sports-coach.net

■ Make sure the athlete feels well enough for the test.

■ Make sure that the athlete has not eaten a heavy meal for approximately 3 hours before the test.

■ The athlete must not consume alcohol the day before the test and on the day of the test.

■ Make sure the athlete has had enough water to drink.

■ The athlete must not smoke for at least 2 hours before the tests.

Performer coaching diaries

Many coaches encourage their athletes to keep training diaries. It is also becoming more common for coaches to keep diaries on coaching and performers' responses to the coaching.

See page 108 in Unit 3 for more information on training diaries

Record progress in fitness training but also keep a record of coaching points so you can reflect on them and evaluate performance and coaching techniques. One way of recording progress and setting out goals is to write a coaching diary and complete it during training and competition.

Day-to-day information that could be recorded

■ How well the coach and the performer feel the coaching is progressing

■ Performance data, including fitness and skills tests.

What a coaching diary should contain

■ Date and detail of each training session

■ The targets or goals for each session, e.g. to improve defending skills

■ Test results and reflections on the performer's successes following coaching points.

■ Competition results

■ Feedback from the coach and reviews.

Table 4.2 Performance profile

Player characteristic	Ideal player (1–10) (A)	Player assessment (1–10) (B)	Area for improvement (A – B = C)
Psychological e.g. confidence	8	4	4
Physical e.g. strength	6	6	0
Technical e.g. penalty flick	10	10	10
Tactical e.g. awareness	10	6	4
Other			

activity

GROUP WORK
4.4

P3

M3

1. On your own, write a briefing paper designed for other coaches. Describe three different coaching techniques that are used to improve the performance of athletes.

2. Now present your paper to the rest of the group by explaining each of the three techniques you described.

activity

INDIVIDUAL WORK 4.5

D2

1. Observe a coaching session and make notes about the effectiveness of techniques you have observed.
2. Present your findings to your fellow students and show your evaluation of three different coaching techniques that can improve the performance of athletes.

Be able to plan a sports coaching session

Items to use when you plan a sports coaching session

- **Aims and objectives of your session** – what are you trying to achieve? Be realistic about your goals and try not to be overambitious. For example, an aim for a coaching session might be to improve the arm action of a swimmer performing the front crawl. An objective is something that leads to an aim. For example, an objective leading to the aim of better front crawl could be to work on the timing of each breath. Aims and objectives should be realisitic, measurable and easy to understand.

- **Targets for the session** – targets are linked to your aims and should be SMART. For example, a performer might have a target to swim one length using their corrected swimming technique by the end of the session.

- **Your role** – what part are you going to play as the coach in this session? Will you be directing procedures throughout as an instructor? Or will you allow the swimmer to work out their own technique?

- **Your responsibilities** – what are you in charge of? Do you have to check for equipment safety? Do you have to manage the session by booking the pool? You will probably have responsibility for the performer's safety and for keeping your session within their capabilities.

- **Assess the participants** – make a note of their ages, gender, number, abilities, and any particular needs. For example, if a performer is asthmatic or diabetic, you will need to plan a session that takes account of their needs.

- **The resources** – what help will you get from other people during the session? What equipment and other physical resources will you need? What financial aspects do you need to consider? You may need to pay for the venue or see that the organising body pays for the venue.

- **Health and safety** – you will have to carry out a risk assessment that considers potential hazards and how to limit their risks. Make sure everyone clearly understands emergency procedures and contingency plans. Plan how to inform all participants of fire safety information, for example, if the session is indoors.

- **Components of the session** – your plan will probably include a warm-up, the main session of coaching and a cooldown. It is good practice to include feedback at the end of the session, feedback from you and from the participants.

remember

Aims and objectives should always be realistic – are you trying to do too much or too little?

remember

SMART = specific, measurable, achievable, realistic, timed.

remember

Good coaches play to their strengths and try to improve their weaknesses. If you are an excellent communicator, use this skill when you give instructions to athletes. If your demonstrations are much more effective than your verbal instructions, you may prefer to use video recordings of performances to help you get your message across.

- **Sequencing** – always plan for one part of a practice to follow in a systematic and complementary manner. Skills need to be built up sequentially so effective learning can happen.

- **Coaching skills and techniques** – select coaching techniques that suit the participants and make them work effectively by using your skills of communication, organisation, analysis, problem solving, evaluation and time management.

Initial planning

Coaching is mainly about providing a safe and ethical environment where a performer is able to do well and feel at ease. That means the performer must be central to the coaching process. Successful coaching sessions require thorough preparation based on the performer's needs.

Consider guidelines from *national governing bodies* and your own experience when planning and preparing sessions. Here are some things to keep in mind:

- **Needs** – including special and medical needs and the potential of the people taking part. Take careful account of who the people are or the type of team you are coaching. Take note of their ability levels and whether some people may need particular help and guidance.

- **Goals** – the participants should achieve specific goals.

> **remember**
>
> Include the performer in the planning process, then they are more likely to be well motivated and respond positively to your instructions.

Figure 4.17 Select techniques that suit you performers

- **Activities** – coaching activities that will help the participants achieve these goals. Consider the nature of the task and the ability of the performers, then select appropriate coaching techniques from those identified earlier.
- **Equipment** – it may be possible to hire other facilities or equipment or to adapt what is already owned.
- **Risks** – consider health and safety hazards and risks.

See page 98 in Unit 3 for more information on goal setting
See page 46 in Unit 2 for more information on health and safety requirements

<table>
<tr><td>*remember*</td><td>You always consider child protection issues.</td></tr>
</table>

Collect accurate and up-to-date information to help you plan the session. Analyse the information and identify the implications for the coaching and the participants. Maintain appropriate. If you cannot meet the coaching needs of any participant, refer them to another competent coach.

Specific information to note

- How many participants are expected
- The physical and mental needs of participants and their potential
- Any medical conditions
- The aims of the programme to which the session belongs
- The preferred learning styles of the participants
- Evaluations and action plans of other relevant sessions.

Specific goals to identify

Identify goals that meet the needs and potential of all the participants; balance the needs of individuals with the needs of the group. Here are some typical goals related to a session:

- Improve physical ability
- Improve mental ability
- Improve skills and techniques
- Provide fun and enjoyment.

Preparation of activities for the session

- Select activities and coaching styles that will motivate the participants to participate fully in the session.
- Choose activities that will enable all the goals to be achieved.
- Plan activities that have realistic timings, sequences, intensity and duration.
- Strike an effective balance of coaching styles.
- Get the resources you need for the session: facilities, equipment, personal clothing, any support from other staff.

activity
INDIVIDUAL WORK 4.6

P4

Design a coaching planner and, using the information above, make a plan for a sports coaching session in a sport of your choice.

Be able to deliver a sports coaching session

remember

Work on material and skills that are appropriate for the needs of the learners. Have different levels of difficulty to challenge all abilities in your group; this is called differentiation.

Meet the participants punctually and make them feel welcome and at ease. Explain and agree the goals that are appropriate for participants to achieve. Check the participants' level of experience, ability and physical readiness to participate effectively and safely. Always make sure that the participants have the correct equipment and clothing.

Include an appropriate warm-up and perhaps explain its value and purpose. Be prepared to revise your session plans if you need to. Flexibility is a sign of a good coach.

For coaching to be effective, explanations and demonstrations need to be technically correct and appropriate to the participants' needs and level of experience. Check the participants' understanding of the activity throughout the session.

Table 4.3 Template for a session plan

Date Venue Duration	Attendance	Equipment needed
Introduction (including aims and objectives)		
Warm-up activities	Drills and games	Cooldown activities
Coaching tips, questions and challenges		Learning outcomes
Evaluation (key points from session, what worked and what did not, modifications for next sessions, etc.)		

activity
INDIVIDUAL WORK 4.7

P5 **M4**

Deliver the sports coaching session you planned in Activity 4.6. Deliver the session with direct support from your tutor or without support.

Use governing body journals for coaching ideas from the following governing body websites for rugby, netball, football and hockey:

www.rfu.com

www.england-netball.co.uk

www.thefa.com

www.englandhockey.co.uk

You will be judged against the following criteria:

- You have adopted an appropriate role.

- You have taken sufficient account of your responsibilities.

- You have given an effective demonstration of skills and techniques.

- You have shown due consideration for health and safety issues, e.g. emergency procedures and contingencies.

- You have made effective use of resources, e.g. equipment and facilities.

- Your session contained the appropriate components, e.g. warm-up, main body, cooldown.

- You have given effective feedback.

- You have used sequencing.

Figure 4.18 Good coaches are always trying to improve their coaching

Review: evaluating coaching sessions

Your review should include an evaluation of:

- how far your aims and objectives were met
- whether your targets were met
- how effective the session was at different points (formative evaluation) and at the end (summative evaluation)
- feedback from participants, observers, your peers, and assessors.

From this review you should be able to identify your strengths and areas for improvement. The final step is to plan for improvement. Identify opportunities and potential barriers that may stop you developing your coaching.

Evaluation is the process of analysing the sessions you have planned and delivered. It can help you identify what went well and what could have been improved. Effective evaluation is essential for making progress in your coaching. Good coaches are always trying to improve what they do. They think about the coaching sessions they have delivered, identify strengths and weaknesses, and learn lessons for the future.

Also consider developments in coaching practice and take part in regular coach education to develop further and add to your coaching skills. This could include attending courses and conferences, reading journals or other relevant publications, and observing or working with other coaches.

Coaching courses are often organised by sports governing bodies and can be found from Sports Coach UK

www.sportscoachuk.org

Review not just how you delivered a session but also how you planned it. Good planning is the key to effective coaching. Problems during a coaching session may have been avoided by putting more thought into the planning.

Take account of how the participants felt about the coaching session. Their views are important and probably more objective than your own. You could ask for their views by *verbal feedback* or a written evaluation. Comments may be affected by *demand characteristics*, when participants report what they think may please the reader, instead of what they actually thought.

Record self-evaluation, evaluation by other coaches and evaluation by the participants. Then act on your findings, otherwise the whole process is meaningless. Coaching elements that received favourable evaluations should be continued and developed. Coaching elements that received poor evaluations should be addressed and become part of an *action plan* to improve. Review your progress and watch how your coaching practice develops; update your personal action plans accordingly.

activity
INDIVIDUAL WORK
4.8

P6

Write a SWOT analysis of your coaching session.

- **Strengths** – what were the best aspects of the session and why? What did you do well and why?
- **Weaknesses** – are there gaps in the coaching session? What did you not do very well and why?
- **Opportunities** – how can you improve the session to benefit the performer?
- **Threats** – what may prevent you achieving possible improvements?

This will form a review of the planning and delivery of your sports coaching session.

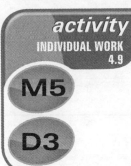

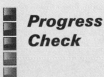

1. Write a detailed evaluation of your session that makes suggestions for developing improvements.

2. Review the feedback about your session from a variety of sources, such as peer assessment and self-assessment. Write a justification for each of your suggestions to improve coaching performance.

Progress Check

1. Identify five roles that a coach has to perform in a sport of your choice.

2. Identify a brief code of conduct for a coach in your sport.

3. Using examples from sport, explain what responsibilities a coach might have.

4. What makes a message communicate effectively?

5. What aspects of sports psychology might be useful for a coach to consider?

6. What is positive reinforcement and how would you use it when coaching a beginner in sport?

7. When is the command style of coaching appropriate in sport?

8. Use practical examples to explain what makes feedback effective.

9. What planning should a coach do before a successful coaching session?

10. How does a coach evaluate the effectiveness of a coaching session?

Sports Development

This unit covers:

- The key concepts in sports development
- Key providers of sports development
- How quality is measured in sports development
- Sports development in practice

Sports development is continuing to include new and varied activities, particularly as we move towards the 2012 Olympics. Sports development affects people from recreational players to elite performer. This unit covers the key concepts of sports development, including the sports development continuum, barriers to participation and associated target groups.

It describes the key providers in sports development so that you can evaluate their structures, functions and roles. It looks at how people learn by their mistakes and how they measure quality in sports development, including the advantages and disadvantages. The last part explores current initiatives in sports development. Have a go at comparing these initiatives and try to offer realistic recommendations for improvement.

grading criteria

grading criteria

To achieve a **Pass** grade the evidence must show that the learner is able to:	To achieve a **Merit** grade the evidence must show that the learner is able to:	To achieve a **Distinction** grade the evidence must show that the learner is able to:
P4 describe two methods of measuring quality in sports development　　　Pg 179	**M4** compare and contrast two different sports development initiatives, identifying strengths and weaknesses　　　Pg 182	
P5 describe two different sports development initiatives　　　Pg 181		

Understand key concepts in sports development

Sports development is about making and helping pathways and structures to enable people to learn basic skills, participate in sports of their choice, develop their competence and performance, and reach levels of excellence.

Sports development builds and helps partnerships to provide appropriate and accessible sporting opportunities for all. Some partners in sports development are local authorities, primary schools, secondary schools, colleges, universities, clubs, governing bodies of sport, community clubs and services, leisure centres, specialist sports facilities, and national organisations such as *Sport England*, the *Youth Sport Trust* and *Sports Coach UK*.

Sport England – for links to sports development case studies

www.sportengland.org

The Sports Council, now called *UK Sport*, saw the need for a coordinated response to sports development and in 1996 it produced the report *Better Quality Sport for All*. This highlighted the need to enable people to learn basic sports skills that could progress to sporting excellence. The strategy had four aims:

- People would develop the skills and competence to enable sport to be enjoyed.
- Everyone would follow a lifestyle that included active participation in sport and recreation.
- People would achieve their personal goals at their chosen level of involvement in sport.
- People would develop excellence and achieve success in sport at the highest level.

The strategy stated that everyone should have the right to play sport. Be it for fun, for health, to enjoy the natural environment or to win, everyone should have the opportunity to enjoy sport.

This continuous improvement would help to achieve personal bests in participants, officials, administrators and high-level performers. The challenge was to make the UK 'the sporting nation'.

> **remember**
>
> Most successful sports development activities involve partnerships – different organisations working together towards similar aims.

Figure 5.1 Everyone should have the opportunity to enjoy sport

Sports development continuum

The framework for sports development is called the **sports development continuum**. It is actually a four-level progression from foundation to excellence via participation and performance. There are many aspects to sports development and the importance of each aspect is largely determined by the level a person has reached. Not everyone will reach excellence and only some will reach performance and become involved in competitive sports.

The continuum helps to assess whether sports provision is appropriate. For example, it can be used to identify target groups and communities where development should be concentrated. It also helps many initiatives against drugs and crime and initiatives to promote healthy lifestyles.

See page 272 in Unit 11 for more information on different groups in society and their barriers to participation

Identifying community groups that need sports development can also lead to regeneration of an area. Do not underestimate the importance of sports development – its influence goes far beyond participation in sport.

Figure 5.2 Sports
development continuum

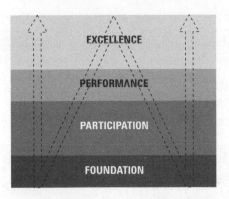

Sports development continuum

Foundation

Foundation is when local authorities work with clubs and schools to develop basic
movement and sports skills. Acquiring good exercise habits with appropriate knowledge
and understanding helps to develop a positive attitude to sports and physical activity.
Here are its goals:

- To increase curriculum time for PE
- To increase the numbers of children taking part in extracurricular sport
- To increase the percentage of children taking part in out-of-school sport
- To generate more positive attitudes to sport, especially by girls
- To increase the percentage of young people taking part in a range of sports on a
'regular' basis.

Figure 5.3 Good exercise
habits foster a positive
attitude to sport

Participation

Sports development tries to make participation as wide as possible. Here are its goals:

- To increase the numbers of people taking part in regular sporting activity
- To reduce the dropout in participation with age
- To reduce barriers to participation.

case study 5.1

A district council's strategy to develop participation in sports

Sport England recognises a total of more than 110 sports; many but not all are played in this district. This council has therefore selected five focus sports where it is possible to develop meaningful action plans for the sport or theme. Here are some areas to include in the action plans: foundation and participation, performance, sports clubs, coaches and volunteers, school sport, funding, facilities, sports equity, competition structure, management plans, contribution to wider social outcomes, target groups. Here are descriptions for three of these focus sports: athletics, basketball and girls' football.

Athletics

A plan for athletics development in the district has been produced. The development group includes representatives from athletics clubs and schools around the district and is working hard to further the development of athletics in the district. The sports development department works closely with schools and clubs to develop opportunities in athletics locally. There is a strong link with the regional development coordinator to enable the delivery of national initiatives and programmes from the governing body, UK Athletics. The sports development department organises coaching courses each year to encourage people to qualify as coaches and to encourage existing coaches to further their coaching development. Courses provided each year are level 1 and level 2.

Figure 5.4 Coaching courses help coaches to improve

Basketball and girls' football

The sports development department works in partnership with primary schools, secondary schools, clubs, the Basketball Association and the Football Association to increase opportunities for young people to try basketball or girls' football and reach their desired level of performance. Through leader awards and governing body qualifications, it recruits and trains coaches to work on the programme throughout the district. Existing and prospective clubs are offered advice and support in developing any aspect of their club in accordance with nationally recognised standards.

Figure 5.5 Girls' football is being developed by schools, clubs and the FA

activity
INDIVIDUAL WORK

1. How does this district enable more participation in competitive sport?
2. How else might the district cater for the foundation stage?

Performance

Performance is the improvement of standards through coaching and training. It relates to competitive sport and encourages people to obtain fulfilment and enjoyment by improving their performance. Here are its goals:

- To increase the numbers of participants trying to improve their sporting skills
- To increase the numbers of club members.

Excellence

Excellence is about reaching the top standards in sport, such as national and international competition. Here are its goals:

- To achieve higher world rankings, better win-loss records, national and international records and individual personal bests
- For English teams to achieve success in international competition.

Link   See page 98 in Unit 3 for more information on individual and team goal setting

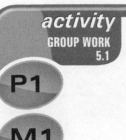

activity
GROUP WORK
5.1

P1

M1

1. Make a poster display describing three examples of the sports development continuum from three different sports.

2. Identify the main strengths and weaknesses of the three examples you identified in the first task. Now write a report that compares and contrasts these three examples.

Barriers to participation

All of us experience barriers to participation, but some people experience many more barriers or much greater barriers.

Our culture in the UK is diverse and we are proud to call ourselves multicultural but in sport there are still examples and practices that move against the sense of **sports equity**. In many ways, sport is a reflection of our society, with norms and values that are historical and cultural.

case study
5.2

Kick racism out of football

'Kick racism out of football' was a slogan adopted by a campaign started in 1993 to cut racial harassment in football by fans and players. The Commission for Racial Equality (CRE) and the Professional Footballers Association (PFA) both backed the campaign.

activity
INDIVIDUAL WORK

1. How can a slogan help to combat racism and encourage participation?

2. Besides racial harassment, what other barriers hinder black players and stop them becoming managers, for example?

A process of **socialisation** can steer us towards certain sports, for instance girls towards netball and dance, boys towards football and wrestling. This makes sports equity very difficult, because there are many social pressures that obstruct a boy who wants to do ballet or a girl who wants to play rugby.

There are also economic barriers to sport. Many people cannot afford the equipment, facilities or membership fees to participate. Some people find it difficult to participate because they cannot afford time away from work and family commitments.

Other barriers to participation

Time

Many people decide not to participate in sport because of work commitments. It is common to hear them say, 'I haven't got the time.' This is legitimate but their perception of their available time is often different from the reality. Getting home from college and watching television all evening is a way of spending your leisure time. A person who does this clearly has some leisure time but they choose to watch television instead of doing a sport.

Figure 5.6 Socialisation can steer boys towards traditionally male activities

Resources

Perhaps you have sports facilities or sports clubs nearby, but it will depend on where you live. The distance to sports facilities and sports clubs has a big effect on whether people participate. One way of increasing participation for people without facilities nearby would be to provide a good transport service to a distant sports facility.

Figure 5.7 Couch potatoes rarely do sport in their leisure time

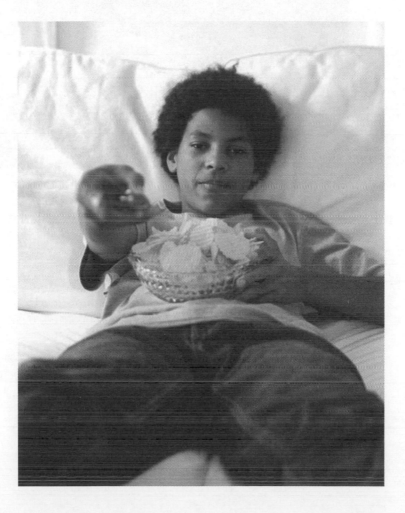

Fitness and ability

Some people think they are not good enough to join in sports activities. This view of themselves may well have arisen from previous experiences, perhaps at school. They may have failed in an activity then felt humiliated and ever after they have seen themselves as a hopeless case. Psychologists call this feeling *learned helplessness*.

Learned helplessness

Learned helplessness is a psychological phenomenon that arises when a person fails on a task and has the failure reinforced. The person then avoids that task and may often say something like this: 'I was hopeless at sport when I was at school, so it's no good me trying again as I'll only fail.'

Figure 5.8 Some opt out of sport because they feel hopeless at it

To overcome this feeling of helplessness and regain confidence, the person needs to experience success in some aspect of sport. After all, it's extremely unlikely they will feel a failure at every sport.

Crime

Reports commissioned by Sport England in 2002 showed that sport is getting youngsters away from crime and helping fight drug abuse. According to these reports, since the first sport development worker was appointed, there has been a 40% reduction in crime levels on Bristol's Southmead estate.

Peer pressure

Peer pressure is a big influence on young people. If you're a young person and your peers do not value sport, it may be very hard for you to value sport. This can form a real barrier to participation. Sport can be a social activity but it can also be isolating if your friends do not value your sport and reinforce non-participation. Thankfully there are many people, young and old, that do value sports participation and who can encourage their peers to participate fully.

Some sports may have more peer group support than others. For example, a group of males may value traditionally male sports such as rugby and football but may not put much value on gymnastics. A group of girls may support each other in traditionally female activities such as dance but may offer less support to one of their friends playing women's football.

Health problems

Some people have health problems that prevent their participation in sport, although many medical practitioners encourage an active lifestyle as much as possible. Most rehabilitation regimes include physical exercise, and sport is an ideal way. There is an increase in obesity in the western world due to our diets and lack of exercise. Embarrassment is a powerful emotion that prevents many people taking the first step to try a sport. People that experience embarrassment need encouragement and the right environment to help them get involved. Joining clubs such as Weight Watchers can encourage some people to take exercise, which may lead to participation in a sport. Others disagree; they say that joining a weight-loss group is demeaning and only reinforces a person's lack of self-esteem. Lack of self-esteem has to be tackled before a person can gain the confidence needed to join other people and participate in sport.

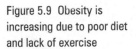

See page 85 in Unit 3 for more information on obesity

Figure 5.9 Obesity is increasing due to poor diet and lack of exercise

Access

Growth in sports facilities has increased access and more low-cost courses are available, but some people still do not have enough money to participate in sport. Here are the most important questions that influence access for many people:

- What is available?
- What is affordable?
- How do I feel about myself?

This is sometimes expressed in three words: *provision*, *opportunity*, *esteem*. Here are the main issues related to access and some examples:

- **Opening times** – may not be convenient for shift workers.
- **Age** – sport is often perceived as a young person's activity and the elderly may feel undignified if they participate.
- **Race** – experiencing racial discrimination may be a reason for lack of confidence to get involved in a predominantly white environment such as a golf club. For example, in Luton a participant's ethnic origin is a huge influence on their choice of sport. Just 2% of Pakistani residents go swimming, compared with 36% of white and Indian people.

Figure 5.10 Racial discrimination should not be a barrier to participation

- **Class** – participation in polo is often by people from the upper middle classes. It is perceived as a posh person's sport.
- **Disability** – facilities may be lacking, such as wheelchair ramps, or inadequate, such as doors that are too narrow.

 See page 273 in Unit 11 for more information on barriers to participation

Figure 5.11 Polo is often seen as a posh person's sport

case study
5.3

Low incomes

People on low incomes living in a disadvantaged community in the north of England demonstrate some of the lowest levels of sports participation ever measured. Some 71% of people from social group DE take part in at least one sport, but in Liverpool it is only 51%. In Bradford, the proportion of children swimming, cycling or walking is less than half the national average. Some 43% of British children play cricket, but in Liverpool only 3% of children play cricket. Yet in Bradford, Liverpool and similar areas the vast majority of children have a very positive view about the value of sport.

activity
INDIVIDUAL WORK

1. Why do low incomes make it difficult for people to participate in sport?
2. What strategies could you use to increase sports participation in low-income areas?

Write a newspaper report as part of a campaign to increase participation and performance in sport. Describe the barriers to participation for individuals from three different target groups. Mention the different levels of the sports development continuum.

Target groups

Effective sports development identifies target groups then develops strategies to increase their sports participation and make it more equal with the rest of society. UK sports organisations have identified groups of people where sports participation is comparatively low.

Sport has a big role in promoting the inclusion of all groups in society. Yet inequalities still exist in sport and are largely the result of cultural influences that go way back into history. There are inequalities of gender, race and disability. Male-dominated sports, such as rugby, were first played at public schools or in male-dominated environments. Rugby is now played by increasing numbers of women but very few rugby coaches are women.

The Macpherson Report on the death of Stephen Lawrence, the success of UK Paralympians, high-profile campaigns such as Let's Kick Racism Out of Football, the Brighton Declaration on Women and Sport, and the evident multiculturalism in British society all highlight the need for more equality of opportunity in sport.

Black Information Link – more information related to the Macpherson Inquiry
www.blink.org.uk

BBC Sport – more information on UK Paralympians
www.bbc.co.uk/sport

Kick It Out – challenges racism throughout the football, educational and community sectors
www.kickitout.org

sportdevelopment.org.uk – the library contains more on the Brighton Declaration on Women and Sport
www.sportdevelopment.org.uk

These groups are generally recognised as being under-represented in sport:

- Black and ethnic minority (BEM) communities
- Disabled people
- Women
- People over age 50
- Young people.

They are not the only groups that are under-represented. Equity concerns fairness and access for all. In sport, as in all society, many individuals and particular groups may feel they are victims of discrimination.

Sports equity

Sports equity is concerned with fairness in sport, equality of access, recognising inequalities and taking steps to address them. It is about changing the culture and structure of sport so it becomes equally accessible to all members of society, whatever their age, ability, gender, race, ethnicity, sexuality or socio-economic status. Sports equity, then, is more concerned with the sport itself.

Figure 5.12 Wider accessibility will require sports to change their culture and structure

The funding agreement between sports authorities and the government has a commitment to ensure that sports governing bodies are 'modernised'. This includes modernising how they address equal opportunities and having minority groups represented among their staff.

activity
GROUP WORK
5.3

M2

Prepare and give a presentation explaining the barriers to participation for individuals from three different target groups at different levels of the sports development continuum.

Methods of development for target groups

For foundation and participation on the sports development continuum

- Use images and photos that illustrate the range of participants currently involved in the sport.
- Run stories and articles in governing body publications that address equity in sport from positive and negative standpoints.
- Get senior sporting figures to make a public statement about how they are going to improve equity in sport.
- Endorse an overall sports equity statement as well as specific equity policy statements for the priority groups – ethnic minorities, disabled people and women.
- Allocate financial resources to equity planning.

For disability sport

- Promote the inclusion of disabled people in the mainstream programmes of national governing bodies of sport, local authorities and other providers.

- Increase funding.

- Raise the profile of sport for disabled people.

For women in sport

- Statistics reveal some inequalities, particularly in the higher levels of coaching and administration.

- Female athletes made up 40% of the British team at the 1996 Olympic Games yet only 11% of coaches were women.

See page 272 in Unit 11 for more information on different groups and their participation in sport

Active Communities

Active Communities is a project aimed at increasing sporting opportunities for priority target groups that have had relatively low levels of participation in sport.

case study **Active Communities**

5.4

Active Communities is a framework of services, products and funding streams provided by Sport England, often in partnership with other organisations and agencies. It assists individuals and organisations to create their own active communities. Five headings reflect the most important issues leading to the development of an active community:

- Promote social justice

- Increase participation in sport

- Develop community sports leaders

- Develop community sports programmes and facilities

- Plan for sport and recreation.

Active Communities brings together the first two stated aims of Sport England's mission statement: to provide opportunities for more people to take part in sport, and to provide more places for people to play sport in their communities. The third aim – to improve standards of performance to help English players win more medals – relies on the successful development of sport in UK communities. According to Sport England, Active Communities is designed to help 'increase and sustain lifelong participation in sport and recreation, and to promote continuous improvement in the delivery of sporting opportunities and services at a local level for all the community'.

activity

INDIVIDUAL WORK

1. What are the three main aims in Sport England's mission statement?

2. How would you use the active communities framework to increase participation in your area?

Gender equity

The Brighton Declaration on Women and Sport provided some principles to increase women's involvement and participation. Here are a few examples:

- Increase awareness of the issues surrounding women's and girls' involvement in sport.
- Support women and girls to become involved in sport at all levels and in all capacities.
- Encourage organisations to improve access to sporting opportunities for women and girls.
- Challenge instances of inequality found in sport and seek to bring about change.
- Raise the visibility of all British sportswomen.

Figure 5.13 The Brighton Declaration proposed principles to get more women into sport

In 1999 the Women's Sports Foundation (WSF) launched a framework that 'aims to create a positive environment in which all women and girls have an equal opportunity and adequate resources to be involved in all areas of physical activity and sport at their chosen level'.

Other strategies for gender equity

- Provide gender awareness training for governing body coaches, leaders and organisers.
- Establish a programme of courses that will recruit women into the management of sport.
- Raise the profile of women in officiating.
- Give financial support to top women athletes so they are on a par with their male counterparts.

case study 5.5 — Sexist protest over women officials

Mike Newell, when he was manager of Luton Town FC, nicknamed the Hatters, told a post-match press conference that Amy Rayner's appointment as a match official was tokenism and political correctness: 'Rayner shouldn't be here. I know that sounds sexist, but I am sexist.' The Hatters' boss claimed that bringing women into the game wasn't the way to improve refereeing and officialdom, and wondered how long it would be before all officials were women.

activity
INDIVIDUAL WORK

1. What sexist attitudes can you find in the above account?
2. This may be one way of raising the profile of women officials, but what other ways are there?

Get Set Go!

Get Set Go! is a personal development programme set up by the WSF. It helps women into sports leadership as coaches, administrators or officials. Governing bodies can identify women for these courses to encourage individuals in coaching and leadership roles.

Performance and excellence

There have been many initiatives by government and sports organisations, such as *Sport England* and *CCPR*, to improve all levels of sports performance from the basics to elite competition. Here are some important initiatives.

High-performance coaching

High-performance coaching (HPC) is run by Sports Coach UK. If you are a coach working in or towards national and international level, you can use the resources and support from HPC. Sports Coach UK work in partnership with other organisations such as the *British Olympic Association* (BOA).

UK Sport – manages and distributes public investment, a statutory distributor of funds raised by the National Lottery

www.uksport.gov.uk

Sports Coach UK – a charitable organisation that develops coaches and coaching throughout the UK

www.sportscoachuk.org

Olympic Movement

www.olympic.org/uk/index_uk.asp

UK Sports Institute

The UK Sports Institute is a network of centres and experts that support the UK's top sportspeople. It is made up of four sports institutes in England, Scotland, Wales and Northern Ireland, plus a central services team in London that is part of UK Sport.

The aim of the UK Sports Institute is to provide elite sportspeople with the support services and facilities they need to compete and win at the highest level. The services are provided locally, where athletes live, work and train.

The central services team provides these services directly to sports: the Athlete Medical Scheme, research and technical development, sports science, sports medicine, performance planning and guidance. There is also IT advice, education and training. The central services team is responsible for the ACE UK athlete career and education programme and the world-class coaching programme.

The English Institute of Sport (EIS) is a network of training facilities and services for elite athletes, managed by nine regional institute boards. A total of £120 million from the Sport England Lottery Fund is being spent on developing 80 built facilities, including centres at the Universities of Bath, Loughborough and East Anglia, as well as bases in Manchester, Sheffield, Gateshead, Lilleshall, Bisham Abbey, Holme Pierrepont and London.

World Class Events Programme

The World Class Events Programme is a UK Sport initiative that spends lottery money on attracting the world's top sporting events. Since 1997 it has supported over 70 world, European and Commonwealth sports events throughout the UK. Each year, UK Sport invests £25 million of lottery funding in world-class programmes and approximately £1.6 million of this goes on world-class major events in the UK. Apart from a few exceptions, the programme supports events on a one-off basis, so that the same events do not receive awards time after time.

Sports colleges

Under a government initiative, some schools are recognised as having expertise in areas such as languages, performing arts and sport. Sports colleges have expertise in sport. They have to develop their links with outside agencies and create an extensive extracurricular programme that includes links with external clubs.

Youth Sport Trust

www.youthsporttrust.org

Specialist Schools and Academies Trust

www.specialistschools.org.uk

Sport England

www.sportengland.org

Figure 5.14 Sports colleges must have extensive links to external sports clubs

activity

INDIVIDUAL WORK 5.4

D1

1. Write a briefing paper analysing the barriers to participation for individuals from three different target groups at different levels of the sports development continuum.

2. Identify and present three effective and realistic solutions to overcome the barriers to participation in a sport of your choice.

Know about key providers of sports development

Main activity providers

- National organisations
- Governing bodies
- Voluntary organisations
- Private sector providers
- Professional providers.

Examples of national organisations are Sport England, Sports Coach UK, the Youth Sport Trust. Local authorities also provide activities; the relevant local authority for the Blackpool area is Lancashire County Council. Governing bodies may be international, national, regional or local.

This section describes an example for each type of provider, giving its structure and its role in sports development. These descriptions will be very useful when you come to evaluate providers.

UK Sport and Sport England

UK Sport

The national sports councils were formed in 1972 and deemed to be independent from the government. They were reorganised to create UK Sport in 1996. UK Sport is as an agency under government direction to provide support for elite sportspeople who have a high level of performance or the potential to reach the top. It distributes government funds, including lottery money, supports world-class performers and promotes ethical standards of behaviour. It has an anti-doping programme to detect the use of performance-enhancing drugs.

UK Sport oversees the work of the four home-country sports councils:

- Sport England
- Sportscotland
- Sports Council for Northern Ireland
- Sports Council for Wales.

---

case study 5.6

Sport England

Sport England was created to give opportunities for people to start in sport, stay in sport and succeed in sport. It is responsible for delivering the government's sporting objectives and works on strategies to make England more active. It encourages people to get involved with sport and physical activity. Sport England distributes funding and invests in a range of sporting projects, including the Active England fund.

Sport England is divided into six working units: the main board and five committees. The main board used to be called the council. It has overall responsibility for the performance of Sport England. It deals with strategy, finance, major projects and performance management. The committees have responsibility for specific tasks and strategies or policies. They report to the main board. The five committees are audit, risk and governance; national investment; marketing and commercial; equity; and staffing and remuneration.

activity
INDIVIDUAL WORK

1. What are the main responsibilities of Sport England?
2. How does Sport England help sports development?

Sport England
www.sportengland.org

Sports Coach UK

Sports Coach UK is a charitable organisation that develops coaches and coaching throughout the UK.

case study
5.7

Sports Coach UK

At a ceremony at Twickenham rugby ground on Monday 11 December 2000, Sports Coach UK became the first sporting organisation to be recognised for its achievements in racial equality by completing the preliminary level of the standard. Four governing bodies of sport were also recognised: cricket, rugby union, rugby league and basketball. To achieve the preliminary level, Sports Coach UK had to commit and show evidence of having:

- made a clear public commitment to achieving racial equality at the highest level;

- developed a written statement or policy on racial equality which links to the governing bodies' aims and objectives;

- developed racial equality action plans or objectives within existing statements and set appropriate racial equality targets;

- communicated the racial equality policy and action plan to all involved in development and delivery of the sport.

activity
INDIVIDUAL WORK

1. How has Sports Coach UK helped in the development of sport?
2. This case study has a big impact on several aspects of the sports development continuum. Which aspects?

Youth Sport Trust

The Youth Sport Trust (YST) was established in 1994 to build a better future for all young people through PE and school sport. A registered charity, it began by providing equipment and resources to help teachers deliver high-quality PE and sport in primary schools. Later it expanded into creating a sporting pathway for all young people aged 18 months to 18 years.

YST believes in these rights for young people:

- **The right to experience and enjoy PE and sport** – YST works with the government, corporate partners and schools to develop educational resources, environments and opportunities for young people.

- **The right to be introduced to PE and sport at a level that suits them** – YST's TOP programmes help young people access quality PE and sport at all stages from early years to secondary school.

- **The right to experience and benefit from positive competition** – YST works with these bodies to help young people benefit from competitive activities: national governing bodies of sport (NGBs), national school sport associations, the National Council of School Sport, Sport England.

- **The right to develop a healthy lifestyle** – YST tries to increase young people's involvement in PE and school sport and supports and encourages them to become more active. Some say this makes a major contribution to the health of the nation.

- The right to progress along a structured pathway of sporting opportunities – YST works to enhance the provision for young people to experience and actively engage in sporting opportunities beyond the school day.

- The right to fulfil their sporting potential – in the run-up to London 2012, YST is working to help young people fulfil their sporting potential as performers and as leaders.

Figure 5.15 The YST tries to increase young people's involvement in PE and school sport

 See page 253 in Unit 11 for more information on sports organisations

Local authorities and sports development

Local authorities recognise the benefits of developing sport for their citizens. They follow the national lead in developing sport for healthy living and its many social and community benefits. Sport plays an important part in raising self-esteem and local authorities develop sport to ensure an overall better quality of life. Local authorities consider their own participation trends in sport and they target their resources and expertise to rectify apparent imbalances in participation rates. This local approach under a national umbrella is a trend to ensure inclusion; in other words, it tries to include people in sport rather than to exclude them from participating.

Best Value

Best Value is an initiative behind the Active Communities programme of Sport England. It aims to improve the provision of sport opportunities for all the community. This aim was encouraged by government policy for modernising local government, set out in the 1998 White Paper *Modernising Local Government: In Touch with the People*. Best Value was designed to improve how local authorities deliver sport to their local communities. According to Sport England, the crucial ingredients of delivering Best Value are the four Cs: challenge, consult, compare and compete.

The value of sport

In its 1999 publication *The Value of Sport*, Sport England highlights the key role of the public sector in enabling and providing sport at the local level. It actively champions the benefits and contribution that sport can make to the broader local authority policy agenda, including health, education, social inclusion, community safety, community regeneration, the economy and the environment.

Methods for sports development

Local authority sports development policies contain a variety of methods to promote and develop sport right across the sports development continuum. Local authorities will support local schools and colleges with help and advice from **sports development officers**. Local authorities also help local organisations to develop sports facilities by giving them financial help and expert advice on strategy and building regulations. Local

---

case study 5.8

Sports development at Birmingham City Council

Sports development officers (SDOs) are personally involved in providing daily and weekly sessions in a wide range of sports, delivering new opportunities and maintaining community sports activities around the city. The city council is committed to increasing opportunities for people from under-represented groups within the community. Women and girls, people from ethnic minority groups and people with disabilities are a focus at all levels of sports development work.

The city council set out to increase participation and develop sporting skills and it recognises that this requires committed, well-trained coaches, teachers and instructors. It is involved in the organisation of a wide range of courses and seminars for coaches at all levels. Particular emphasis is placed on vocational qualifications through links with governing bodies of sport, colleges and training agencies.

The city council views sports development as working with others to form partnerships. The council works with voluntary organisations and statutory bodies to develop sport and events of special interest for the people of Birmingham. There is a network of strong partnerships, working together with voluntary sporting organisations. Key partners include the Sports Council, the National Coaching Foundation, the Central Council for Physical Recreation, governing bodies of sport, Birmingham Sports Advisory Council and several organisations in Birmingham's business community. The sport development team has focused on the sports development continuum:

- **Foundation** – work in association with clubs and schools developing sporting skills with children of primary school age. The acquisition of good exercise habits provides a basis for personal development and future participation in sport.

- **Participation** – sports clubs and other voluntary organisations are the essential partners in creating a wide participation level for all ages, if only for reasons of enjoyment, fitness or a simple desire to get involved in sport. The development of school–club links and the process of supporting community sports clubs with the help of leisure centre managers is an important part of the council's strategy.

- **Performance** – coaching schemes are an essential part of sports development in Birmingham, providing opportunities for participants to achieve their potential and obtain fulfilment and enjoyment from improving their performance. School holiday courses, weekly sessions and close links with local governing bodies of sport are a strong feature at this level.

- **Excellence** – the council runs sports development–led programmes and, more particularly, it has created partnerships to provide increased opportunities for participants of national and international calibre to emerge.

---

activity
INDIVIDUAL WORK

1. What is the role of this provider related to the participant level of the sports development continuum?

2. What are the main focus groups for this provider?

authorities often run coach education programmes, including coaching courses at all levels. To increase participation and interest in sport, they run taster sessions in sports, summer schools, and competitions and tournaments in a wide variety of sports. These sports development methods are often targeted at the groups highlighted earlier (page 158), including disaffected youth to encourage social inclusion.

National governing bodies

Most sports that we know today were developed and organised in the late nineteenth century. The participants needed to agree rules and regulations for their sports, so they met and formed their own committees called national governing bodies (NGBs), such as the *Football Association* (FA), the *Lawn Tennis Association* (LTA), the *Amateur Swimming Association* (ASA) and the *Rugby Football Union* (RFU). There are over 265 governing bodies in the UK. The teams and clubs then pay a subscription to the governing body. They in turn administer the sport nationally, organise competitions and organise the national team. There are still many amateur positions in each governing body, but increasing numbers of staff are paid a salary.

Figure 5.16 Rugby union is played to RFU rules

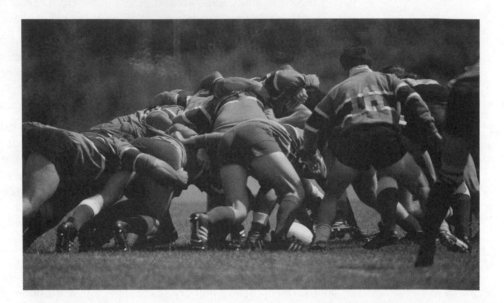

The NGBs are also members of international governing bodies, such as the Union of European Football Associations (UEFA) and the Fédération Internationale de Football Association (FIFA). These international bodies control and organise international competitions.

Figure 5.17 International football may be organised by FIFA

Strength

case study 5.9

Sports development at the British Judo Association

The British Judo Association (BJA) club recognition scheme was introduced to recognise and reward examples of good practice in judo clubs. It will also spread best practice in management and coaching across the country.

An integral part of this scheme is the Sport England Clubmark, created in partnership with national governing bodies with the aim of accrediting sports clubs that are committed to providing a safe and effective environment suitable for children and young people. Although the Sport England Clubmark specifically recognises clubs that work with children and young people, the BJA has developed its recognition scheme as a whole-club development programme. This means that it is also relevant to those working with adults and is comprehensive, regardless of membership size, facility status or how often the club meets.

Figure 5.18 The BJA has a scheme to reward good practice in judo clubs

The scheme has three levels: bronze, silver and gold. Working through the scheme, a club is able to provide the best quality of service to members by creating a specifically trained workforce of coaches, officials and administrators. This will also ensure the club is best placed to develop judo opportunities in partnership with local agencies, such as local authorities. This is an example of a governing body developing its sport from the foundation level all the way to excellence.

activity
INDIVIDUAL WORK

1. How has this governing body ensured that its sport continues to be developed?
2. What partnerships have been used to deliver this development?

Institute for Sport, Parks and Leisure – more examples of governing body schemes
www.ispal.org.uk

Voluntary organisations

The voluntary sector is the largest in UK sport. It has long been the backbone of sport in the UK and only very recently has sport taken on a much more professional footing. However, volunteers and their organisations continue to be very important in running sport across the UK. It is estimated that there are over 6 million people in sport's voluntary sector. The people who work in these organisations such as hockey clubs, rambling organisations and climbing associations are rarely paid and the organisations are not profit-making. Many voluntary organisations try to make some money so their activities can be improved and expanded but no individual makes a profit. These voluntary organisations rely on public and private funds to survive.

See page 258 in Unit 11 for more information on voluntary organisations and other sports organisations

The role of voluntary organisations in sports development is that they often support local needs. For example, a local athletics club tries to get as many people as possible involved in athletics and tries to attract people of different ages and from different socio-economic backgrounds. It enters a team in the local leagues and holds training sessions for its members.

Figure 5.19 Athletics clubs often help with sports development for all ages

Private sector

The private sector provides sport, often according to local needs. It is involved in sports development by getting as many involved as possible, to raise attendance levels and improve profits. Unlike a voluntary organisation, a private organisation aims to make money for the organisation and the people who run it. An example of a private club is a health and fitness club that provides the equipment, health and fitness instruction, and often beauty treatments as well as personal training, an increasingly important area.

activity

GROUP WORK 5.5

P3

Make three poster presentations, one on each of three sports development providers in the UK. Each presentation should describe the structures and roles of the provider.

Other sports development organisations

National Association for Sports Development

The National Association for Sports Development (NASD) was created on 1 April 2000 to provide support and professional development for sports development workers. It worked in partnership with the Institute of Sport and Recreation Management (ISRM) until September 2006, when it was united with the Institute of Leisure and Amenity Management (ILAM) to create the Institute for Sport, Parks and Leisure (ISPAL).

English Federation for Disability Sport

The English Federation for Disability Sport (EFDS) is a national body that develops sport for people with disabilities in England. It works closely with other national disability organisations recognised by Sport England:

- British Amputee & Les Autres Sports Association
- British Blind Sport
- British Deaf Sports Council
- British Wheelchair Sports Foundation
- Cerebral Palsy Sport
- Disability Sport England
- English Sports Association for People with Learning Disabilities.

EFDS has a four-year national plan, *Building a Fairer Sporting Society*, which outlines the inclusion of disabled people in the identified national priority sports of athletics, boccia, cricket, football, goalball and swimming. It is also involved in the development of coach education and training opportunities that are accessible to disabled people and cover the technical issues of coaching disabled people.

Here are the objectives of EDFS:

- The creation of programmes for grass-roots participation by disabled people.
- The delivery of a rationalised programme of championships and events for disabled people.
- The establishment of a talent identification system for disabled players and athletes.
- The establishment of regional and national training squads for disabled players and athletes.

Disability Sport
www.disabilitysport.org.uk
English Federation of Disability Sport
www.efds.net
Disability View – online magazine
www.disabilityview.co.uk
Disability Now – online disability-related newspaper
www.disabilitynow.org.uk
Youreable.com – information, products and services for disabled people
www.youreable.com

Figure 5.20 EFDS develops sport for people with disabilities

Sports development officers

Sports development officers aim to improve access to sport and physical activity and develop interest in them. They organise sporting projects, information and training for competitive and leisure participants to increase levels of participation in all areas of society and all cultures.

The role involves working in partnership with a wide range of organisations to use local resources efficiently and to develop regional and national initiatives.

The role often involves:

- promoting sport and health in general
- developing a specific sport, known as *sport-specific development officers*
- the development of disability awareness within sport.

Sports development officers often get involved in a range of activities, such as:

- identifying sport, recreation and health initiatives
- overseeing strategic planning and implementation
- coordinating and delivering relevant activities and events
- employing and training coaches, volunteer staff, etc.
- evaluating and monitoring activities using performance indicators
- maintaining records and producing written reports
- attending local, regional and national meetings, seminars and conferences
- checking venues
- promoting events
- liaising with clubs, schools, professional bodies and sports governing bodies
- developing a range of partnerships to enhance provision and support
- managing resources and a budget
- identifying potential opportunities for external funding
- maintaining links with county, regional and national sporting representatives
- working within organisation guidelines, e.g. equal opportunities, health and safety
- occasionally offering coaching, where coaching awards are held.

A specialised post, such as a disability sports development officer, may also involve:

- training and educating coaches, volunteers and facilities staff in disability issues (experts in disability awareness may well be called on, where appropriate)
- using information and publicity to ensure people with disabilities are more aware of the sporting opportunities available to them

- organising sport-specific activities
- maintaining inclusiveness on the agenda
- encouraging and motivating participants to gain coaching qualifications, so that developments are sustainable.

---

case study

5.10

SDO conditions of service

The hours of a sports development officer (SDO) may vary from week to week. There will be some unsocial hours to cover times when most people are able to take part in leisure activities. SDOs may be based in an office during the day, carrying out the administrative part of the job, and spend the evenings and weekends visiting community groups, schools, events, sports venues and meetings.

The work involves a lot of local travel for SDOs and regional travel for sport-specific development officers (SSDOs), so a driving licence is likely to be required. Although SDOs will not usually join in the activities they have organised, they may have to be present to ensure they run smoothly. This can involve being outside in all weathers. Salaries vary depending on experience and on the specific job, but just as a guide, they may be between £16000 and £25000 per year.

---

activity

GROUP WORK

1. Why do SDOs often work unsocial hours?
2. Suggest the three most important aspects of sports development in the work of an SDO?

---

activity

INDIVIDUAL WORK

5.6

M3

Choose three sports development providers and write a detailed evaluation of their structures, functions and roles.

Understand how quality is measured in sports development

Methods of measuring quality

Quest

Quest is the UK quality scheme for sport and leisure. It originated in the early 1990s through the British Quality Association Leisure Services Subcommittee, chaired by the Sports Council, which became UK Sport. After a feasibility study commissioned by the Sports Council, the subcommittee identified very strong support for a sport- and leisure-specific scheme that set clear standards and encouraged continuous improvement.

The standards were widely consulted on and the scheme was rigorously piloted before it was launched in September 1996. Quest is endorsed and financed by the four home-country Sports Councils and supported by a wide range of industry organisations. The development of quality standards for service delivery in sports development was crucial to continuous improvement and self-assessment.

The *Model Survey Package* is a guidance manual produced by Sport England that assists local authorities in carrying out market research in their localities. It gives practical guidance on how to carry out statistically sound surveys of sports facility customers and people using parks and other outdoor recreation sites, and how to do household surveys.

case study 5.11

The best SDU in the country

A sports development unit (SDU) was recognised as the highest-scoring sports development team in the country, topping the table with an impressive Quest rating of 84%. The way it delivers sports development is in four different strands: schools, community, sports, health.

There is a sports development manager and four senior sports development officers (SDOs); each senior SDO looks after one of the four disciplines. There are 12 SDOs, all externally funded. The first steps along the path of continuous improvement towards Quest accreditation began with best value. This process, which required all local authority departments to question the fundamental principles behind their service delivery, proved to be a highly effective tool for the sports development unit.

The unit has a vision of continuous improvement that encourages everyone to get involved, everyone to take responsibility for their own success and everyone to enjoy being part of a successful team that wins recognition for its achievements. The Quest process has also made a difference to some individual management styles. It makes you think about how you deal with people and how decisions are made that affect not only your team but the wider community you're working with. Key decisions are made by the team, and the leadership is democratic.

activity
INDIVIDUAL WORK

1. What is the meaning of 'best value'?
2. Why did this sports development unit receive a high Quest rating?

Here are some criteria used by many organisations for assessing their own effectiveness:

- **Value for money** – a cost-benefit analysis is based on financial and human resources using objective measures for the costs and rewards. The problem is that many rewards, e.g. participation rates, may not be obvious and may also have an effect in the long term rather than the short term.

- **Achievement of aims and objectives** – all sports organisations have stated aims and objectives, which are largely measurable. There are normally short-, medium- and long-term assessments of these aims and objectives.

 Link

See page 98 in Unit 3 for more information on goals and goal setting

- **Consultation** – feedback on performance is not necessarily about statistics related to success and participation rates. There can also be some very useful feedback from officers of the organisations, other partner agencies as well as the sports participants and the general public. This can take the form of a questionnaire or an interview. Many organisations hire a market research team to gather relevant information in a valid and reliable way.

remember

To obtain reliable feedback there needs to be wide consultation between all those involved in sports development.

Investors in People

The performance of a sports organisation can be measured using Investors in People (IiP) standards. Here are the characteristics of an organisation that fulfils the requirements of the IiP award:

- A strategy for improving the performance of the organisation is clearly defined and understood.
- Learning and development are planned to achieve the organisation's objectives.
- Strategies for managing people are designed to promote quality of opportunity in the development of the organisation's people.
- The capabilities required by managers to lead, manage and develop people effectively are clearly defined and understood.
- Managers are effective in leading, managing and developing people.
- People's contributions to the organisation are recognised and valued.
- People are encouraged to take ownership and responsibility by being involved in decision-making.
- People learn and develop effectively.
- Investment in people improves the performance of the organisation.
- Improvements are continually made to the way people are managed and developed.

Figure 5.21 How IiP improves performance. Courtesy Investors in People

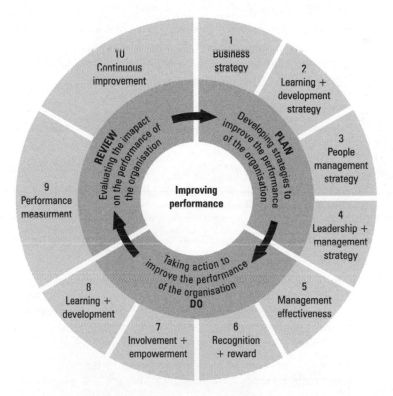

Investors in People UK
www.iipuk.co.uk

case study
5.12

Sports organisations invest in people

London Sports Forum for Disabled People is a registered charity promoting the sporting interests of disabled young people and adults in the area. Its purpose is to ensure that all disabled people, including people with learning disabilities, physical impairments, visual impairments and hearing impairments, have more opportunities to get involved in sport and physical activity at a level of their choice.

The forum enables participation, promotes the sporting interests and needs of disabled people, and works to enable organisations and groups to improve opportunities across the whole of the area. Its track record of excellent and effective management was recognised in 2006 when it received accreditation from Investors in People (IiP). The IiP accreditation recognises the effective structures that guide the forum's work and that help ensure its staff receive the development and guidance they need to continue working towards their vision of sport achieving equality.

The IiP award recognises the quality of this organisation in four key areas:

- **Commitment** – an Investor in People is fully committed to developing its people in order to achieve its aims and objectives.

- **Planning** – an Investor in People is clear about its aims and its objectives and what its people need to do to achieve them.

- **Action** – an Investor in People develops its people effectively in order to improve its performance.

- **Evaluation** – an Investor in People understands the impact of its investment in people on its performance.

activity
INDIVIDUAL WORK

1. What aspects of the forum's work are recognised by IiP accreditation?
2. What aspects of the sports development continuum are covered by the forum?
3. Undergoing IiP assessment could have disadvantages for the forum. Suggest some of these disadvantages.

Charter Mark

Figure 5.22 Charter Mark is a quality award for public services

Charter Mark is a government quality award for public services that can prove excellence in customer services. It is awarded for three years with annual maintenance visits to ensure compliance. It can help everyone in a sports development organisation to improve customer service. Organisations that achieve the standard are permitted to display the Charter Mark logo.

An organisation has to provide evidence, which is then qualified to make sure the organisation reaches Charter Mark standards. Six areas are investigated:

- Set standards and perform well
- Actively engage with your customers, partners and staff
- Be fair and accessible to everyone and promote choice
- Continuously develop and improve
- Use your resources effectively and imaginatively
- Continue to improve opportunities and quality of life in the communities you serve.

case study

5.13

Assessment by Charter Mark

Assessment for the UK government's Charter Mark lasted for two days, although the assessor had already spoken to many partner organisations before he even began the on-site visit. It was an extremely vigorous and exhausting assessment, where the sports development unit had to go through all 63 criteria and give evidence to justify how they met Charter Mark's standards. The assessment also included interviews with staff and users, visits to sessions in a variety of settings around the borough, and face-to-face interviews with other partners.

activity
INDIVIDUAL WORK

1. How could an organisation concerned with sports development show evidence of engaging actively with customers?

2. How might an organisation concerned with sports development show that they are being fair and accessible to everyone and that they promote choice?

Clubmark

According to Sport England, about 60% of young people belong to a sports club outside school. Sport England views the influence of sports clubs as being crucial for the development of talent within a safe setting.

Clubmark is Sport England's quality accreditation for clubs with junior sections, across all sports. The national governing bodies (NGBs) accredit clubs that comply with minimum standards in these four areas:

- The playing or participation programme
- Duty of care and child protection
- Sports equity and ethics
- Club management.

Clubmark accreditation is designed to demonstrate to partners, parents and young people that Clubmark-accredited clubs treat young people well. This accreditation also encourages clubs to enthuse young people to be active and to enjoy a healthy lifestyle. Clubs are also encouraged to enable young people to use their leisure time with creativity and to make the most of their sporting talents. Clubmark also recognises clubs that identify and support the development of the most talented young sportspeople.

Over 2000 accredited clubs have been awarded Clubmark in over 20 sports. Sport England aims to increase the number of accredited clubs to 5000 by 2012. To maintain high standards, all organisations involved in awarding Clubmark accreditation have been required to have a licence since March 2006.

Introducing Clubmark – more information on Clubmark and case studies on its holders

www.clubmark.org.uk

NGB schemes

National governing bodies (NGBs) of sports have developed schemes to maintain the quality of their sports development. Swim 21 is an example.

case study 5.14

Clubmark

A sports club wanted to be seen as giving high-quality coaching and applied for Clubmark. All members of the club had to work as a team to be accredited. This included coaches, players and parents or carers. The club put together a portfolio of their work, called a Clubmark folder. The club obtained templates from the Clubmark website. All members were given a membership pack with clear guidelines and players were issued with identity cards. This showed that members were well guided and supported and that there was rigorous checking of adults who were working with young people. The club was successful in attaining the award and can advertise its Clubmark accreditation. Accreditation means the club can apply for more funding and has given its staff greater pride in their work.

activity
GROUP WORK

1. What are the main benefits of Clubmark accreditation?
2. Clubmark accreditation is based on what criteria?

Swim 21

The Amateur Swimming Association (ASA) launched Swim 21 in 2002 and amended it at the beginning of 2006. It aims to accredit 800 clubs by March 2009. Swim 21 links with Sport England's Clubmark scheme and is the ASA's quality mark for clubs across its aquatic activities. It was developed for clubs to help athletes, teachers, coaches and administrators achieve their full potential. It focuses on the needs of athletes and aims to give them the best possible support and environment.

Swim 21 is a quality accreditation. It recognises nationally and regionally the clubs that are committed to providing safe, effective and quality services to their members. Clubs that wish to gain this quality award should be able to show quality in one or more of these areas:

- Teaching
- Skill development
- Competitive development
- Performance.

Here are some of the benefits of NGB accreditation such as Swim 21:

- Publicity, promotion, recognition and profile
- More members
- More coaches
- More officials and volunteers
- Increased opportunity to secure funding
- A more organised and better-resourced club
- School–club links
- Greater support from the NGB
- Club sustainability and development
- Participants and players make achievements and develop.

Amateur Swimming Association – more details on Swim 21
www.britishswimming.org

activity
GROUP WORK
5.7

P4

Each member of your group should write a briefing paper that describes two methods of measuring quality in sports development, then they should present it to the rest of the group.

Purposes of quality measurement

Benchmarks or quality schemes are to ensure that the sports organisation is performing well against its stated objectives. For example, if an organisation such as a sports club or a local authority is trying to increase participation in a particular sport, it needs to know how well it is doing. These measurements can lead to *Improvement* because the strengths and weaknesses of any scheme can be assessed.

The strengths can be built on and developed and the weaknesses can also be worked on to limit any negative effects. Quality measurement can also lead to *standardisation* across organisations. For example, the Quest scheme ensures that quality measurements across sports are the same, hence fair for all.

Quality of measurement is also an excellent way of making individuals and organisations *accountable*; in other words, they have to give reasons for their successes and their failures. It can lead to overall improvement because if you know that your work is being measured, then you know that the way you are carrying out the work is also measured and this may motivate you to work harder and be more effective.

Organisations gain many benefits by attempting to attain quality awards, as illustrated by the case studies in this unit. Here are some of the main benefits:

- **Increased funding from different sources** – a club that has attained a quality mark can often apply immediately for more money.

- **Benchmarking** – this tells an organisation how well it is doing and may highlight areas for improvement. It involves measuring the organisation against similar organisations across the country.

- **Improved coaching and performance** – these quality measures can motivate individuals in an organisation and make it concentrate on sports development to raise performance standards.

- **Recognition** – the outside world can recognise the high quality of a club, a voluntary organisation or a local authority and will raise the status of that organisation. This may help it to attract the best coaches and performers.

There are more advantages than disadvantages to measuring quality like this, but here are the two main disadvantages:

- **Cost** – applying for an award and gathering the evidence can cost a lot of money and use up a lot of staff time. An organisation may have to show that it operates certain procedures and this may mean employing more staff or buying in further resources or expertise.

- **Time** – it often takes a long time to put together a bid for an award and collect the required evidence, and it can divert staff from their main job of sports development.

activity
INDIVIDUAL WORK
5.8

M2

Write an evaluation of the two measurement methods you described in Activity 5.7. Identify their strengths and weaknesses in your evaluation.

Know about sports development in practice

This unit has shown many examples of sports development in action. Sports development is constantly changing and can be heavily influenced by political and economic decisions. This makes it dynamic but can also lead to some disjointed initiatives that waste public money and devalue its role. Yet the vast majority of sports development is worthwhile and has a direct impact on the aspects identified in the sports development continuum.

Link

See page 148 in this unit for more information on the sports development continuum

At the time of writing, many sports development activities are being introduced, both nationally and locally. Here are descriptions of some current initiatives. These descriptions will help you to compare and contrast initiatives and to recommend realistic improvement.

Current initiatives

London 2012

Many sports development initiatives are related to the 2012 Olympic Games that will be held in London. In February 2006 UK Sport published its submission to the government on options for increased funding for elite athletes in the run-up to London 2012.

In the Budget on 22 March 2006, Chancellor Gordon Brown announced additional 2012 performance funding of £200 million, an average of £33.5 million per year. This enables *UK Sport* to start working towards fourth place in the 2012 Olympic medal table and first place in the Paralympic medal table.

On 1 April 2006 UK Sport took on the full responsibility for all Olympic and Paralympic performance-related support in England. This includes the identification of talent right the way through to performing at the top level. UK Sport will operate a *world-class performance pathway* at three levels: podium, development and talent.

remember

There are many aspects to sports development and the importance of each aspect is largely determined by what level you are working at on the sports development continuum.

Figure 5.23 London 2012 has led to many sports development initiatives

World Class Podium

World Class Podium will support sports with realistic medal chances in 2012. Athlete places on this scheme are allocated to a sport based on results at the last games, competitive track record, medal capability in the future, and demonstrated ability to constantly produce high-quality athletes. Support is provided to athletes.

World Class Development

World Class Development is for Olympic athletes about six years away from a medal, less for Paralympic athletes. Other sports are eligible for funding if they are not yet funded by World Class Podium and where there is performance evidence that they have the potential to win a medal in the next Olympic/Paralympic cycle.

World Class Talent

World Class Talent will support the identification of athletes who have the potential to progress with the help of targeted investment. Its funding will allow sports to identify the athletes with all the right attributes to compete effectively on the world stage. It will look at how sports can identify new athletes and how talent can be transferred across sports. Olympic athletes will be a maximum of eight years away from gaining a medal, less for Paralympic athletes.

Figure 5.24 World Class Podium aims for more British medallists in 2012

activity

INDIVIDUAL WORK 5.9

P5

Using the previous examples or examples from earlier in the unit, describe two different sports development initiatives.

Awards for All

Awards for All is a lottery grants scheme for local communities. There are different schemes for each of the four UK countries. Awards for All England is supported by the Arts Council England, the Big Lottery Fund, the Heritage Lottery Fund and Sport England. Grants of £300 to £10 000 are awarded for people to take part in art, sport, heritage and community activities, and projects that promote education, the environment and health in the local community.

You can apply if you are a not-for-profit group or if you are a parish or town council, school or health body; if you have a bank account that requires at least two unrelated people to sign each cheque or withdrawal; and if you can use the grant within one year.

Here the aims of Awards for All:

■ To extend access and participation by encouraging more people to become actively involved in local groups and projects, and by supporting activities that aim to be open and accessible to everyone who wishes to take part.

■ To increase skill and creativity by supporting activities that help to develop people and organisations, encourage talent and raise standards.

■ To improve the quality of life by supporting local projects that improve people's opportunities, health, welfare, environment or local facilities.

A project that is likely to meet the aims of Awards for All is a training and activities programme to involve more disabled people in sport and to provide sports facilities with qualified coaching for young people on an urban estate.

Awards for All – lottery grants scheme for local communities
www.awardsforall.org.uk

activity
GROUP WORK 5.10
M4

Make a PowerPoint presentation that compares and contrasts two different sports development initiatives.

Big Lottery

The Big Lottery Fund was launched on 1 June 2004, following the merger between the New Opportunities Fund and the Community Fund. Created by the National Lottery Act, the Big Lottery Fund hands out half the good causes money from the National Lottery and aims to improve communities and the lives of people most in need. Sports development projects may receive money from the Big Lottery Fund.

The five sports councils – UK Sport, Sport England, Sportscotland, the Sports Council of Northern Ireland and the Sports Council of Wales – are responsible for distributing National Lottery grants and government funding for sport. Sport England uses National Lottery money to increase sports participation at community level and national level:

■ **Community investment** – decisions about Sport England lottery grants over £10 000 are made locally by the nine regional sports boards. Eligible projects are assessed against the priorities in each region's sports plan and the National Framework for Sport.

■ **National investment** – Sport England is investing £315 million of lottery money through the national governing bodies of 32 key sports and other key national partners.

case study 5.15

Sports development by Everyday Swim

Everyday Swim is an initiative in sports development that aims to identify and remove barriers that discourage people from swimming. It is led by the Amateur Swimming Association (ASA), which is the national governing body for swimming. The initiative has funding and support from Sport England.

Olympic gold medallist Duncan Goodhew agreed to be Everyday Swim's ambassador. The project aims to get people into swimming and aquatic activities, whatever their ability, and to keep them interested. It covers all appropriate aquatic activities, such as water polo, aquafit and casual swimming. The project is evaluated nationally and locally to ensure progress is shared across all areas, and evidence is gathered for future development.

Projects focus on different aspects of swimming provision, such as community use of a 50 m swimming facility, better access to swimming for rural communities, and frequent non-competitive swimming for children. The ASA will invest with local partners who can offer at least 1:1 funding for a project. Partners are asked to match funding for two years at between £50 000 and £150 000 per year.

activity
INDIVIDUAL WORK

1. Besides the examples given here, how could funding help to develop swimming in a local community?

2. What are the main disadvantages of such initiatives?

UK Sport is responsible for high-performance sport in the UK and supports world-class athletes and events plus ethically fair and drug-free sport. Through its World Class Performance programme, UK Sport distributes lottery funding as grants to governing bodies of sport to invest in performance directors, coaches and sporting services; and as personal grants to athletes as a contribution to basic living costs, personal training and sports equipment costs.

On 6 July 2005 London won the competition to host the 2012 Olympics and Paralympics. Some of the public funding will come from the National Lottery.

activity
INDIVIDUAL WORK
5.11

D2

Write a detailed report analysing two different sports development initiatives. Make clear and realistic recommendations for improvements to these initiatives. Present your recommendations to the rest of the group.

***Progress
Check***

1. What is the sports development continuum?

2. Use examples from sport to describe the participation stage of the sports development continuum.

3. What target groups are related to sports development and why are they targeted?

4. Define sports equity.

5. Describe some of the barriers that prevent participation in sport and give examples of how they are being dismantled.

6. Name two providers of sports development and describe their structures and roles.

7. What role do the UK sports institutes play in sports development?

8. Explain Sport England's Best Value initiative.

9. Describe the two methods to measure the quality of sports development in the UK.

10. Describe fully a current sports development initiative in your own sport.

Fitness Testing for Sport and Exercise

This unit covers:

- A range of laboratory- and field-based fitness tests
- The practice of health screening
- Preparing for appropriate fitness tests then conducting them
- Analysing the results of fitness tests

Fitness for sport is vital for good performances and to prevent injury. In individual and team sports, fitness testing is carried out regularly to assess strengths that can be reinforced and weaknesses that can be addressed.

Fitness is also important for the general public and is often an integral part of the work of a health or leisure club. Effective fitness testing is needed to create a meaningful training or exercise programme. The overall effectiveness of a training or exercise programme can be assessed with more fitness tests at the end of the programme.

This unit will help you acquire the skills, knowledge and understanding to safely select and carry out fitness testing on an individual. It will help you analyse test results and give feedback on fitness tests to individuals. It begins with a range of laboratory- and field-based fitness tests and outlines their advantages and disadvantages. It explains the importance of health screening and health monitoring.

It shows you how to select an appropriate test, how to prepare for it and how to conduct it safely so it gives valid results. It shows you how to analyse fitness against normative data so you can give effective feedback to people.

grading criteria

To achieve a **Pass** grade the evidence must show that the learner is able to:	To achieve a **Merit** grade the evidence must show that the learner is able to:	To achieve a **Distinction** grade the evidence must show that the learner is able to:
P1 describe one test for each component of physical fitness, including advantages and disadvantages Pg 200	**M1** explain the advantages and disadvantages of one fitness test for each component of physical fitness Pg 202	**D1** evaluate the health screening questionnaires and health monitoring test results and provide recommendations for lifestyle improvement Pg 210
P2 prepare an appropriate health screening questionnaire Pg 204	**M2** describe the strengths and areas for improvement for two contrasting individuals using information from health screening questionnaires and health monitoring tests Pg 210	**D2** analyse the fitness test results and provide recommendations for appropriate future activities or training Pg 217

grading criteria

To achieve a **Pass** grade the evidence must show that the learner is able to:	To achieve a **Merit** grade the evidence must show that the learner is able to:	To achieve a **Distinction** grade the evidence must show that the learner is able to:
P3 devise and use appropriate health screening procedures for two contrasting individuals Pg 210	**M3** justify the selection of fitness tests commenting on suitability, reliability, validity and practicality Pg 215	
P4 safely administer and interpret the results of four health monitoring tests for two contrasting individuals Pg 209	**M4** compare the fitness test results to normative data and identify strengths and areas for improvement Pg 215	
P5 select and safely administer six different fitness tests for a selected individual and record the findings Pg 214		
P6 give feedback to a selected individual following fitness testing, describing the test results and interpreting their levels of fitness against normative data Pg 217		

Understand a range of laboratory-based and field-based fitness tests

If done properly, fitness tests can be useful in establishing the strengths of the performer and the weaknesses or areas for development. These tests can also be a useful monitoring device to see how well the fitness programme is working and also how hard the performer is working. The test results can then be used to inform and update the next stage of the fitness programme. For example, it may be discovered that speed is an issue and the performer shows low scores related to speed. The training programme would then be modified to incorporate much more speed work. Fitness testing is often used as a screening device for selection to a particular team, because it may be indicative of that individual's potential.

Norms are provided for some of the tests given below, but they are notoriously invalid because they rarely consider all the variables present. It is interesting to refer to norms but it is better to work to your own benchmarks for improvement. The following tests are for specific physical fitness components; each has advantages and disadvantages.

See page 80 in Unit 3 for more information on fitness components

Strength tests

Grip dynamometer

Description

Dynamometers such as the handgrip dynamometer measures the strength of the handgrip to give an objective measure of strength. It is generally accepted that there is a strong correlation between handgrip strength and overall strength, although other variables may invalidate this method for overall strength measurement.

Figure 6.1 Grip dynamometer

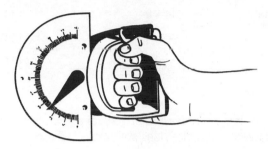

Method

Adjust the handgrip to fit the subject's hand. The subject should stand, holding the dynamometer parallel to the side of the body, with the dial facing away from the body. Ask them to squeeze the handle as hard as possible without moving their arm. Three trials are recommended with a 1 min rest between each trial.

Norms

Here are national norms for 16–19 year olds showing the average of three trials with the favoured hand. Another method is to record the better of two trials for each hand.

Table 6.1 Grip dynamometer – average of three trials for 16–19 year olds with favoured hand

	Average grip (kg) with favoured hand	
	Male	Female
Excellent	>56	>36
Good	51–56	31–36
Average	45–50	25–30
Fair	39–44	19–24
Poor	<39	<19

These adult norms are the average of the best scores for each hand.

Table 6.2 Grip dynamometer – adult norms

	Grip norm	
	Male	**Female**
Excellent	>64	>38
Very good	56–64	34–38
Above average	52–56	30–34
Average	48–52	26–30
Below average	44–48	22–26
Poor	40–44	20–22
Very poor	<40	<20

remember
Consider that the non-dominant hand usually scores about 10% lower. For a valid test, use the same hand or an average score of both hands.

remember
The starting weight is important because the maximum weight should be lifted within five attempts.

Validity
The validity of this test as a measure of general strength has been questioned, as the strength of the forearm muscles does not always represent the strength of other muscle groups.

Advantages
This is a simple and easy test that usually indicates general strength levels. All it requires is a dynamometer and it is relatively safe and quick to administer.

Disadvantages
The dynamometer must be adjusted properly for the hand size of the athlete. If this is not done accurately, the test lacks validity.

1RM tests

One rep max (1RM) tests are for strength and are based on the maximum weight that can be moved a distance in one repetition. The bench press for one rep max can be carried out as a test for upper body strength. This test measures the maximum strength of chest muscle groups.

1. Do a warm-up with about 10 reps of light weights, followed by a 1 min rest then perform two warm-up sets of 2–5 reps with slightly heavier weights, with a 2 min rest between sets.

2. Have a 2 min rest then perform the test by doing the 1RM attempt with correct bench-press technique.

3. If the lift is successful, rest for another 2 min.

4. Increase the load by 10% and attempt another lift.

5. If the lift attempt fails, rest for 2 min then attempt a lift using a weight about 5% lower.

6. Increase or decrease the weights until a maximum lift is performed.

Sports Coach – more information on weight training
www.sportscoach.co.uk

Good scores
Here are what most people agree are good 1RM scores:

■ Males – 1.25 × body weight

■ Females – 0.8 × body weight.

Table 6.3 Rep max bench press scores for adults

	Weight lifted per body weight (kg/kg)
Excellent	>1.60
Good	1.30–1.60
Average	1.15–1.29
Below average	1.00–1.14
Poor	0.91–0.99
Very poor	<0.90

Validity
For people with less experience of lifting weights, the results can vary with technique rather than strength. The muscle energy systems also change when reps are changed, which also affects the score. Therefore the test may become invalid.

Advantages
The equipment is found in most gyms and health clubs. The test is simple to perform and does not require much technical expertise.

Disadvantages
People performing the test must be taught the correct technique, otherwise it can be very dangerous. Variations in technique may affect the score. The level of motivation could also affect the score, so it is better to let people motivate themselves.

Figure 6.2 1RM for a bench press is a good indication of upper body strength

Squat

The squat is considered the most convenient leg strength test to predict sprinting and jumping ability.

Good scores

Here are what most people agree are good 1RM scores:

- Males – 2 × their body weight
- Females – 1.5 × their body weight.

Hamstring and quadriceps strength

Hamstring and quadriceps strength records the 1RM for each leg in leg curl and leg extension exercises. Divide your leg curl score by the leg curl extension to find the ratio for each leg. For each leg, the curl score should be at least 75% to reduce the chance of injury.

Speed measurements

Speed can be measured by the 30 m sprint test. This should be on a flat non-slip surface to prevent accidents. The sprint should be from a flying start back from the beginning of the marked-out stretch. The time is taken from the beginning of the 30 m stretch to the end.

Approximate norms

Table 6.4 Approximate norms for intermediate-level team players (30–35 m sprints)

	Approximate 30–35 m sprint norm (s)	
	Male	**Female**
Very good	<4.80	<5.30
Good	4.80–5.9	5.30–5.59
Average	5.10–5.29	5.60–5.89
Fair	5.30–5.60	5.90–6.20
Poor	>5.60	>6.20

Validity

The conditions must remain similar for each test. Do the same warm-up each time you do the test. Sprint technique may affect times and the level of motivation may invalidate results. The timing procedure should be standardised, and this is probably the weakest part of the test. The timer should be the same person for each subject's test.

Advantages

It is easy to administer and requires no special equipment.

Disadvantages

The timing can be unreliable. It could be dangerous without an appropriate warm-up and if the surface is slippery. Give athletes appropriate footwear to avoid injury. Weather conditions can affect the results.

Power measurements

Power can be assessed by using the vertical jump test, often called the Sargent jump test. Commercial jump test boards can be fixed to the wall, which makes it easier to achieve standardised measurements.

Ask the subject to jump vertically, using both feet, and touch the calibrated scale on the board with one hand. Note the position of the touch. Have the subject do this three times then record the highest touch position.

remember

Give athletes an appropriate warm-up and have them do a practice sprint. Encourage the athletes to continue running hard through the finish line. To obtain valid results, use the same encouragement each time you do the test.

Figure 6.3 Speed can be measured using a sprint test

If there is no test board, the subject stands side on to a wall and stretches up with the hand closest to the wall, keeping their feet flat on the ground. Put a chalk mark on the wall at the level of the subject's fingertips; this is the static reach height. Ask the subject to stand slightly away from the wall. Now ask them to jump vertically as high as possible and to touch the wall at the highest point of the jump. Make a note of this height. The score for this attempt is the difference between the static reach height and the jump height. Ask the subject to make three attempts and record the best of their three scores.

A timing mat measures the duration a subject's feet are off the mat then uses it to calculate jump height. To be accurate, the subject's feet must land on the mat while their legs are almost fully extended.

Approximate norms

Table 6.5 Leg jump norms for adult sportspeople

	Leg jump norm (cm)	
	Male	**Female**
Excellent	>70	>60
Very good	61–70	51–60
Above average	51–60	41–50
Average	41–50	31–40
Below average	31–40	21–30
Poor	21–30	11–20
Very poor	<21	<11

Sargent jump calculation

Overall leg jump power can be calculated approximately using this equation:

$$\text{Power (W)} = 2.21 \times \text{body weight (kg)} \times \sqrt{\text{jump distance (m)}}$$

Figure 6.4 Power can be measured using the vertical jump test

Advantages

It is simple and quick to perform and, apart from a wall, it requires no facilities.

Disadvantages

It can cause injury if the landing area is uneven. Jumping technique can obscure the results, so the technique must be taught and remain constant.

Standing broad jump test for power

The standing broad jump test for power measures the explosive strength of the leg muscles. The subject stands behind a line marked on the ground with feet slightly apart. Use a 2 ft (0.61 m) take-off and landing, and ask the subject to swing their arms and bend their knees to drive themselves forward. The subject attempts to jump up and forward as far as possible, landing on both feet. The subject has three attempts. The jump is measured from the take-off line to the nearest point of contact on the landing. Record the longest jump out of the three attempts.

Approximate norms

Table 6.6 Standing broad jump norms for adults

	Standing broad jump norm (cm)	
	Male	Female
Excellent	>250	>200
Very good	241–250	191–200
Above average	231–240	181–190
Average	221–230	171–180
Below average	211–220	161–170
Poor	191–210	141–160
Very poor	<191	<141

Advantages
It is a simple test that does not take long to perform.

Disadvantages
Jumping technique can obscure the results, and unless the test and retest technique are identical, the results will be invalid. Lack of a standardised technique may mean that quoted norms are invalid.

Wingate test for anaerobic capacity

The Wingate test measures anaerobic capacity using a cycle **ergometer**, which is a static exercise bike with alterable resistance to effort. Ask the subject to warm up by cycling on the ergometer. When their heart rate is 150 beats per minute (bpm), set an appropriate cycle workload on the ergometer – men 0.083–0.092 kg per kilogram of body weight, women 0.075 kg per kilogram of body weight. Now tell the subject to pedal as fast as they can for 30 s. The ergometer measures the number of revolutions of the pedals every 5 s.

Calculations
At the end of the test, the power output is calculated as follows:

$$\text{Output (W)} = 11.765 \times \text{load (kg)} \times \text{number of revolutions per 5 s}$$

This is a maximal test, so check that the subject is fit and healthy enough to complete it.

The peak power (PP) output, observed during the first 5 s of exercise, indicates the capacity to generate anaerobic energy. Here is the way to calculate it:

$$PP = \frac{\text{force} \times \text{distance}}{\text{time}} = \frac{\text{force} \times (\text{number of revolutions} \times \text{distance per revolution})}{\text{time}}$$

Note that 5 s = 0.0833 min.

Figure 6.5 Anaerobic capacity can be measured using the Wingate anaerobic cycle test

Approximate norms

Table 6.7 Power norms for active adults on the Wingate test

Rank (%)	Power norm (W)	
	Male	Female
90	822	560
80	777	527
70	757	505
60	721	480
50	689	449
40	671	432
30	656	399
20	618	376
10	570	353

Validity

A cycle ergometer test is more specific to cycling sports, so generalising the results to other activities is less reliable. The test scores can reliably determine peak anaerobic power, anaerobic fatigue and total anaerobic capacity.

Advantages

Comparatively reliable tests can be performed indoors in controlled conditions.

Disadvantages

The results are less relevant for non-cycling activities. The results can be affected by a performer's motivation levels, the reliability of the equipment and the accuracy of its calibration.

Cardiovascular endurance

A person's endurance fitness is indicated by their $V_{O_2 max}$, the maximum amount of oxygen they can take in and use in 1 min. The potential $V_{O_2 max}$ of an individual can be predicted using the multistage fitness test, sometimes called the bleep test or the beep test. It is a shuttle run that gets progressively more difficult.

The test is published on audio CD by Sports Coach UK, formerly the National Coaching Foundation. Subjects run a 20 m shuttle as many times as possible and they must turn at each end of the run in time with the bleep on the tape. The time interval between the bleeps gets shorter as the test goes on, so the subject has to run the 20 m faster and faster. When the subject cannot keep up with the bleeps, they are deemed to have reached their optimum level.

The level reached by the subject is recorded and used as a baseline for future tests, or it can be compared with national norms.

Safety factors

According to health and safety guidelines issued by the British Association of Advisers and Lecturers in Physical Education (BAALPE), a person experiencing shortness of breath, chest pains, palpitations or light-headedness should stop exercising immediately and should be sensitively advised to seek advice from a medical doctor or general practitioner (GP). The teacher or coach should observe the subject all through the test, especially if the subject has low physical fitness.

Figure 6.6 A person's potential V_{O_2max} can be predicted using the bleep test

National team scores

Table 6.8 National team scores on the multistage fitness test

	National team score	
	Male	**Female**
Basketball	L11–S5	L9–S6
Hockey	L13–S9	L12–S7
Rugby league	L13–S1	
Netball		L9–S7
Squash	L13–S13	

Norms for $V_{O_2\,max}$

Table 6.9 Maximal oxygen uptake norms

	Maximal oxygen uptake norms (cm³kg⁻¹min⁻¹) for age range (years)					
	18–25	**26–35**	**36–45**	**46–55**	**56–65**	**65+**
Men						
Excellent	>60	>56	>51	>45	>41	>37
Good	52–60	49–56	43–51	39–45	36–41	33–37
Above average	47–51	43–48	39–42	35–38	32–35	29–32
Average	42–46	40–42	35–38	32–35	30–31	26–28
Below average	37–41	35–39	31–34	29–31	26–29	22–25
Poor	30–36	30–34	26–30	25–28	22–25	20–21
Very poor	<30	<30	<26	<26	<22	<20
Women						
Excellent	56	52	45	40	37	32
Good	47–56	45–52	38–45	34–40	32–37	28–32
Above average	42–46	39–44	34–37	31–33	28–31	25–27
Average	38–41	35–38	31–33	28–30	25–27	22–24
Below average	33–37	31–34	27–30	25–27	22–24	19–22
Poor	28–32	26–30	22–26	20–24	18–21	17–18
Very poor	<28	<26	<22	<20	<18	<17

Validity

It is suitable for sports teams and school groups, but not for populations where a maximal exercise test would be contraindicated. It has a high correlation to actual $V_{O_2 \, max}$ scores.

Advantages

It can be performed cheaply on large groups of athletes in one session. It continues to maximum effort, whereas many other tests of endurance capacity stop before reaching maximum effort.

Disadvantages

Practice effects can skew the results. The motivation levels of the subjects can influence the amount of effort expended. The scoring can be subjective as some scorers may be more lenient than others. Environmental conditions can often affect the results, especially if the test is completed outside.

---

case study 6.1

Top bleep scores

At their peak fitness, it is rumoured that David Beckham (football), Lance Armstrong (cycling) and Neil Back (England rugby player) achieved a top score of 23 in the bleep test. Professional rugby flankers mostly score 12 or 13, and prop forwards score about 10. The UK national women's rugby seven-a-side team that went to Hong Kong in spring 2001 averaged over 11, with a range from 9 to 12.

activity
INDIVIDUAL WORK

1. How do bleep test scores for athletes correspond to their values of $V_{O_2 \, max}$?

2. Name some positions in your sport and say what level of aerobic fitness each requires.

Muscular endurance

remember

If you are suffering from any injury or illness, you should consult a doctor before doing the muscular endurance test.

Testing the endurance of a particular muscle group can assess an individual's muscular endurance. Sports Coach UK has devised the abdominal conditioning test to test the endurance of the abdominal muscle group by measuring the number of sit-ups (curl-ups) a person can perform by keeping to a bleep on an audio cassette. When the person cannot complete any more sit-ups in time with the bleep, they are deemed to have reached their optimum level. This test can be used as a benchmark for training or used for comparison with national norms.

Approximate norms

Table 6.10 Muscular endurance test norms

Stage	Cumulative sit-ups	Standard	
		Male	**Female**
1	20	Poor	Poor
2	42	Poor	Fair
3	64	Fair	Fair
4	89	Fair	Good
5	116	Good	Good
6	146	Good	Very good
7	180	Excellent	Excellent
8	217	Excellent	Excellent

Figure 6.7 Lance Armstrong
is rumoured to have
achieved all 23 levels in the
bleep test

Validity
The test must be conducted by using the standardised instructions. The results can be affected by a person's level of motivation to do the test.

Advantages
Simple and quick, it requires minimal equipment and large groups can be tested in one go.

Disadvantages
A person's technique can affect the results; for example, a curl-up with the feet held increases the involvement of the hip flexor muscles, making the test less valid as a measure of abdominal strength.

Press-up test

Full-body press-ups
1. The subject lies on the mat with their hands a shoulder width apart and their arms fully extended.
2. They lower their body until their elbows reach 90°.
3. They return to the starting position with their arms fully extended.
4. Do not hold the subject's feet.
5. The press-up action should be continuous with no rest.
6. Ask the subject to complete as many press-ups as possible.
7. Record the total number of full-body press-ups.
8. Female athletes can use the modified press-up position to assess their upper body strength.

Modified press-ups

1. The subject lies on the mat with their hands a shoulder width apart, their knees bent and their arms fully extended.
2. They lower the upper body until the elbows reach 90°.
3. They return to the starting position with their arms fully extended.
4. Do not hold the subject's feet.
5. The press-up action should be continuous with no rest.
6. Ask the subject to complete as many modified press-ups as possible.
7. Record the total number of modified press-ups.

Figure 6.8 Female athletes can use the modified press-up to assess their upper body strength.

Approximate norms

Table 6.11 Full-body press-up norms

	Number of full-body press-ups for age range (years)				
	20–29	30–39	40–49	50–59	>60
Excellent	>54	>44	>39	>34	>29
Good	45–54	35–44	30–39	25–34	20–29
Average	35–44	25–34	20–29	15–24	10–19
Fair	20–34	15–24	12–19	8–14	5–9
Poor	<20	<15	<12	<8	<5

Table 6.12 Modified press-up norms

	Number of modified press-ups for age range (years)				
	20–29	30–39	40–49	50–59	>60
Excellent	>48	>39	>34	>29	>19
Good	34–38	25–39	20–34	15–29	5–19
Average	17–33	12–24	8–19	6–14	3–4
Fair	6–16	4–11	3–7	2–5	1–2
Poor	<6	<4	<3	<2	<1

Validity

The test's validity depends on how strictly it is conducted and the subject's level of motivation to perform the test. Published tables relate the results to potential level of fitness and the correlation is thought to be high.

Advantages
This test is easy and quick to perform and requires no equipment.

Disadvantages
The deciding factor can be the subject's level of motivation, not their fitness. Poor technique could invalidate the results and may lead to injury.

Flexibility measurement

Flexibility can be measured using the sit and reach test. The objective is to measure the athlete's lower back and hamstring flexibility. The subject sits on the floor with legs outstretched in a straight position. The subject reaches as far forward as possible but keeping the legs straight and in contact with the floor. The distance is measured between the ends of the fingers and the feet (pointing upwards). More accurate measurements can be obtained using a sit and reach box. The measurements can be used to assess future training needs and to compare a subject's performance with national norms.

Approximate norms

Table 6.13 Sit and reach test norms for 16–19 year olds

	Number of sit and reaches	
	Male	Female
Excellent	>14	>15
Above average	11–14	12–15
Average	7–10	7–11
Below average	4–6	4–6
Poor	<4	<4

Validity
The test's validity depends on how strictly it is conducted and the subject's level of motivation to perform the test. Published tables relate the results to potential level of fitness and the correlation is high. This test measures the flexibility of the lower back and hamstrings only, and is valid only for these body parts. For reliable results, use an appropriate warm-up and follow the same procedures each time.

Advantages
It is simple and quick to perform. Extensive data is available for comparison.

Disadvantages
Variations in arm and leg length can obscure the results. Most norms are based on no previous warm-up, but the best results will be achieved after a warm-up or if the test is preceded by a test such as the endurance test. Consequently, there is a need for a consistent method of administrating the test.

Figure 6.9 Lower back and hamstring flexibility can be measured using the sit and reach test

Body composition by skinfold measurement

Measurements are made using a skinfold caliper from the areas around the biceps, triceps, subscapular and suprailiac. The measurements are added together and recorded to compare with national norms or, more importantly, to assess training or weight management programmes.

Measurements are usually made at three to nine anatomical sites around the body. For consistency, they are usually made on the right side only. The tester pinches the skin at the appropriate site to raise a double layer of skin and the underlying adipose tissue but not the muscle. The skinfold calipers are then used 1 cm below and at right angles to the pinch, and a reading is taken after 2 s. To ensure accurate measurements, take the mean of two separate measurements.

Table 6.14 Percentage body fat for male and female athletes by sport

	Body fat (%)	
	Male	Female
Baseball	12–15	12–18
Basketball	6–12	20–27
Canoe or kayak	6–12	10–16
Cycling	5–15	15–20
Field and ice hockey	8–15	12–18
Gymnastics	5–12	10–16
Rowing	6–14	12–18
Swimming	9–12	14–24
Tennis	12–16	16–24
Track runners	8–10	12–20
Track jumpers	7–12	10–18
Track throwers	14–20	20–28
Triathlon	5–12	10–15
Volleyball	11–14	16–25

Validity
Measurements often contain errors, so it is usually inappropriate to convert skinfold measurements to percentage body fat. It is best to monitor and compare body fat measures taken from several sites. Record them, leave a time interval, then record them again and see how they have changed.

Advantages
Skinfold measurement is often used to assess body composition. It is simpler than other techniques such as hydrostatic weighing. Beyond the price of the skinfold calipers, the costs are minimal.

Disadvantages
The reliability of skinfold measurement can vary from tester to tester depending on their skill and experience.

remember
It is wise to have another person present. Have female testers for female subjects and male testers for male subjects.

activity
GROUP WORK
6.1

P1

Produce an information booklet that describes a test for each component of physical fitness, including advantages and disadvantages.

Link   See page 53 in Unit 2 for more information on child protection

Body composition by hydrostatic weighing

Hydrostatic weighing measures the water displacement when a subject is submerged in water. It is often known as hydrodensitometry. Record the dry weight of the subject in light bathing clothes. Now ask them to sit on a modified seat above a tank of water and get them to expel all air from their lungs. Lower the subject into the tank using the hoist equipment until all their body parts are under the water. Measure their weight in the water.

Calculation

The body density in kilograms per litre (kg/dm^3) is calculated as follows:

$$\text{Body density} = \frac{W_a}{(W_a - W_w)/D_w - (RV + 0.1\ dm^3)}$$

where:

W_a = body wight in air (kg)

W_w = body weight in water (kg)

D_w = density of water (kg/dm^3)

RV = residual lung volume (dm^3)

Validity

The measurements have high validity but the wet and dry weights need to be accurate.

Advantages

Underwater weighing is the most accepted test of body density and is recognised as extremely accurate.

Disadvantages

The equipment for underwater weighing is very expensive. University research departments usually have weighing tanks but there is limited access for the general public.

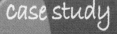

case study 6.2

Hydrodensitometry

Hydrodensitometry shows that a client has too much body fat. The client wants to lose weight and improve their overall fitness.

activity

INDIVIDUAL WORK

1. What other tests would you ask the client to take?
2. What are the disadvantages of hydrodensitometry when testing for body fat?

Body composition by bioelectric impedance

A small electric current is passed through the body from the wrist to the ankle. The subject lies on their back on a non-conducting surface, legs apart and arms away from the body. A pair of electrodes are placed on the subject's hand and wrist, and another pair on their ankle and foot. Compared with other tissue, fat has a greater resistance to the flow of electric current, so the higher the **bioelectric impedance**, the greater the percentage of body fat.

Validity
The validity of the results is high but it requires well-controlled conditions to get accurate and reliable measurements.

Advantages
It is simple and quick to perform.

Disadvantages
The equipment is expensive. The subject's level of hydration, their body temperature and the time of day affect the impedance measurements.

activity
GROUP WORK
6.2

M1

Using the booklet you produced in Activity 6.1, explain the advantages and disadvantages of one fitness test for each component of physical fitness.

Understand the practice of health screening

Health screening is an essential part of training and fitness testing for sport and general exercise. Fitness and exercise professionals always advise people to get checked out by a GP before starting a new exercise regime, and they make sure people go through the induction process in a health and leisure facility with a qualified fitness instructor or personal trainer.

Procedures

If the health and fitness of a subject is improving, then an initial assessment of various aspects of health and physical performance allows the subject and the professional to monitor progress. This screening process can include basic assessment of body composition, cholesterol, blood glucose and iron levels, which could be linked to a nutritional analysis, particularly if the subject's overall goal is weight management.

Health and fitness professionals are also able to monitor the subject's physiological responses to physical activity and therefore recommend specific effort levels based on heart rate, which can then be monitored by the subject or by the health and fitness professional during exercise. The more elite the sportsperson, the greater the depth of analysis and it may assess extra parameters specific to the sport, such as strength or power.

Here are some typical measurements for health screening:

- Body mass index (BMI)
- Blood pressure
- Cholesterol
- Glucose
- Resting heart rate
- Hydration
- Flexibility.

case study 6.3

A local authority guide for preventing sports-related injuries

General prevention guidelines

Before beginning an exercise programme or training for an athletics event, follow a few simple guidelines to help prevent injuries:

Prevent injuries with a complete examination

■ Have your doctor review your medical history.

Prevent injuries with proper attire and equipment

■ Make sure your equipment fits properly (helmet, tennis racquet grip, etc.).

■ Make sure you wear quality shoes designed for your sport or foot type (good arch support, durable heel, etc.).

■ Obtain necessary mouth guards or face masks for collision sports.

Prevent injuries by training and playing smart

■ Avoid overuse injuries such as tendonitis and stress fractures by beginning slowly then gradually increasing the time and intensity of your workouts.

■ Acclimatise yourself to the environment. Avoid heat- or cold-related stresses.

■ Limit your workout session to two hours. Allow adequate time to recover from a training session.

■ Maintain hydration or fluid levels. Drink plenty of water before, during and after practice or competition.

Prevent injuries by training correctly

■ Address all aspects of fitness, muscle strength, endurance, cardiovascular fitness and flexibility.

■ The minimum training requirement is two times per week to see improvement in aerobic or anaerobic activity.

■ Noticeable improvements in strength and endurance take three to four weeks.

■ Your pre-season conditioning programme should begin six weeks before the start of your sports season.

Prevent injuries by proper warm-up and stretching

■ Warm-up prepares the body for performance, decreases the potential for soft tissue injury, and helps reduce delayed-onset muscle soreness that can follow exercise.

■ Warm-up should consist of 15 min of submaximal sport-specific exercise. This activity increases the body's heart rate, body and muscle temperature, and muscle elasticity.

Prevent injuries by stretching

■ Stretching prepares your muscles for activity and prevents injuries from tight soft tissue structures such as muscles and tendons.

■ Static stretches should be slow and sustained – no bouncing or jerking. You should not feel pain while stretching. Stretch the entire body. No sport involves just part of the body. Stretch each body part two or three times for 20–30 s.

activity
INDIVIDUAL WORK

1. What is the meaning of 'playing smart'?

2. A guide like this, what part does it play in health screening?

case study 6.4 — Pre-screening questionnaire

According to Standard 5 of the Fitness Industry Association (FIA) code of practice, fitness professionals should offer an appropriate pre-screening questionnaire and exercise induction procedure for members and keep a record for each facility user.

activity
INDIVIDUAL WORK

1. What is the meaning of 'an appropriate pre-screening questionnaire'?
2. Why is it important to keep records for each facility user?

Fitness Industry Association
www.fia.org.uk
Fitness Industry Education – for fitness industry courses
www.fitnessindustryeducation.com

Questionnaires

Questionnaires should be designed to obtain as much information as possible so that safe exercise and fitness testing can be carried out by different individuals.

David Lloyd Leisure – for private fitness clubs and their health screening
www.davidlloydleisure.co.uk

activity
INDIVIDUAL WORK 6.3

P2

Using the above examples of questionnaires as a basis but without copying them, prepare an appropriate health-screening questionnaire.

> **remember**
>
> If you are not a trained medical practitioner, the screening process is one that identifies possible problems that must be dealt with by a suitably qualified medical practitioner. Do not comment or give advice on medical problems – leave it to the doctors.

Client consultation

Clients complete questionnaires during a health-screening consultation. Listen to the client during the consultation and note any potential problems, such as high blood pressure in the family.

As you carry out the health-screening procedure, make the client feel comfortable about the process and ensure that you use the right non-verbal communication. In other words, show that you are interested through your body language and maintain eye contact. To maintain confidentiality, make sure your consultations cannot be overheard. Personal information you collect from the client is confidential, so do not divulge it to anyone else unless you think the client is in danger, but get permission from the client first.

Health-monitoring tests

Heart rate

When screening heart rate, be familiar with the factors affecting heart rate, such as medication, stress, illness, time of the day, caffeine, food, alcohol, altitude and temperature. Cardiac drift is the increase in heart rate while you exercise with a constant workload. Your heart rate can increase by up to 20 beats per minute during exercise lasting about 20–60 min, even when the workload or work rate does not alter.

Figure 6.10 Health screening – sample questionnaire 1

Health screening – sample questionnaire 1

Take a few minutes to fill in this questionnaire. The information you provide will help us develop a programme to suit your needs.

Current physical activity

1 a) During the last week, on how many days did you walk continuously for at least 30 minutes?

Think about all the walking you have done, including any leisure walking, walking to and from home, and any purposeful walking

On .... days last week

b) On those days, on average, how long did you walk for each day?

.... minutes

2 a) During the last week, on how many days have you done any kind of housework, gardening, DIY or building work?

On .... days last week

b) On those days, on average, how long did you spend doing these things on each day?

.... minutes

3 a) During the last week, on how many days did you take part in any sport or activity?

For example, swimming, cycling, aerobics, dance, yoga, sports, or working out at a gym

On .... days last week

b) On those days, on average, how long were you active for each day?

.... minutes

4 a) At the moment, what would prevent you from becoming more active?

Tick whichever ones apply to you

Injury ❑	Dislike sport/exercise ❑	Lack of transport ❑
Poor health ❑	Family commitments ❑	Cost of facilities ❑
Distance to facilities ❑	Work commitments ❑	No one to do it with ❑
Not aware of facilities/classes available ❑	Facilities not available when I can attend ❑	

Other *(Please state)* ....

....

b) Which of the following best describes you? *Please tick only ONE*

I am not interested in pursuing a healthy lifestyle or being physically active ❑

I have recently been thinking about becoming regularly active ❑

I am intending to change my behaviour and to become regularly active within the next six months ❑

I have recently changed my behaviour and I am active on a regular basis ❑

I have been regularly active for at least six months ❑

Health needs

5 How would you describe your general health?

Very good ❑   Good ❑   Fair ❑   Poor ❑   Very poor ❑

6 a) In the last 12 months, roughly how many days have you been absent from work due to personal illness or injury?

.... days

b) Do you suffer from any long-term medical illnesses, such as diabetes, back pain or stress?

Yes ❑   No ❑

c) If yes, what long-term illness do you suffer from? *(Please state)* ....

d) Is this long-term condition the reason for most of your sickness absence?

Yes ❑   No ❑

7 How would you describe the following when you are at work? (*Please tick*)

	Very good	Good	Fair	Poor	Very poor
Energy levels	❑	❑	❑	❑	❑
Mood	❑	❑	❑	❑	❑
Concentration	❑	❑	❑	❑	❑
Stress levels	❑	❑	❑	❑	❑

Figure 6.11 Health screening – sample questionnaire 2

Health screening – sample questionnaire 2

PRE-TRAINING HEALTH SCREENING QUESTIONNAIRE

Name .... Gender ....

Date of birth ....

Address ....

Email ....

If you are between the ages of 15 and 69 and are intending to take part in physical activity or regular sport/exercise and you are new to exercise, the questions below will give an indication as to whether you should consult a doctor before you start. If you are over the age of 69 and you are not used to physical activity, you should consult your doctor first in any case. All information you record on this form will be treated with utmost confidentiality, it will be stored in a secure place and made available to you at any time.

Please state YES or NO

Q1   Has your doctor ever said you have a heart condition and/or should only participate in medically supervised physical activity?

Q2   Do you ever feel pain in your chest during physical activity?

Q3   Have you experienced chest pains when not doing physical activity?

Q4   Do you suffer with palpitations?

Q5   Do you experience dizziness or fainting?

Q6   Have you ever been told you have high blood pressure or are you taking medication for blood pressure or any other heart condition?

Q7   Do you have any existing bone or joint problem that could be made worse by physical activity?

Q8   Do you experience shortness of breath during only mild exertion?

Q9   Do you suffer from either asthma or diabetes mellitus?

Q10 Are you currently taking any prescribed medication we need to be made aware of? If so, what?

....

Q11 Are you pregnant or have you given birth in the last 6 weeks?

Q12 Have you recently undergone surgery or are you carrying any injury?

Q13 Are you aware of any other reasons why you should not participate in physical exercise without medical supervision? If so, what?

....

If you have answered YES to any of **Q1 to Q13**, we will require you to obtain written consent from your doctor before agreeing to undertake any form of fitness testing, physical activity, training or exercise with you. We suggest you talk to your doctor by phone or in person before you begin becoming more physically active and certainly before you undertake any form of formal fitness assessment. Tell your doctor about this questionnaire and which questions you answered YES to.

You may be able to do any activity you want as long as you begin slowly and build up gradually, or you may need to restrict your activities to those which are safe for you. Talk with your doctor about the kinds of activity you wish to participate in and follow his/her advice.

Please state YES or NO

Q14 Is your blood pressure known to be higher than average (over 120/80)?

Q15 Is your level of cholesterol known to be high?

Q16 Do you smoke regularly? If so, how many? ....

Q17 Is there any history of coronary heart disease or coronary artery disease in your parents or siblings before the age of 55?

On induction recheck:

Blood pressure reading

Resting heart rate

If you have answered YES to two or more of **Q14 to Q17**, for safety reasons we will restrict any programme of exercise to a moderate intensity unless you obtain written consent from your doctor to exercise at a higher intensity. Moderate intensity is a level at which you are able to comfortably sustain exercise for up to at least 60 minutes (usually not exceeding 65% of your maximal heart rate).

IMPORTANT NOTE

If you proceed with a programme of physical activity and, during that period, your health changes so that you would subsequently answer YES to any of the above questions, inform us immediately, as you may need to change or even suspend your physical activity or exercise plan. If you feel unwell because of a temporary illness such as cold or flu, it is advisable to stop training and recover properly – wait until you are better.

CLIENT DECLARATION

I have read, fully understood and completed this questionnaire. The answers I have given are accurate to the best of my knowledge.

Signed ....

Date ....

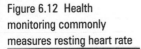

See page 23 in Unit 1 for more information on the function of the heart
See page 105 in Unit 3 for more information on the heart's response to training and exercise

On its own, a client's heart rate is not an accurate indication of fitness for exercise; it is only one part of the health screening process.

Heart rate provides a useful indication for monitoring a client's reaction to training. A heart rate monitor is a useful method for recording heart rate during exercise.

Follow these steps to calculate a client's resting heart rate (RHR):

1. Find a quiet, private venue for your assessment.

2. Get the client to lie down or sit down and ask them to relax.

3. After 5–10 min use a heart rate monitor to take their pulse rate in beats per minute. Use this as the client's resting heart rate.

Manual method of measuring resting heart rate

The manual or palpitation method is used at the wrist (radial artery) and the neck (carotid artery).

See page 24 in Unit 1 for more information on the circulatory system

Always use your fingers to take a pulse, not your thumb, particularly when recording someone else's pulse, as you can sometimes feel your own pulse through your thumb.

To take your resting heart rate at the wrist, place your index and middle fingers together on the opposite wrist, about 1/2 inch (13 mm) on the inside of the joint, in line with the index finger. Feel for a pulse. When you find a pulse, count the number of beats you feel in a 1 min period. You can estimate the rate per minute by counting over 10 s and multiplying this figure by 6, or over 15 s and multiplying by 4, or over 30 s and multiplying by 2.

Normal RHR ranges from 40 bpm up to 100 bpm; an ideal rate is 60–90 bpm. The average RHR for a man is 70 bpm and the average RHR for a woman is 75 bpm.

Figure 6.12 Health monitoring commonly measures resting heart rate

Blood pressure

A measuring instrument called a sphygmomanometer is placed where the subject cannot see the results. Blood pressure is recorded after the subject has rested quietly for 5 min. The client sits with one an arm resting so the elbow is approximately at the level of the heart. The cuff is attached, the pressure is then increased to approximately 180 mm Hg. The stethoscope is placed over the brachial artery in the cubital fossa.

The pressure is released at a rate of approximately 2 mm Hg per second. Record the pressure when the first sound is heard (systolic pressure) and the pressure when all sound disappears (diastolic pressure). The units for blood pressure are millimetres of mercury (mm Hg). Normal blood pressure for men and women is usually considered to be 120 for systolic pressure and 80 for diastolic pressure.

Approximate norms

It is common for blood pressure to increase in stressful conditions. If you suspect that the subject has become stressed, repeat the test when the subject has relaxed.

Table 6.15 Blood pressure norms

	Blood pressure (mm Hg)		
	Acceptable	Borderline	High
Systolic	<140	140–160	>160
Diastolic	<85	85–95	>95

Lung function

Lung volumes can vary with age, gender and body height. One way to measure lung function is by using a spirometer and measuring forced vital capacity (FVC) and forced expired volume in 1 second (FEV1). Both are measured with full expiration. The client must fill their lungs completely and seal their lips tightly around the mouthpiece of the spirometer. The subject then empties their lungs as hard as they can, as fast as they can. The best of two trials is usually recorded.

> **remember**
>
> Seek medical advice if a subject's blood pressure falls in the high category.

Figure 6.13 Refer your client to a doctor if their blood pressure is high

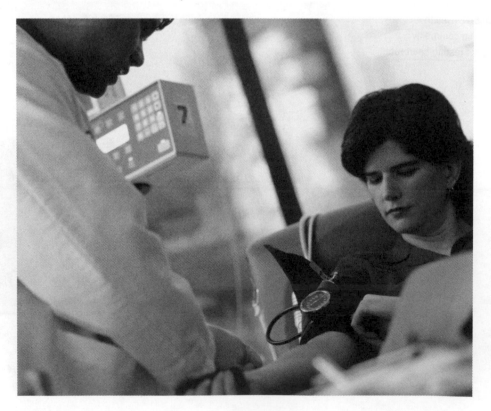

Lung function tests do not usually predict fitness and exercise performance. The peak flow test is a simpler and cheaper way to measure lung function:

1. On the gauge of the peak flow meter, put the pointer to zero.
2. The client takes a deep breath, places the mouthpiece of the peak flow meter in their mouth and closes their lips tightly around it.
3. The client then breathes out as hard as they can, as fast as they can – forcibly rather than slowly.
4. Record the value on the gauge before moving the pointer back to zero.
5. Take at least three measurements.
6. Record the peak expiratory flow (PEF) in litres per minute (dm^3/min).

remember

Peak flow is often used as an indicator of asthma.

Waist/hip ratio

The waist/hip ratio measurement is often used to determine the risk of coronary artery disease associated with obesity. The waist measurement is taken at the narrowest waist level, or at the midpoint between the lowest rib and the top of the hipbone (iliac crest). The hip measurement is taken at the level of the greatest protrusion of the gluteal muscles.

Link

See page 85 in Unit 3 for more information on heart disease and body composition

You can use any units of measurement as long as you use the same units to measure the waist and the hip. The waist/hip ratio is dimensionless – it is just a number.

Table 6.16 Waist/hip norms

	Waist/hip norm	
	Male	**Female**
Acceptable		
Excellent	<0.85	<0.75
Good	0.85–0.90	0.75–0.80
Unacceptable		
Average	0.90–0.95	0.80–0.85
High	0.95–1.0	0.85–0.90
Extreme	>1.0	>0.90

activity

INDIVIDUAL WORK 6.4

P4

Safely administer and interpret the results of four health-monitoring tests for two contrasting individuals.

Body mass index

remember

The BMI does not apply to elderly clients, pregnant women or highly trained athletes.

The body mass index (BMI) is a measure of body composition. It is calculated by taking a client's weight and dividing by the square of their height:

$$BMI \ (kg/m^2) = \frac{body \ weight \ (kg)}{height^2 \ (m^2)}$$

The higher the BMI, the more body fat is present. However, other issues such as body type should also be considered.

BMI norms

Table 6.17 BMI norms

	BMI (kg m^{-2})
Underweight	<20
Healthy range	20–25
Overweight	25–30
Obese	>30

case study 6.5 — Body mass index

Here are a client's height and weight measurements:

Height 1.7 m

Weight 70 kg

activity
INDIVIDUAL WORK

1. What is the client's body mass index (BMI)?
2. Is this BMI acceptable for general fitness?

activity
INDIVIDUAL WORK 6.5

P3

M2

Using the results of health-screening questionnaires and health-monitoring tests, describe the fitness strengths of these two clients and the areas where they could improve their fitness:

1. A male aged 50 who is not a sportsman.
2. An active female aged 18.

activity
INDIVIDUAL WORK 6.6

D1

Write a report that evaluates the questionnaires and health-monitoring results and recommend lifestyle improvements for your clients.

Be able to prepare for and conduct appropriate fitness tests

First of all, select the right test for the client. A range of tests would cover the main areas of fitness.

 Link

See page 80 in Unit 3 for more information on components of fitness

This section describes how to prepare for a variety of tests. Each test is covered using three headings:

- Preparation
- Purpose
- Method.

See page 98 in Unit 3 for more information on goal setting

Prescribe a specific exercise or training programme based on test results and the appropriate benchmark. After the tests, educate the client about health and fitness issues, such as the dangers of smoking, the need for a healthy diet and the need for more general activity each day.

Multistage fitness test

Preparation
The written pre-test precautions provided with the test indicate that a valid test requires the subject to reach maximal effort. If there are doubts over the ability of any client to take part in the test, advise the client to seek medical advice beforehand.

Clients with an injury or illness should not do the test. The test starts very slowly, so there is a gentle warm-up as the test progresses. But besides this built-in warm-up, it is advisable to do very light jogging and gentle stretching before commencing the shuttle runs.

Ideally, clients should be medically screened for the absence of cardiac abnormalities before they do vigorous and sustained physical activity. The test requires a flat, non-slip surface, marking cones, a measuring tape, a pre-recorded audiotape with a tape recorder and recording sheets.

Purpose
The objective of the multistage fitness test is to monitor the development of the client's maximum oxygen uptake. The level of endurance fitness is indicated by the client's $V_{O_2 max}$, which is the maximum amount of oxygen they can take in and use in 1 min. The potential $V_{O_2 max}$ of a client can be predicted using the multistage fitness test.

Method
1. Measure and mark out a 20 m area and mark each end with marker cones.
2. Warm up the client with jogging and stretching.
3. When the tape indicates, the client starts to jog the 20 m shuttle.
4. The client places one foot on or beyond the 20 m markers at the end of each shuttle.
5. If the client arrives at the end of a shuttle before the bleep, they must wait for the bleep then start running again.
6. The client keeps running for as long as possible. They should stop when they cannot keep up with the bleeps on the tape.
7. If the client fails to reach the end of the shuttle before the bleep, they should be allowed two or three further shuttles to see if they can regain the required pace. If they still cannot keep up, they should stop.
8. Record the level and number of shuttles completed when the client stops.
9. Warm down the client with some stretching exercises.

Harvard step test

Preparation
To prepare for the Harvard step test, you need a gym-type bench about 45 cm high. A stopwatch is also required along with a recording sheet. Putting the body under stress by exercising to exhaustion is sometimes inappropriate. Health screening is vital to ensure safe practice.

Purpose

To monitor the development of the client's cardiovascular system.

Method

The client steps up and down on the bench once every 2 s for 5 min or until exhaustion – when the client cannot maintain the stepping rhythm. The client sits down immediately after the test and the total number of heartbeats is counted in the intervals 1 to 1.5 min after finishing, 2 to 2.5 min after finishing, and 3 to 3.5 min after finishing. The score is obtained from this calculation:

$$\text{Score} = \frac{\text{test duration (s)}}{2 \times \text{total number of heartbeats in the recovery periods}} \times 100$$

Approximate norms

Table 6.18 Harvard step test norms

	Test score (s)
Excellent	>90
Good	80–89
High average	65–79
Low average	55–64

Maximal treadmill protocol

Preparation

The client should be screened for health and fitness problems. If there are no issues, then the test is suitable. The client will need to warm up gently and perform appropriate stretching exercises. Use a treadmill where the speed and grade of slope can be adjusted. You will also need a stopwatch and recording sheets.

Purpose

To monitor the development of the client's general endurance related to $V_{O_2\,max}$.

See page 81 in Unit 3 for more information on $V_{O_2\,max}$

Method

The athlete walks on a treadmill until exhaustion. At timed stages during the test, the grade of slope (%) of the treadmill is increased as follows:

- Active and sedentary men
  - Treadmill speed set at 3.3 mph (1.5 m/s)
  - Start – grade set at 0%
  - After 1 min – grade raised to 2%
  - After 2 min – grade is increased by 1%
  - Every minute thereafter – grade is increased by 1%.
- Active and sedentary women
  - Treadmill speed set at 3.0 mph (1.3 m/s)
  - Start – grade set at 0%
  - After 3 min – grade is increased by 1%
  - Every 3 min thereafter – grade is increased by 2.5% (1.4°).

The stopwatch is started when the test begins and stopped when the client is unable to continue.

Figure 6.14 A treadmill is a simple way of controlling exercise loads in fitness tests

Calculation

$$V_{O_2\,max} = 1.44T + 14.99$$

where T is the total time in minutes to do the test.

 See page 195 in this unit for tables of $V_{O_2\,max}$ norms

1RM tests

Purpose

To measure the maximum strength of various muscles and muscle groups.

 See page 188 in this unit for more information on how to prepare and conduct the tests

activity
INDIVIDUAL WORK
6.7

P5

Select a person then choose six different fitness tests and safely administer them. Record the results.

remember

The client should warm up with 10 reps of a light weight, then after 1 min rest perform two heavier warm-up sets of 5 reps, with 2 min rest between sets. The subject should rest for 2 min, then perform the 1 RM attempt with proper technique.

For the following tests, see details earlier in the unit on preparation, purpose and conduct of the tests:

- Grip dynamometer – strength test
- Vertical jump – muscular power test
- Wingate test – anaerobic capacity test
- Sprint tests – speed
- 1 min of press-ups or sit-ups – muscular strength endurance tests
- Skinfold calipers – body composition
- Bioelectric impedance analysis – body composition
- Hydrodensitometry – body composition.

Health and safety

Always do health and safety checks before a testing session. Check that the equipment works properly, check there is an adequate supply of safety equipment such as first-aid kits, and do an adequate warm-up.

For maximal endurance testing on elderly and special populations – only after medical clearance has been given – have medical assistance close at hand as well as adequate resuscitation equipment.

Any person aged over 35, particularly anyone overweight or with a history of high blood pressure and heart disease, should consult a medical practitioner before doing vigorous testing.

See page 202 in this unit for more information on health screening

All clients that are not accustomed to exercise should complete a physical readiness questionnaire and receive adequate health screening.

See page 64 in Unit 2 for more information on health and safety risk assessments

remember

Terminate a fitness test if the client experiences undue stress, if the client asks for it to be terminated, if the equipment malfunctions or if you think there is a threat to the client's well-being.

Here are the steps to follow:

1. Identify what is to be measured.
2. Select a suitable measurement method or test.
3. Collect the data.
4. Analyse the data.
5. Decide on an exercise or fitness programme.
6. Implement the programme.

In step 2, select a test that is valid and appropriate for your client. All tests should have these four characteristics:

- **Specific** – the test should assess a client's fitness for one activity or exercise.
- **Valid** – the test should measure what it is supposed to measure.
- **Reliable** – the same test run in the same way should produce the same results.
- **Objective** – the test results should be independent of the tester.

activity
INDIVIDUAL WORK 6.8

M3

Create a poster to justify your selection of fitness tests in Activity 6.7. Comment on their suitability, reliability, validity and practicality.

---

remember

These factors may affect the reliability of a test: how much sleep the client had before the test, their emotional state and level of motivation, the accuracy of the measurements (times, distances, etc.), temperature, noise and humidity, time of day, caffeine intake, other people present, the skill of the tester.

Consider these points when you conduct any test:

- Each test should measure one factor only.
- The test should not require any technical competence on the part of the client – the simpler the better.
- The client should understand what is required, what is being measured and why it is being measured.
- The test procedure should be strictly standardised to ensure consistency.

Results from testing clients can be used to:

- create an appropriate training or exercise programme
- predict future performance or fitness levels
- indicate weaknesses
- measure improvements
- evaluate whether training was successful
- motivate the client.

Recording information

Monitor the exercise programme so you can maintain progression in training. Serious sports performers may keep a training diary. The test results can be recorded by you and separately by your client.

activity
INDIVIDUAL WORK 6.9

M4

Take the results you obtained in Activity 6.7 and compare them with national norms to identify areas of strength and areas for improvement. Present your findings as a briefing.

Link   See page 108 in Unit 3 for more information on training diaries

Here some items that may be included in test records:

- Client's health
- Physiological data – body weight and resting heart rate
- Time trials – speed, speed endurance, endurance
- Muscular endurance – chins, push-ups, dips
- Maximum strength – maximum repetitions
- Explosive strength – vertical jump
- Flexibility or mobility – sit and reach test.

Be able to analyse the results of fitness tests

Normative data

Perhaps you have already compared your client's results or your own results with Tables 6.1 to 6.18. Normative results, or norms, are average results from a particular cohort or group of people. Unless otherwise stated, the norms in this unit are relevant to most of the population aged 18–50. Normative data can be quoted for more narrow groups of people, such as women aged 18–30 or males who regularly participate in exercise. Always compare like with like; in other words, take your test results and compare them with norms for people of similar age, gender, etc.

Feedback to clients

Think about how you will give any feedback on test results. Will it be verbal feedback or will it be written feedback? Most clients find it most satisfying to receive a combination of verbal and written feedback – a written report they can take away and reflect on plus a verbal explanation from the coach that puts the results into context. Whenever you give feedback, try not alarm your clients unnecessarily. You may have to warn a client about their health or refer them to a doctor, but that does not necessarily mean they are ill.

Figure 6.15 Most clients like a combination of verbal and written feedback

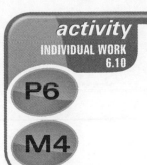

activity
INDIVIDUAL WORK
6.10

P6

M4

Give verbal and written feedback to the person who did the fitness tests in Activity 6.7. In your feedback, describe the test results and interpret the person's fitness levels against normative data.

remember

Refer clients to a qualified doctor for medical diagnoses. Most people who give fitness test results are not qualified to give medical diagnoses. If in doubt, always refer the client to a doctor.

Tell the client their test results in a way they can understand. For most clients, it is meaningless to give them lots of data with no explanation. Here are some items to include when you tell a client their test results:

■ The tests you carried out

■ The client's results and any appropriate norms

■ Overall levels of fitness for that type of client

■ Strengths and areas for improvement

■ A list of recommendations.

The list of recommendations should include a programme the client can follow with minimum disruption to their life. It may be linked to nutritional and lifestyle advice.

 Link

See page 105 in Unit 3 for more information on the FITT method

activity
INDIVIDUAL WORK
6.11

D2

Write a report to analyse the results of the fitness tests. Look beyond the basic facts and recommend some appropriate activities or training for the future. Your recommendations should include information on frequency, intensity, time and the type of activity.

 *Progress Check*

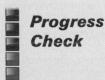

1. What test can be used to measure flexibility?
2. Describe a strength test.
3. What are maximal fitness tests and submaximal fitness tests?
4. Choose a fitness test then name two of its advantages and two of its disadvantages.
5. What important features should be included in any health-screening questionnaire?
6. Give details of two health-monitoring tests.
7. How would you prepare and conduct a test for speed?
8. What health and safety aspects would you always include in any fitness test?
9. Why would you terminate a fitness test before completion?
10. What is normative data?

Practical Team and Individual Sports

This unit covers:

- Using a range of skills, techniques and tactics in selected team and individual sports
- The rules and regulations of selected team and individual sports
- Assessing your own performance in selected team and individual sports
- Assessing the performance of other teams and other individuals in selected sports

These units will help you improve your sports performance as an individual or as part of a team. It provides opportunities to refine you skills, to investigate team and individual tactics, and to review and analyse your performance. It investigates the rules and regulations of team and individual sports and reinforces the health and safety aspects for all participants.

grading criteria	To achieve a **Pass** grade the evidence must show that the learner is able to:	To achieve a **Merit** grade the evidence must show that the learner is able to:	To achieve a **Distinction** grade the evidence must show that the learner is able to:
	P1 describe skills, techniques and tactics required in two different team/individual sports Pg 232	**M1** explain skills, techniques and tactics required in two different team and individual sports Pg 232	**D1** analyse identified strengths and areas for improvement in own performance in two different team/individual sports, and justify suggestions made in relation to personal development Pg 243
	P2 demonstrate appropriate skills, techniques and tactics in two different team/individual sports Pg 232	**M2** explain the application of the rules and regulations of two different team/individual sports in three different situations for each sport Pg 241	**D2** analyse identified strengths and areas for improvement in the performance of a team/individual in a team/individual sport, and justify suggestions made in relation to the development of a team/individual Pg 246
	P3 describe the rules and regulations of two different team/individual sports, and apply them to three different situations for each sport Pg 241	**M3** explain identified strengths and areas of improvement in own performance in two different team/individual sports, and make suggestions relating to personal development Pg 243	

grading criteria	To achieve a **Pass** grade the evidence must show that the learner is able to:	To achieve a **Merit** grade the evidence must show that the learner is able to:	To achieve a **Distinction** grade the evidence must show that the learner is able to:
	P4 using two different methods of assessment, identify strengths and areas of improvement in own performance for two different team/individual sports Pg 243	**M4** explain identified strengths and areas for improvement in the performance of others in a team/individual sport, and make suggestions relating to the development of a team/individual Pg 246	
	P5 using two different methods of assessment, identify strengths and areas for improvement in the performance of others in a team/individual sport Pg 246		

Be able to use a range of skills, techniques and tactics in selected sports

Team sports

Some typical team sports are association football, basketball, cricket, hockey, netball, rugby union, rugby league, rounders, volleyball and lacrosse.

Individual sports

Some typical individual sports are cross-country, golf, gymnastics, judo, swimming, trampolining, badminton, tennis, squash and table tennis.

Skills and techniques for team sports

Some skills and techniques for team sports are passing, throwing, receiving, catching, shooting, movement, turning, intercepting, tackling, footwork, marking, dodging and creating space.

The football pass

Passing techniques in football are important for keeping possession and controlling the game. The easiest and best method for short passes is to use the inside of the foot. This ensures that a flat surface strikes the football.

The instep of the foot can be used for long passes and the heel can be used to pass behind. The outside of the foot can be used to pass the ball quickly to the side, or to bend the ball to pass it around an opponent. Passing drills develop a player's techniques and help them use space effectively. For good passing, the player's head should be over the ball and their body should be well balanced.

Long balls can be highly effective if your team has tall players with strong heading ability or fast forwards who can run behind the defence, but there is a high risk of losing the ball to your opponents. Accurate short passes with supporting runs into space allow a team to keep possession and build an attack. Ideally you want to approach the ball at an angle of about 30° so that you have room to swing through with your kicking leg.

Position your non-kicking foot close to the side of the ball, use your arms for balance, keep your head still and keep your eyes on the ball. Keeping your ankle firm, bring your kicking foot through and strike the centre of the ball with the side of the foot. Striking the centre of the ball will keep the ball on the ground. The aim is to make contact with the centre of the ball or above the centre of the ball. With this type of passing you are looking to keep the ball low so it is easy for a teammate to control.

The weight you put on the pass is important. Follow through with your kicking leg to increase the power of the pass. Vary the weight of the pass to suit the distance you want to cover. Your ability to judge the weighting of pass will improve with experience. There are many soccer drills for passing skills, and one of the most enjoyable is a game of three, four or five a side played in a small area, such as one-quarter of the pitch. Using a confined area forces players to keep moving to find space.

Figure 7.1 Passing is a way to keep possession and control the game

case study 7.1   Football pass

Players such as David Beckham and Steven Gerrard frequently use the drive pass during a game. Others often lose the ball through poor technique.

activity
INDIVIDUAL WORK

1. How would you describe the drive pass in football?
2. In what situations would you use the drive pass?

Football Association
www.thefa.com
Scottish Football Association
www.scottishfa.co.uk
Fédération Internationale de Football Association
www.fifa.com
Union of European Football Associations
www.uefa.com
Women's football
www.thefa.com\womens

The hockey pass

The push pass is the best way to pass the ball over a distance of about 10 m. It is a quick and accurate way of getting the ball to a teammate. The push pass can also be disguised to deceive your opponents.

The hands on the hockey stick should be about 30 cm apart, with the left hand near the top of the stick and the right hand further down. Keep your eyes on the ball, with your feet apart and knees bent and make sure your back foot is in line with the ball.

Keep your stick in contact with the ball as you begin to shift your weight from your back foot to your front foot. Follow through, keeping your stick in contact with the ball for as long as possible and increasing the speed of your stick head as you near your front foot.

To gain more power and pace, stay low and side on to the target and follow through firmly with your stick; it should finish pointing towards the direction of the pass.

Figure 7.2 The push pass is quick and accurate

Hockey Network
www.hockey-net.co.uk
Welsh Hockey Union
www.welsh-hockey.co.uk
England Hockey
www.englandhockey.co.uk

Skills and techniques for individual sports

Some skills and techniques for individual sports are take-offs, landings, grips, swings, throwing, attacking and defending shots, serves, footwork, rotation and turns.

Gymnastics: basic floor skills

Backward roll

- The momentum for the backward roll is gained by pushing with the arms. A very common error is to roll over one side of the head.
- The gymnast must place their hands flat on the floor, fingers towards their shoulders as they roll back.
- A good drill to establish this is to have the gymnast roll back, place their hands flat on the floor by their head and roll back to a stand.
- Doing a backward roll down an incline with a mat will help develop a feel for the skill or *kinaesthesia*.
- The gymnasts should land on their feet, not on their knees.

Forward roll

- To start the roll, the gymnast needs to squat knees together and place both hands flat on the floor in front of them.
- The gymnast should then tuck their head down while pushing with their legs and should keep some weight supported with their arms.
- Gymnasts should be encouraged to stand up without pushing on the floor with their hands.
- A good drill is to encourage the gymnast to rock onto their back and roll up to their feet keeping their arms straight out in front.

Handstand

- One of the most important skills in gymnastics is a good handstand. The handstand is often the basis of other skills in gymnastics.
- The handstand should stretch or extend as much possible. The gymnast should be stretching upwards towards the ceiling and staying hollow.
- A gymnast should be able to look at their toes while in a handstand. Doing this requires the handstand to be tight and hollow.

Basic blocking skills for vaulting

- Set up a vault board and a large mat or stacked mats about level with the gymnast's shoulders.
- The gymnast punches to a handstand then falls to a hollow with only a couple of steps. Arms should be kept next to the ears, body positions tight.
- With the stacked mats work block to back. Full run approach, punch off the board, block through a handstand on the mats to land flat on the mats. It is very important to maintain proper body position. Shoulders should be completely open.

- Work on arm swing to block against a wall. Gymnasts could stand near a wall, lean in with an arm circle and block off the wall with straight arms. Really focus on blocking through the shoulders.

- Handstand shoulder shrugs. From a handstand facing the wall, shrug up and down without bending the arms.

- Hand bouncing on a sprung floor or on mats. Kick to a handstand block then continue to bounce on the hands. Before trying this, check that the gymnast has a strong handstand.

Gymnastics Library

www.gymnasticslibrary.com

British Gymnastics

www.british-gymnastics.org

Figure 7.3 Gymnasts require skills on apparatus and the floor

remember

Skills are often learned by progressing from simple skills to more complex skills.

Improving swimming technique

This section is adapted from a 2006 article by Matt Luebbers at www.swimming.about.com

Factors that affect swimming speed include technique, fitness, joint flexibility and the size of your hands and feet. There are several swimming skills you can work on to get faster in the water. These skills can also make you more efficient – you might go at the same speed but use less energy. To increase your swimming speed, decrease your swimming drag or increase your swimming force. The first steps to faster swimming are body positioning, water catching and grabbing, pressing and rotating.

Body positioning

The body needs to be in the best possible position to minimise the drag of the water and to increase the power available from muscles through good biomechanical leverage. While swimming, the body should be straight and long, and parallel to the water surface. You should be looking down, sideways or up to the side as you breathe, but never forward. If you look forward, your legs will tend to drop towards the bottom, and you will lose your parallel alignment with the water. The top of your head always points towards your destination.

Water catching and grabbing

Put your hand and forearm in a position that allows you to grab the water. Reach forward and down when swimming and point your fingertips towards the bottom of the pool, point your elbow up towards the sky or out towards the side, and think of everything from the elbow joint down the forearm and through the fingertips as one large paddle.

Pressing

Press on the water with the largest muscles available. For most swimmers that means the muscles in the chest and back, not the arms or shoulders. Feel a pocket develop in the armpit as you apply force to the water. As you press on the water, your back and chest muscles pull your arms from ahead of you to under and behind your chest. Imagine grabbing the water first, then pressing on the water. Feel your body surge forward over your arms as you press.

Rotating

To make full use of the grab and the press, rotate your body about an axis from the top of your head through your neck, back and legs. When your arm is grabbing, rotate your body so the grabbing arm side is under water and the opposite side is above the water, or at least closer to the water surface than the grabbing side. Rotate your body

Figure 7.4 Swimming speed depends on fitness, joint flexibility and hand size

as one unit, from shoulders through hips, with the hips and shoulders in line with each other. Having grabbed the water, press on the water and rotate your body as you press, moving it slightly ahead of the press.

Swimming Teachers' Association
www.sta.co.uk
Amateur Swimming Association
www.britishswimming.org
Swimclub.co.uk – online swimming forum
www.swimclub.co.uk

Tactics for team sports

Some tactics for team sports are attack, defence, set plays, team formations, movement, communication and phases of play. Tactics have to be relevant to your own sport.

Cricket tactics

The captain places fielders in positions designed to get the batsmen out by being in the right places to take catches, and to prevent runs being scored by the batting side. Taking wickets is crucial to winning the game, so there will almost always be several fielders in positions to take catches: slips, gully, silly point, silly mid-off, silly mid-on, short leg and leg slip.

CricInfo
www.cricinfo.com
ABC of Cricket
www.abcofcricket.com

More dispersed or varied fielding positions in the outfield are designed to prevent runs, while several fielders are also in positions to take an occasional catch. Examples include point, cover, mid-off, mid-on, midwicket and square leg.

Figure 7.5 Field placement is a key tactic in cricket

Figure 7.6 Cricket field positions

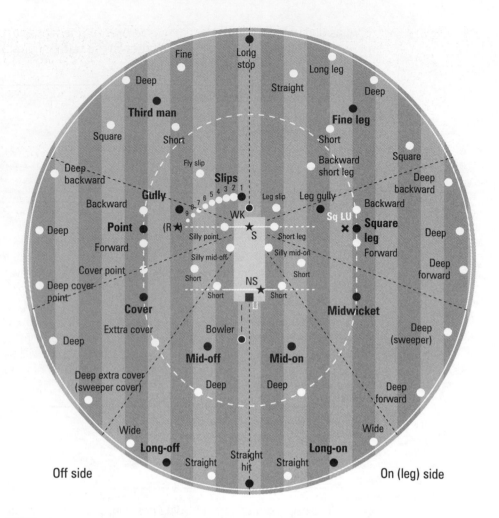

Off side   On (leg) side

● Mandatory fielder: bowler and wicket-keeper (WK)
● Traditional primary position of the region
○ Variations of, or additions to, the primary position
✗ Umpire (U) and square leg umpire (Sq LU)
★ Batsman: striking (S), non-striking (NS), runner (R)
- - - Approximate regions
– – – 33-yard circle
——— Boundary

Short: nearer batsman
Silly: very near batsman
Deep: further from batsman
Wide: further from line of pitch
Fine, straight: nearer line of pitch
Square: nearer line of batsman's crease
Backward: behind batsman's crease
Forward: in front of batsman's crease

Positions in the outfield are mainly used to prevent runs. They include third man, deep point, deep cover, long-off, long-on, deep midwicket, deep square leg and fine leg. All are called defensive fielders. With fielders in the outfield, the bowler can tempt the batsman with bouncers, challenging them to hook the ball clear of the fielders and setting up possible catches.

Fields can be described as attacking, to take wickets, or defensive, to prevent runs. Field placements also depend on the type of bowler. A standard attacking field for a fast bowler may include three or four slips, one or two gullies and perhaps a short leg or a silly point. It can also include mid-off, mid-on and fine leg. Remaining fielders can be placed at cover, point, midwicket or square leg.

A defensive field for a fast bowler will have one or two slips, then almost a full ring of infielders: gully, point, cover, mid-off, mid-on, midwicket and square leg. A fine leg and perhaps a third man cover the boundary behind the batsman, while outfielders forward of the batsman will vary depending on the batsman's tendency to hit in certain directions.

case study 7.2

Cricket field

A close slip, gully, and two or more other close catchers: silly point, silly mid-off, silly mid-on, short leg and a leg slip are all placed. The rest of the fielders form an infield ring.

activity
GROUP WORK

1. What sort of field placement does this describe?
2. What type of bowler would it suit?

Netball tactics

The aim of these tactics is to create smooth passages of play in and around the goal circle and to maximise scoring opportunities.

How to develop correct movements

- Place marker cones in the goal circle, 1 m apart.
- Facing down court and using a running step, the shooter makes figures of eight, working around the cones.
- Add the other shooter, coaching the need to keep a balanced circle. This is an exercise in spatial awareness and positioning, crucial aspects of effective play.
- Then add a pass from a feeder who is stationary.
- Take the cones away but try to keep the figure-of-eight pattern going as much as possible.
- Use chest and bounce passes and vary the distance, height and strength of each pass.
- Coach the need for forward or diagonal backward movement to take a pass.
- Then add one player as a defender.
- The ball starts in the circle, passes out to the moving feeder, who passes to the free player, who shoots for goal with normal defending and rebounding.
- Coach the need for eye or ball faking by the feeder before the ball is passed.
- Then add another feeder, such as wing attack (WA) or centre (C).
- The ball travels from the centre with the pass going to the WA. Both shooters are in the circle moving in a figure-of-eight pattern with one defender marking the players.
- The ball is passed in and out of the circle three times before a shot is attempted.
- Coach the importance of cooperative play between the players with appropriate body language and good eye contact.
- Next the goal attack (GA) stands out of the circle and could receive the centre pass.
- To vary this, ask for the ball to be passed to the GA before it enters the shooting circle.
- Give the number of times the ball must be passed between the players before a shot is attempted.
- Add defenders and build up into a centre-pass strategy with options of passing in and around the circle.

case study 7.3

Netball team

A netball team have a problem distributing the ball quickly to outplay opponents. They are often too slow in catching and passing the ball and often lose possession. The coach is seeking ways of improving team tactics but this problem is preventing development.

activity
GROUP WORK

1. What tactics might the coach wish to employ?
2. What individual techniques could be improved to help these tactics?

Figure 7.7 Netball tactics can maximise scoring opportunities

 England Netball
www.england-netball.co.uk
International Federation of Netball Associations
www.netball.org
Netball Skills – many links to other netball sites
www.netballskills.com

Tactics for individual sports

Some tactics for individual sports are attack, defence, movement, communication and phases of play.

Badminton tactics for doubles play

The basic service is the low one. The server should follow it to the net to cover any replies and to force the receiver to lift the return to the server's partner in the rear court. High serves are used for variety and, since the receiver will have a chance to hit downwards, the server should retreat for defence to a position that is level with their partner in mid-court. The same system should be applied during rallies; if you or your partner lift the shuttle so it can be hit downwards by your opponent, then adopt the side-by-side defensive formation. But if the shuttle is above net height, hit it downwards and adopt the front-and-rear formation.

In the side-by-side defensive formation, the aim is to play shots the opposition will not be able to attack. These shots are usually drives through the front player or net shots in front of them. When you attempt a shot like this, as soon as the shuttle reaches a position on your opponent's side from where it cannot be attacked – at or below net height – the striker should immediately move in towards the net. This converts a defensive position into an attacking position. When conversion shots are not feasible, lift the shuttle deep to the rear of the court to allow time to cover the next shot.

Suppose you are the rear-court player in the front-and-rear attacking formation. You should keep hitting downwards in a straight direction so your partner knows roughly where the shuttle will be played. Use a variety of pace and angles to force your opponent into making a weak reply for your partner. Lift the shuttle only under exceptional pressure, because your partner at the net will be an easy target to attack. Your partner, the net player, should be looking to intercept any replies that pass within reach. Their racket must be kept above net height so the shuttle can be taken as early as possible. If the shuttle cannot be killed, it should be played tight to the net to force the opposition to lift it again, thereby maintaining the attack. When attacking, play cross-court shots only occasionally, as they put your partner out of position and create space for your opponents to exploit.

Badminton tactics for mixed doubles

The basic formation for mixed doubles involves the woman covering the forecourt and the man covering the mid-court and the rear court. To help assume this position, when the man is serving, the woman should stand in front of him on his non-racket side. As with level doubles, the low service is favoured, although a variety of high serves to the woman may often be used to force her away from her forecourt position.

The role of the woman in mixed doubles is similar to the role of the net player in level doubles; she must stand in the forecourt with her racket up and ready to intercept any shot she can take in front of her. As soon as the shuttle has gone past her, it becomes the responsibility of the man. Whenever possible, she should hit the shuttle downwards to force the opposing man to reach forwards to lift it.

The man's main objective should be to take the shuttle as early as possible and to strike it downwards or at least flat to prevent the opposition from attacking his partner. He must also avoid lifting it, as his partner at the net will have little time to react to a shuttle struck down at her. When a pair are forced to lift, the woman should always position herself across the court from where the opposition are hitting. This will give her slightly more time to sight the shuttle, as it will have to travel a greater distance to reach her.

Badminton England
www.badmintonengland.co.uk
Badzone – badminton club directory
www.badzone.co.uk

Figure 7.8 Badminton tactics are based on court positioning

case study 7.4

Badminton tactics

During a game of badminton the doubles team realise that their opponents are exploiting one of the team member's weakness in their backhand. The opponents keep scoring points and the game is turning against them.

activity
GROUP WORK

1. What tactics could be employed to combat the opposing team's strategies?
2. How might the team communicate with each other to change tactics?

Tennis tactics for doubles play

In doubles, the server normally serves from about midway between the centre and the doubles sideline. There are good reasons for serving from elsewhere: to serve to the receiver's backhand, to be deceptive, if your serve works well from a wide angle. Serve from various places to add variety to your game.

Returning serve is tougher in doubles than in singles, because you have a partner at the net. It is better to get the first serve in and let your partner finish off the return. Try to achieve a high percentage of first serves. If you are partnering the server, you normally stand about midway between the centreline and the doubles sideline. Don't stand too close to the net. If you get an easy volley, you should step towards the net.

Good doubles players never play one up, one back. They try to get both players up to the net so they control the point. When they get to the net, they normally go to the net together. When driven from the net, because they are lobbed over their heads or because the opponents are about to pound an overhead, they back up to the baseline together.

Signals

Some tennis partnerships or teams give signals to share tactics in doubles play. Usually the server's partner signals if they wants to cross. A fist behind the back usually means they are staying, and an open hand means they are crossing. Sometimes a team will give signals to show where they want the server to aim their first serve. Teams that don't signal can get together and talk.

Verbal communication and calls

There should sometimes be verbal communication between the players. Here are some examples: Mine! I got it! Yours! Take it! Bounce it! No! Switch! Try not to call for a ball just after the ball bounces, as that may be heard as a line call. If your partner calls for the ball, you must let them have it, no matter how easily you can play it or how tough it looks for them. A volley, including an overhead, belongs to the person at the net, unless they are called off it. Get into the habit of calling for the ball by calling for the overheads that are obviously yours. Call 'Yours!' when the lob is obviously going to your partner, then they won't worry if they hear you nearby.

Figure 7.9 Communication is very important when playing doubles

Lawn Tennis Association
www.lta.org.uk
Tennis.co.uk
www.tennis.co.uk

---

activity
INDIVIDUAL WORK
7.1

P1

P2

1. Choose two different sports, either two team sports (Unit 7) or two individual sports (Unit 8) and describe the skills, techniques and tactics for each one. Write out the descriptions and make a portfolio for each sport. This portfolio can be used for writing up your practical sessions and for your teacher to attach observation records.

2. Do a demonstration for the rest of the group that shows them appropriate skills, techniques and tactics of your chosen sports. Include your planning and observation assessments in your portfolio.

---

activity
INDIVIDUAL WORK
7.2

M1

Write a detailed explanation of your skills, techniques and tactics for your two chosen sports. Make your explanations by putting your ideas into game situations. Include your explanations in each of your sport portfolios.

Understand the rules and regulations of selected sports

For your selected sports you should know and understand the written laws or rules produced by the governing body. There are also unwritten rules that largely relate to sportsmanship and sports etiquette.

---

case study
7.5

Injured player

In a football match, a shot hits a defender and rebounds to the attackers, who regain control in midfield. The defender has fallen to the ground, injured by the impact of the ball. An attacking team player who has the ball hesitates, wondering what to do while an injured player is in obvious pain on the floor.

---

activity
GROUP WORK

1. What should the attacking player do as part of the etiquette of the game?
2. What then do the defending team do?
3. What other examples are there of unwritten rules related to etiquette for your sport?

Rules for selected team sports

Men's lacrosse

Rule 19 on numbers of players

19.1 Ten players shall constitute a full team. There shall be 1 goalkeeper, 3 defenders, 3 midfielders and 3 attackers.

19.2 If, because of injuries or men out of the game due to expulsion fouls, a team cannot keep 10 players in the game, then it may continue the game with fewer than 10 players, but no exceptions will be made to the regular rules for this situation.

Rule 20 on substitutes

20.1 A team may have up to 3 substitutes.

20.2 Only 13 players in a squad may dress in team uniform for a game. Any others in the squad who are in the bench area must wear alternate strip or tracksuits.

Rule 21 on captains

21.1 Each team shall designate a captain or co-captains, and they shall act as the representatives of their team on the field of play during the game. Where a team designates co-captains, one of them shall be designated the official representative of that team on the field.

21.2 The privilege of the captains to act as the representatives of the team on the field does not grant them the right to enter into argument with an official or to criticise any decision of an official.

21.3 Should the captain leave the field of play, either he or his coach should designate to the nearest referee the name and number of the replacing captain. If a team is without a designated captain at any time during the play of the game, then one of the referees may designate an acting captain.

Women's lacrosse

New major foul

A player must not use her crosse and/or her body with force in a dangerous and/or intimidating manner, and/or show disregard for the safety of an opponent. Dangerous follow-through has been added to fouls requiring a mandatory yellow card.

Carding procedure for personal/misconduct fouls

a. A player receiving a yellow card must leave the field for 2 minutes of lapsed playing time. A substitute may take her place.

b. A player receiving a second yellow card (yellow and red card shown together), is suspended from playing for the remainder of the game. Her team must *play short for 5 minutes of lapsed playing time before a substitute may enter the game.

c. A player receiving a single red card is suspended from the remainder of the game, and her team must *play short for 10 minutes of lapsed playing time before a substitute may take her place.

Carding procedure for delay of game and/or persistent minor fouls

a. Green card to captain (minor foul penalty).

b. Green/yellow card to player who fouled (major foul penalty).

c. Green/red card to player who fouled (major foul penalty; team must *play short for 5 minutes of lapsed playing time before the player or substitute may enter the game).

*Teams must play short below/goal side of the restraining lines at both ends of the field.

Volleyball

- Six players on court.
- First team to 25 points wins.
- Of the six players, three are to the front and three to the back.
- The back player at the left is the server.
- You must serve from behind the back line.
- The serve must be hit with the hand.
- After serving, the server moves back onto court to help their team.
- The serve is allowed to clip the net on the way over, but must not touch the antenna or pass over or outside the antenna.
- Once the ball has been served, any player can move anywhere on court and even chase the ball out of court if needed.
- If the serve is going out, leave it to hit the floor; if you touch it before it lands, you must play the ball back.
- The serve is not allowed to touch the roof.

Volleyball.com – information on all aspects of the sport
www.volleyball.com
About volleyball
www.volleyball.about.com

Rounders

- Games are played between two teams of 6 to 15 players.
- Bowlers must bowl underarm at a height between the knee and head of the batter and without letting the ball bounce, go wide or go straight at the bowler.
- One rounder is scored if (i) the fourth post is reached before another ball is thrown or (ii) if the fourth post is reached on a no-ball.
- Half a rounder rounder is scored if (i) the fourth post is reached without hitting the ball, (ii) the second post is reached after hitting the ball, (iii) there is obstruction by a fielder or (iv) there are two consecutive no-balls.
- The most common ways to be out are caught by a fielder, stumped at a post before reaching it or running inside a post. There are other ways of getting out but these are the most common.
- When at a post you must remain in contact with that post.
- When the bowler has the ball in their square, you cannot run between posts.
- You cannot have more than one batter at each post.
- You must touch the fourth post on getting home.

National Rounders Association
www.nra-rounders.co.uk

Rugby league

The aim of the game is to score more points than the other team. Each team is given six tackles or chances to score. If, after six tackles, they have not scored, then the ball is handed over to the other team who then also have the chance to score with their six tackles. The ball must be passed backwards and you cannot knock the ball forwards, except by kicking it.

A game of rugby league consists of two halves of 40 min, with injury time added on at the end of each half. In between the two halves, there is a 10 min interval after which both teams change ends and attack the half they were defending. A hooter or whistle will indicate the start and finish of the half. Play is only allowed to continue after the whistle or hooter sounds if the ball is still in play. The half will immediately end once a tackle is made or the ball goes out to touch. Time can be extended for a penalty kick or a kick at goal.

Rugby league is played on a pitch no more than 100 m long and 68 m wide. Most colts and juniors will play on pitches smaller than this. The pitch is covered in several markings to indicate the different lines in the game. The three most important lines are the goal lines, the deadlines and the halfway line. There are also several 10 m markings from the touchline on the pitch to show where scrums and restarts should be taken.

Rugby Football League
www.therfl.co.uk
World of Rugby League
www.rleague.com
Rugby League in New Zealand
www.rugbyleague.co.nz

Figure 7.10 Pitch dimensions for rugby league

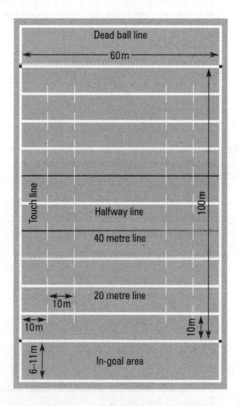

Rugby union

Rugby union is a fifteen-a-side football game; it can also be played seven-a-side, when it is called sevens. The goalposts on a standard pitch are 5.64 m (18 ft 6 in) apart and have a crossbar, which is 3 m (10 ft) above the ground. The ball is oval and is approximately 28–30 cm (11–12 in) long and 58–62 cm (22–24 in) in circumference. The game is controlled by a referee and two touch judges.

In senior competitions a game has two 40 min halves with a 5 min interval. Points are scored in the following ways:

- **Try** – scored by a player grounding the ball in the opponent's in-goal area, worth 5 points.
- **Conversion** – after scoring a try, the scoring team can attempt a conversion, worth 2 points. A player takes a kick at goal in line with where the ball was grounded.
- **Penalty** – most penalties are scored by place kicks, worth 3 points.
- **Drop goal** – the ball is kicked on the half-volley in open play, worth 3 points.

Rugby Football Union
www.rfu.com
All Blacks – a rugby team in New Zealand
www.allblacks.com
Scottish Rugby
www.scottishrugby.org
Welsh Rugby Union
www.wru.co.uk
Irish Rugby Football Union
www.irishrugby.ie

Basketball

In basketball there are three main ways of scoring points. A player scoring inside the three-point line scores two points, but if he scores outside the line, he picks up three points. In the case of fouls and penalties, players throw the ball from a specified spot straight in front of the basket, and only pick up one point. Basketball is a non-contact game but there is often some contact when players rebound or jump to catch the ball under the basketball hoop.

Two referees officiate down the sides of the court to monitor play, a scorekeeper records the score and any fouls, and a timekeeper keeps track of stoppages, timeouts and the resetting of the 24 s shot clock.

Basketball players aren't allowed to hold the ball or use two hands while running, and must dribble it by batting it from one hand to the floor and back again. If they hold the ball for more than two stops while moving, it is called travelling, and control of play is awarded to the opposing team.

A shot can be made by throwing the ball from a distance in a high arc into the hoop or basket. The lay-up shot is where a player is moving towards the basket and lays the ball up and into the basket, typically off the backboard. The finger roll is an underarm version of the lay-up that propels the ball into the basket without using the backboard. The slam dunk is where a player jumps very high and throws the ball downwards, straight through the hoop.

England Basketball
www.englandbasketball.co.uk
British Basketball League
www.bbl.org.uk
US National Basketball Association
www.nba.com

Figure 7.11 Basketball has rules on shooting, passing and dribbling

Rules for selected individual sports

Golf: the water hazard

One of the important things to remember about a water hazard is that if the ball is touching or is inside the boundary lines, then it is in the hazard. It does not matter that the ball is high and dry or that there is no water to be seen; if the area is defined as a water hazard, then golf's Rule 26 applies and the ball is in water.

If the ball is lodged in the branch of a tree overhanging a water hazard or lies on a bridge across a stream, then the margins of a water hazard extend vertically upward. Therefore, even if it is high and dry, the rules say that it is in the hazard. Here are some things you are not allowed to do in a water hazard:

1. Ground the club or test the condition of the hazard.
2. If there is water, you must not touch the water with the club, except during the forward movement of the club when making a stroke.
3. You must not touch or move a loose impediment, except during the forward movement of the club when making a stroke.
4. You cannot touch the ball for the purpose of identifying it.
5. You cannot declare the ball unplayable.
6. You cannot claim relief from immovable obstructions.
7. You cannot claim relief from burrowing animals, reptiles or birds.
8. You cannot play a provisional ball.

You may do the following:

- You may play the ball as it lies.
- You may remove movable obstructions; these are artificial things such as cigarette packets, bottles and rakes.

UK Golf – reference site for courses and clubs
www.uk-golf.com
Golf.com – golfing news and information
www.golf.com

case study 7.6 — Golf etiquette

A golf player who is a novice wishes to know the basics related to etiquette in golf. The player does not wish to be embarrassed by doing the wrong thing in certain situations, such as talking when someone else is taking a shot.

activity
GROUP WORK

1. What are the main codes of etiquette to follow when another player is taking a golf shot?
2. Give examples in your own sport where etiquette plays a part?

Judo

Scoring

If either player fails to score ippon (the equivalent to a knockout in boxing) during the bout, then the scores picked up during the bout for incomplete moves will be taken into consideration.

- **Throws** – partial scores are given if the opponent does not land largely on their back, or if their landing is not hard enough or fast enough.
- **Pins** – a pin broken before 25 s but after 10 s is awarded partial points.
- **Submission** – a failed attempt at forcing a submission by an armlock or strangle does not score points.

Here are the scores in order of quality from highest to lowest:

- **Ippon** – this is signalled by the referee with an arm straight up; it ends the contest.
- **Waza-ari** – this is signalled by an arm out at shoulder level. Two waza-aris by the same person are considered the same as ippon and end the contest.
- **Yuko** – this is signalled by an arm at 45° out from the side.
- **Koka** – this is signalled by an arm against the side.

In judo it is always the highest quality score that wins. For example, a single waza-ari would beat two yukos and a koka.

It is only if an ippon has not been scored by the end of the timed bout that the scores come into play. The player with the highest score wins. If they tie, the referee and two judges decide who is the winner using a majority decision.

Penalties

Players are expected to play by the rules and attack continuously. Penalties can be given for a number of reasons; here are some examples:

- Intentionally going out of bounds or pushing an opponent out
- Refusing to attack or not showing enough aggression
- Performing dangerous acts intended to injure
- Deliberately going to the floor.

Penalties in judo are severe, with contestants punished in different ways, ranging from a koka for small offences to an ippon for the most serious. A repeat of any transgression results in the next penalty up; the lower penalty is removed. The score is given to the opponent.

Here are the four possible penalties from lowest to highest:

- **Shido** – koka is awarded to the opponent.
- **Chui** – yuko is awarded to the opponent.
- **Keikoku** – waza-ari is awarded to the opponent.
- **Hansokumake** – ippon is awarded to the opponent.

Four warnings result in disqualification.

International Judo Federation
www.ijf.org
British Judo
www.britishjudo.org.uk
Judo Information Site
www.judoinfo.com

Squash

Scoring rules

2.1 Only the server scores points. The server, on winning a rally, scores a point; the receiver, on winning a rally, becomes the server.

2.2 A match shall consist of the best of three or five games at the option of the organisers of the competition. The player who scores nine points wins the game, except that on the score reaching eight all for the first time, the receiver shall choose, before the next service, to continue that game either to nine points (known as 'Set one') or to ten points (known as 'Set two'). In the latter case the player who scores two more points wins the game. The receiver shall clearly indicate this choice to the Marker, Referee and the opponent.

The Marker shall call 'Set one' or 'Set two' as applicable before play continues. The Marker shall call 'Game ball' to indicate that the server requires one point to win the game in progress or 'Match ball' to indicate that the server requires one point to win the match.

World Squash Federation
www.worldsquash.org
England Squash
www.englandsquash.co.uk
Squash Player – online journal
www.squashplayer.co.uk

Table tennis

In table tennis, sometimes called ping-pong, two opponents (singles) or two teams of two opponents (doubles), play a match of games and points. Bats made of wood covered in rubber are used to hit a celluloid ball 40 mm in diameter. The game is played over and on a table with a 15.25 cm high net. The ball is hit by each player onto the opponent's side of a table that is 2.74 m long, 1.525 m wide and 76 cm high.

- A player or team wins a point when the opponent or opponents cannot hit the ball with a bat over the net and onto the other side of the table.

- A game is won by being the first player or team to win 11 points, and to be at least two points ahead of the opponent or opponents.

- If both players or teams have won 10 points, then the first player or team to get a two-point lead wins the game.

- A match can be any odd number of games, but is usually the best of five or seven games. In a five-game match the first player or team to win three games is the winner, and in a seven-game match the first player or team to win four games is the winner.

English Table Tennis Association
www.englishtabletennis.org.uk

Figure 7.12 Table tennis is a popular game for singles or doubles

activity

INDIVIDUAL WORK
7.3

P3

M2

1. Make your own booklet on the rules and regulations of two selected team sports (Unit 7) or individual sports (Unit 8). At the end of your leaflet, create a section headed 'Notes for Guidance' and describe three different situations that may lead to the rules being used.

2. Observe an official such as a referee or umpire and write a report on their performance. Show the application of the rules and regulations of two different team sports (Unit 7) or individual sports (Unit 8) in three different situations for each sport.

Be able to assess performance in selected sports

When you assess your performance or other people's performance in a team or individual sport, use the most accurate means that you can. Performance assessment should be specific to the sport you are performing and should consider the application of skills, as well as the techniques and tactics you use. An overall assessment should include your achievements or how successful you are. Assessments should identify strengths that can be reinforced and areas for improvement that can be worked on by appropriate goal setting or target setting.

Assessments can be based on **objective performance data**, which considers results you have achieved or performance outcomes such as goals scored or shots saved in team sports, distance thrown or distance jumped in individual sports.

case study

7.7

ProZone for professional footballers

ProZone is a technique for collecting objective video evidence and statistics on player performance used by most Premiership football clubs. It collects footage using specially placed cameras around the football stadium. During a match it can measure a player's speed, the distance they cover, where they are most active, where they make most tackles, and so on.

Here is some **ProZone** data about a striker during a game. He covers around 11 km during a match: 4000 m walking, 4000 m jogging, 1500 m running, 1000 m light sprinting and 500 m sprinting. Nearly 10% of the time is spent in the defence, 30% of time is spent in and around the opposing team's penalty box. The player heads the ball 5 times, uses his chest 10 times and his feet touch the ball 100 times.

activity

GROUP WORK

1. How can this objective evidence be used to assess performance?
2. What targets could be set if a player's pitch coverage is unsatisfactory?

Figure 7.13 Footballers use video recordings to improve their performance

Assessments can also be based on **subjective observations**. These assessments involve an observer, normally the coach, who makes judgements on what they see. For example, an athletics coach might watch a high jumper and assess their technique by watching the take-off. The observer's judgements could then be fed back to the athlete.

See page 134 in Unit 4 for more information on validity and reliability
See page 186 in Unit 6 for more information on validity and reliability

Software such as Kandle and Dartfish are now an integral part of performance assessment.

Kandle
www.kandle.co.uk
Dartfish
www.dartfish.com

However the assessment evidence is collected, it has to be analysed before it can be used by the performer and the coach. A typical method of analysis is SWOT analysis.

SWOT analysis

- **Strengths** – What is going well? What well-learned skills do you have? What techniques have you mastered and what tactics do you successfully employ?

- **Weaknesses** – What is going wrong? Are you poor at specific skills or techniques? Have you used tactics that are not successful?

- **Opportunities** – What can you do next time to improve? Will you try to do more practice? Can you watch others and learn from them?

- **Threats** – What barriers are there in taking up these opportunities? You may not know how to get help and the right advice. You may not have enough time to develop your skills, techniques and tactics.

remember

Observations of performance may not be accurate. Sports performances often happen very quickly and important information might be missed. An observer may be biased and then their assessment may lack validity.

activity

INDIVIDUAL WORK 7.4

P4

Having talked to your coach or equivalent, identify strengths and areas for improvement in your own performance on two different team sports (Unit 7) or two different individual sports (Unit 8). Then use two other ways of assessing your own performance and compare the results. Write a report showing your results.

activity

INDIVIDUAL WORK 7.5

M3

D1

Write an application for sponsorship. Explain your identified strengths and areas for improvement. As part of your application, produce an action plan that relates to improving your own performance in two different sports. Based on your application, ask someone to give you a mock interview where you have to justify your suggestions.

Performance analysis

Performance analysis often includes video evidence of a performer doing a sport. The analysis can be quite simple, such as highlighting the performer's main strengths and weaknesses, or it can be deeper, such as notational analysis. The greater the depth, the more reliable the analysis.

Notational analysis

Notational analysis involves taking notes about the performance of a person or team during an activity. The notes provide important information for assessing what went well and what needs improvement; see SWOT analysis (page 242).

Notational analysis may consider statistics related to the activity or game, such as how many shots on target or how many successful passes. Tennis coaches, for example, may record the numbers of aces, double faults and forehand winners. The results of these analyses can highlight areas of concern or may give important information that the coach can use to develop a player's tactics. There is always the danger of the performer being affected by this type of observation. If you know that you are being watched and judged, your behaviour may change; you may show off more, lose concentration or change the way you play.

See page 308 in Unit 16 for more information on observed behaviour
See page 186 in Unit 6 for more information on validity and reliability of tests

Analysis model

For any analysis to be successful there needs to be a sequence of events.

All analysis must lead to an evaluation of what is going wrong and what is going right, what needs to be praised and what needs to be developed. The next stage is to formulate a plan with realistic goals. Following the plan, there needs to be practice or performance. The player's performance in the next match is observed then a new five-stage analysis is begun.

Once you have evaluated performance, use a process of development or ways to improve skills, techniques and tactics. Aims and objectives are important. They are based on the strengths and weaknesses identified from your analysis (page 242).

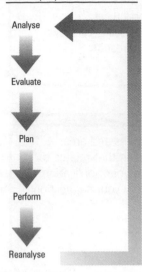

Figure 7.14 Analysis is a five-step cycle

Analyse

↓

Evaluate

↓

Plan

↓

Perform

↓

Reanalyse

Technical weaknesses might include shooting in netball or extension in a trampolining move. Tactical weaknesses may include marking players in hockey or outwitting your opponent in judo.

Training

The planned training programme should be set out week by week, session by session. Each training session should also be planned and structured to suit the development of specific techniques and tactics. Each training session should also involve a warm-up and a cooldown appropriate to the activity. All this should be written clearly as part of the programme.

Technical development

Each training session should include specific activities to improve the targeted technique or skill. For example, if the target is to improve shooting in netball, then each session should have an element of shooting with specific activities such as shooting with and without pressure.

Tactical development

Each training session should also include tactical development. Techniques could be practised against performers at different levels, from the less skilled to the very skilled. Each session could have activities that vary to reflect real game situations. If appropriate, tactics can be developed individually then in small groups then in a full game situation.

Recording documentation

The programme must be planned and recorded, and so must the development of the programme; in other words, record what happens in each session and what adaptations can be brought into the next training session. Perhaps dribbling in basketball was planned to be non-opposed in the first two sessions, but after one session you are ready for an opponent, so you adapt your programme accordingly.

Here are some recording documents:

- Diary
- Logbook
- Portfolio
- Video
- Audio
- Observation record
- Feedback sheets
- Written feedback on skill learning.

Figure 7.15 Weak judo tactics may lose you points

Goal setting

Goal setting is the identification of objectives; the objectives can be short-term, medium-term or long-term. Goal setting is a useful strategy and is widely used in sport for training and performance. Goals can be set by a performer on their own or a coach on their own, but they tend to more effective if the coach and performer set them together. Goal setting is a proven way to increase motivation and confidence and to control anxiety.

Two types of goal are set for sportspeople:

- **Performance goals** – these goals are related directly to the performance or technique of the activity.

- **Outcome goals** – these goals are concerned with the end result, such as whether you win or lose.

Goal setting following evaluation is important if you wish to continue to develop technical and tactical skills. Goals should include long-term elements and short-term elements. For example, suppose you achieve only 60% of successful drops in badminton. After

---

case study 7.8

Goals to improve hockey performance

A member of the national women's hockey team realised that her close control of the ball under pressure was inadequate for international games. She set the goal of being able to collect and distribute a firmly struck ball without hesitation and under pressure from an opponent.

---

activity

INDIVIDUAL WORK

1. How would you make her goal even more SMART?
2. What short-term goals could she concentrate on at first?

Figure 7.16 Goal setting can improve performance

your training programme you do an evaluation and decide that your training sessions should involve more practices under pressure in a realistic environment. A short-term goal would be to spend 10 min of every session practising the drop. A medium-term goal would be that, in competition, 70% of drops will be successful after six weeks and 80% of drops will be successful by the end of the season. Goals are more effective if they have been agreed by all interested parties. For example, get your coach or instructor to agree your goals and write a joint statement.

All goals should follow the SMART principle.

- S = specific
- M = measurable
- A = achievable
- R = recorded
- T = timed.

 Link   See page 312 in Unit 16 for more information on goal setting

activity
INDIVIDUAL WORK
7.6

P5

Observe teams or individuals. Use two different assessment methods and identify strengths and areas for improvement in the performance of a team in a team sport (Unit 7) or an individual in an individual sport (Unit 8).

activity
INDIVIDUAL WORK
7.7

M4

D2

Explain and justify any suggestions for developing a team (Unit 7) or an individual (Unit 8) by assuming the role of a scout reporting verbally and in writing to a selector. Write a report or give a presentation of your findings.

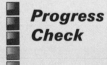 ***Progress Check***

1. What are the differences between skills, techniques and tactics in sport?
2. Choose two sports, team or individual. Consider each sport separately and say what skills it uses the most.
3. Name two different techniques in a sport of your choice. What makes these techniques effective?
4. Consider your own sport. What are its tactics for attack and defence?
5. In what ways does communication form part of tactics in your sport?
6. What is etiquette in sport? Give two examples of etiquette in your sport.
7. What makes an effective performance assessment in sport?
8. What is performance profiling?
9. What is a SWOT analysis?
10. What are SMART goals?

Sport and Society

This unit covers:

- How the development of sport has influenced its organisation
- The sports industry in the UK today
- Contemporary issues affecting sport
- Cultural influences and barriers that affect participation in sports activities

Sport can have a big effect on society and society can have a big effect on sport. This unit explores how sport has evolved, with a particular focus on UK sport. It describes the development of sport from pre-industrial times to the rationalisation of our major sports. It also covers the key organisations that influences sport in the UK.

The UK sports industry is divided into public, private and voluntary sectors. This unit looks at the functioning of the three sectors and considers contemporary issues such as sport and the media, sport and racism, sport and health improvement. It covers the cultural factors that influence sports participation, such as gender, ethnicity and social class, and describes initiatives that break down barriers to participation.

grading criteria

To achieve a **Pass** grade the evidence must show that the learner is able to:	To achieve a **Merit** grade the evidence must show that the learner is able to:	To achieve a **Distinction** grade the evidence must show that the learner is able to:
P1 describe the development and organisation of sport from its pre-industrial origins to the present day Pg 253	**M1** explain the development and organisation of sport from its pre-industrial origins to the present day Pg 257	**D1** evaluate the effects of four contemporary issues on sport Pg 272
P2 describe the scale, structure and provision of the sports industry in the UK today Pg 260	**M2** explain the effects of four contemporary issues on sport Pg 270	**D2** analyse the barriers to sports participation Pg 276
P3 describe the effects of four contemporary issues on sport Pg 266	**M3** explain three cultural influences on sports participation Pg 272	**D3** evaluate three strategies or initiatives which relate to sports participation Pg 282
P4 describe three cultural influences on sports participation Pg 272	**M4** explain the barriers to sports participation Pg 275	

Understand how the development of sport has influenced how it is organised

The development of sport

Sport has had a major influence on our society. It has prepared people to go to war, to hunt for food or to improve their fitness for work. In medieval times, the peasants had little time or energy for anything except working the land, but there were some opportunities for activities such as mob football, which brought out whole villages on holy days and festivals.

The development of mob football

Mob football was a mass game with very few rules. It was played just a few times a year by people in a village or by one village against another. The games were rather like football or rugby and were often extremely violent, so violent that people nearby would barricade their homes during matches. The idea was to force a ball into the centre of the opposing village or into a specific part of one village, such as the marketplace or the village square.

Many theories have been put forward to explain how mob football originated. Earlier versions of mob football, like Shrovetide football, had vague rules restricting only murder or manslaughter. Some historians think that the game originated in Britain around the third century as a celebration over the defeated Romans. Others claim that the game was originally played with the severed head of a vanquished Danish prince. The game may also have been a pagan ritual in which the ball, representing the sun, had to be conquered and driven around the field to ensure a good harvest. There is evidence of early rugby being played in teams between married men and bachelors.

According to one theory, mob football was introduced to England during the Norman invasion from France. A similar game is known to have existed in Normandy not long before mob football appeared in England. There are written records of unfortunate and even fatal incidents that occurred because of mob football. Two instances dating from 1280 and 1312 describe deadly encounters caused by playing with a sheathed knife on the belt. Such examples probably stimulated the development of unwritten laws and principles.

On 13 April 1314 King Edward II issued one of the first recorded prohibitions, because of the impact that 'this hustling over large balls' had on the merchant life. Edward III also tried to stop 'futeball' in 1349, followed by Richard II, Henry IV, Henry VI and James III. The game was frowned upon by the bourgeoisie due to its unchristian nature and its lack of regulations.

Figure 11.1 Mob football was a mass game with very few rules

The ruling classes also had their activities, which eventually became the sports that we know today. For instance, hunting was very popular with those who owned the land and the aristocracy. This was an exclusive activity for the upper classes because they had the land and the money. They also had more time on their hands than the lowly peasants.

Cockfighting goes back to medieval times and often took place in a pit approximately 14 ft (4.3 m) square with an 8 in (200 mm) high fence. Cockfighting was generally an upper-class sport, which is probably why it survived way into the nineteenth century. It was finally made illegal by Act of Parliament in 1849. There was a great deal of gambling on these cruel spectacles. The lower classes often participated in 'throwing at cocks', which traditionally happened on Shrove Tuesday. The cockerel was tied to a stake and you would have to pay to throw sticks or stones at it, from about 20 ft (6 m). If you knocked the bird over and picked up the stick before the bird picked itself up, you could claim the bird as your own and charge others to throw at it.

case study 11.1

Cockfighting in the Midlands over 250 years ago

Here is a report in a Birmingham newspaper of 1746: 'This is to give notice that there will be a main of cocks fought at Duddeston Hall near Birmingham betwixt the gentlemen of Warwickshire and the gentlemen of Worcestershire for four guineas a battle and forty guineas the main. To weigh on Monday 9th June and fight the two following days.'

activity
INDIVIDUAL WORK

1. Who were involved in cockfighting and why?
2. What similar activity did the peasants participate in?

In the nineteenth century, the upper classes began to attend schools called public schools. The word 'public' suggests they were open to anyone, but in fact they were almost exclusively for the upper classes and initially just boys. Sports were developed in these public schools; the popular ones are the forerunners of what we play now.

Figure 11.2 Many sports were developed in public schools

Parents of early nineteenth-century public schoolboys were concerned about the treatment of their boys who, under the prefect–fagging system, were experiencing brutality and bullying. Schools had to take action or face the prospect of parents taking their children elsewhere. Thomas Arnold, headmaster at Rugby school, wanted his pupils to grow up as moral Christian gentlemen, so he revised the fagging system and promoted more regulated sports, which provided exercise and encouraged healthy competition. By 1845 the pupils at Rugby wrote down the rules of football at their school to ensure fair play. In the Rugby version, handling the ball was allowed, but in 1849 pupils at Eton created a rival game, restricting the use of hands.

The pupils took their games with them to university, but many played different versions. Cambridge University had four goes at achieving a common set of rules during the 1840s and 1850s. Eventually, in 1863, it decided on a set of rules where handling the ball was outlawed. At the end of that year, players from around the country came together to form the Football Association (FA) and the Cambridge rules were adopted.

The formation of the FA matched the desire for order that was becoming increasingly important at that time. Other sports followed suit and the Amateur Athletic Club (AAC) was formed in 1866, the Rugby Football Union (RFU) in 1871 and the Lawn Tennis Association (LTA) in 1888. There were mainly social aspects to these organisations, as most were formed in pubs, but they did establish rules and competition arrangements.

See page 232 in Unit 7&8 for more information on rules and regulations of major sports

You can find out about the history of sports from their governing bodies:

Football Association

www.thefa.com

Rugby Football Union

www.rfu.com

Lawn Tennis Association

www.lta.org.uk

Tennis competitions were organised before the creation of a governing body. The first Wimbledon championships were held in 1877, 11 years before the launch of the LTA. In 1858 Major Henry Gem marked out the first court on a lawn in Edgbaston. Major Walter Wingfield is said to have developed the modern game of tennis, although some academics disagree about this. He patented a game called Sphairistike, which used a 'new and improved court for playing the ancient game of tennis'. Wingfield sold sets of his game for five guineas; they included balls, four racquets and netting to mark out the court. The name 'lawn tennis' replaced the name Sphairistike.

case study 11.2 — Cricket past and present

In 1861 an English touring team travelled to Australia for the first time. Seven years later a team of Aboriginals toured England, although the first official Test match was not until 1877, when Australia beat England in Melbourne. Australia won their first Test in England in 1882 and the *Sporting Times* published its famous mock obituary: 'In affectionate remembrance of English cricket which died at the Oval on 29th August, 1882. Deeply lamented by a large circle of sorrowing friends and acquaintances.. The body will be cremated and the ashes taken to Australia.' The 'body' is reputed to be one of the bails, and England and Australia have played for the Ashes ever since.

activity
INDIVIDUAL WORK

1. How can we link today's cricket competitions with historical information?
2. What does the mock obituary reveal about how cricket was viewed in 1882?

Golf's rules were first written in the eighteenth century, but the Open Championship was first played in 1861. Before 1861 there had been separate competitions for amateurs and professionals (pros) as the pros did not fit in with sport's image of a gentlemanly game. The Marylebone Cricket Club (MCC) hired professionals for bowling and fielding so the 'gentlemen' could practise their batting. This distinction between amateur batsmen and professional bowlers led to the annual matches between gentlemen and players. They ran from 1806 right up to 1962 and the two sets of players used different facilities and were not expected to mix off the pitch.

Spectators became more important as interest in sport grew. Transport developments also helped. Factory owners, who once did all they could to prevent their workers playing sports, now realised that sport could keep their workers healthy and loyal. Many employers encouraged the formation of works teams.

case study 11.3 — Formation of teams from factories

Dial Square, formed by workers at the Royal Arsenal in Woolwich in 1886, went on to become Arsenal FC. West Ham was formed by the workforce at Thames Iron Works in 1895. Newton Heath, founded by workers from the Lancashire and Yorkshire Railway Company, went on to become Manchester United.

activity
GROUP WORK

1. Why did factory owners encourage sports teams?
2. Name some famous teams in your area and say how they started out.

After the mid nineteenth century, sport really started to develop quickly. One major factor that influenced the development and participation in sport was the amount of leisure time available.

Increased leisure time

Before the industrial revolution most of the work was on the land and there was no real distinction between work and leisure. Agricultural work was dictated by the seasons and there was no set amount of free time for the workers. The growth of factories and machinery within the factories meant that working hours were long and pay was poor. It was quite common for a worker to work 72 hours per week, so they had very little time and energy to do sport.

The Saturday half-day was very important in providing a short period when sport could take place. Skilled workers were given this half-day before the labourers but by the late nineteenth century, most workers had more time for sport and leisure. Even with the extra time, workers did not have much taste for active sport because of their working and living conditions.

There was considerable deprivation and poverty, but sports clubs did begin to be developed. Factory owners recognised that a happier workforce was a more effective workforce and encouraged the development of sports clubs. Owners of larger factories would also pay for their workers to have an annual excursion, such as a trip to the seaside. This was the beginning of the seaside holiday.

By 1965 a typical working week was 40–45 hours. Today it is about 37 hours, which makes it much easier for workers to get involved in sport. The law states that holidays should be at least four weeks per year, which also makes it easier for people to watch sport and take part in it.

Figure 11.3 Factory owners paid for their workers to have a daytrip to the seaside once a year

Public transport and car ownership

Until the twentieth century, most people travelled on foot or on horseback. There was some boat transport on rivers and canals, but it was the development of roads, the bicycle, the railways and eventually the motorcar that enabled people to travel. The railways, in particular, were very important for the development of seaside resorts, plus they allowed sports fixtures to be played around the country and spectators to go to watch them.

Figure 11.4 Transport has had a big effect on leisure activities

Cars began to be mass-produced in the twentieth century and now most households own a car. Compared to 50 years ago, it is much easier for people to go to play sport or watch it being played.

activity

INDIVIDUAL WORK 11.1

P1

Draw a timeline showing significant moments in the development of sport. For example, you could show the development of rugby and its evolution into rugby union and rugby league.

Key sports organisations

Department for Culture, Media and Sport

The Department for Culture, Media and Sport (DCMS) is a government department that has responsibility for government policy related to sport. Along with the Treasury, it decides how much taxpayers' money is spent on sport and what to spend it on. It has a secretary of state, a minister for sport, a minister for the arts and a minister for creative industries and tourism. In the year 2000/2001, for instance, the budget for the department was approximately £1 billion, 90% of which went directly to service providers in cultural and sporting sectors.

According to the Central Council of Physical Recreation, in 2006 the budget was approximately 1.6 billion; this includes about £25 million for coaching, £6 million for talent scholarships, £20 million per year for facilities at community amateur sports clubs and a guarantee on maintaining levels of funding through the World Class Performance programme.

Department for Culture, Media and Sport

www.culture.gov.uk

UK Sport – provides coaching resources related to social science

www.uksport.gov.uk

UK Sport

The national sports councils were formed in 1972 and deemed to be independent from the government. They were reorganised to create UK Sport in 1996. UK Sport is as an agency under government direction to provide support for elite sportspeople who have a high level of performance or the potential to reach the top. It distributes government funds, including lottery money, supports world-class performers and promotes ethical standards of behaviour. It has an anti-doping programme to detect the use of performance-enhancing drugs.

UK Sport delivers its services through five departments:

- Performance services
- International relations and major events
- UK Sports Institute
- Corporate services
- Drug-free sport.

Figure 11.5 UK Sport supports world-class performers

UK Sport oversees the work of the four home-country sports councils:

- Sport England
- Sportscotland
- Sports Council for Northern Ireland
- Sports Council for Wales.

UK Sports Institute

The UK Sports Institute (UKSI) aims to provide the very best sportspeople with appropriate facilities and support. It provides sports science advice, coaching expertise and top training facilities. It comprises a number of centres around the UK. Each home-country sports council is responsible for developing the sports institutes in its area.

Sports Coach UK

Sports Coach UK (SCUK), formerly the National Coaching Foundation, is there to guide the development and implementation of a coaching system for all coaches in the UK. Its activities include:

- running coaching courses
- administering coaching qualifications
- providing coaching resources
- working with governing bodies to raise the quality of coaching schemes
- producing a national register of coaches to ensure an ethical and secure coaching structure, especially for child protection.

Sports Coach UK

www.sportscoachuk.org

Youth Sport Trust

The Youth Sport Trust (YST) has created a sporting pathway for all children through a series of linked schemes called TOP programmes. YST is responsible for the development of sport for young people. It is a registered charity established in 1994. It has developed schemes to encourage young people from 18 months to 18 years to follow a healthy and active lifestyle.

National governing bodies

The majority of sports that we know today were developed and organised in the late nineteenth century. The participants needed to agree rules and regulations for their sports, so they met and formed their own committees called national governing bodies (NGBs), such as the Football Association (FA) the Lawn Tennis Association (LTA), the Amateur Swimming Association (ASA) and the Rugby Football Union (RFU). There are over 265 governing bodies in the UK. Teams and clubs pay a subscription to their governing body. They in turn administer the sport nationally, organise competitions and organise the national team. There are still many unpaid positions in each governing body, but increasing numbers of staff are paid a salary.

The NGBs are also members of international governing bodies, such as the Union of European Football Associations (UEFA) and the Fédération Internationale de Football Association (FIFA). These international bodies control and organise international competitions.

Figure 11.6 The LTA is the national governing body for tennis

Central Council of Physical Recreation

The Central Council of Physical Recreation (CCPR) is the umbrella organisation for the NGBs and representative bodies of sport and recreation in the UK. Its aim is to promote, protect and develop the interests of sport and physical recreation. CCPR is completely independent of government control and has no responsibility for allocating funds.

European Non-Governmental Sports Organisation

The European Non-Governmental Sports Organisation (ENGSO) is an increasingly effective organisation that represents the views of sports bodies throughout Europe and works towards raising the status of sport in Europe.

European Parliament Sports Inter Group

There is no legal basis for sport in the Treaty of Rome, so sport has little status in the European Parliament. The European Parliament Sports Inter Group provides a forum for MEPs to meet and discuss factors affecting sport in Europe.

European Social Fund

The European Social Fund (ESF) is an important source of funding for activities to develop employability and human resources. It provides up to 45% of the costs of a project, which is then 'matched' by funding from other sources. One of ESF's most important objectives is to improve economically disadvantaged areas and areas adjusting to changes in their industrial and service sectors. ESF is an important source of funding for sports-related employment in the UK.

British Olympic Association

Formed in 1905, the British Olympic Association (BOA) supplies the delegates for the National Olympic Committee (NOC). It is responsible, among other things, for planning and executing the Great Britain team's participation in the Olympic Games. Great Britain is one of only five countries that have never failed to be represented at the Olympics since 1896.

British Olympic Association
www.olympics.org.uk

Figure 11.7 The IOC owns all the rights to the Olympic symbol and the games

International Olympic Committee

The International Olympic Committee (IOC) was created by the Paris Congress in 1894. It owns all the rights to the Olympic symbol and the games. It is the world body that administers the Olympic Movement. Its headquarters is in Lausanne, Switzerland. Members are appointed to the IOC and are responsible for selecting the host cities of the Olympic Games, summer and winter.

---

activity
INDIVIDUAL WORK
11.2

M1

Explain the development and organisation of sport from its pre-industrial origins to the present day.

Know about the sports industry in the United Kingdom today

Scale of the sports industry

The sports industry has grown rapidly over the past 10 years. A massive amount of money has been invested in sport and sports-related goods and services. Sport today is heavily commercialised with worldwide potential. Widespread TV coverage has enabled businesses to promote their products across the globe.

Sponsorship is an important part of sport, with many sponsors spending millions of pounds to have their brand name or logo emblazoned on an athlete's shirt.

---

case study
11.4

Sponsorship

It was forbidden to display advertising logos and names during the 2002 Commonwealth Games in Manchester. This instruction was curiously ignored when David Beckham played a part in the opening ceremony. The fact that he is also a professional football player, rather than a Commonwealth athlete, illustrates the power of big business.

---

activity
GROUP WORK

1. What conflicts are illustrated in the case study?
2. Who are the main sponsors of your main sport and what do they get in return?

The Fitness Industry Association (FIA) reports that consumer spending on sport participation has not increased in line with the UK economy since reaching its peak of £3.6 billion in 2003. It declined to £3.45 billion in 2004 and 2005. Membership of health clubs rose to nearly 12% of the adult population in 2005.

Figure 11.8 David Beckham helped open the 2002 Commonwealth Games

Over the past 30 years the UK has changed from a manufacturing economy to a service economy, with an explosion in the leisure industry. Along with growth in health-related businesses, there has also been growth in support businesses, such as private physiotherapy practices and nutritionists.

Sport-related employment has also risen significantly, with over half a million jobs created during the past 10 years. More people are now employed in the sports industry than in the chemical, agricultural and coal industries.

case study 11.5 — Football League clubs

Football League clubs are turning to gambling to stave off bankruptcy. Up to 20 clubs are in talks with gaming operators about opening casinos in their grounds.

activity — GROUP WORK

1. Besides gambling, in what other ways are Football League clubs trying to raise money?

2. What are the issues related to sports clubs and casino partnerships?

British Association of Sport and Exercise Sciences
www.bases.org.uk
Sport England – promotes sport and invests in sport
www.sportengland.org
Leisure Jobs UK
www.leisurejobs.com

There is a growing business in health and fitness clubs and personal trainers have become fashionable, not just for the very rich. They give a personal training and motivation service to clients who want to train in the right way and who want someone to push them to achieve better fitness levels. Personal trainers advertise in many health and fitness clubs.

Employment opportunities have increased in the sport and leisure industry. Here are some examples of jobs: coach, trainer, administrative staff, physiotherapist, massage specialist, leisure centre manager, entertainer, grounds maintenance worker, corporate hospitality worker. There has been huge growth in the sports manufacturing industry, largely because sportswear is so fashionable.

case study 11.6 — Consumer spending and sport

Despite competition from other leisure activities, sport continues to be one of the UK's most popular pastimes. Sport makes a big contribution to the country's economy; it employs just under 2% of the workforce and is worth twice as much as the entire British agriculture sector. Over the past 10 years there has been a significant shift in British consumers' attitudes towards healthy living. Staying fit and maintaining a healthy diet have quickly moved up many people's priorities and this appears to have contributed greatly to increased sports participation.

activity
INDIVIDUAL WORK

1. What are the main reasons for high consumer spending on sport?
2. In what ways do participation rates affect spending?

Structure of the sports industry

Sports organisations in the UK can be divided into public, private and voluntary. Public organisations are funded by the government from taxes. Organisations in the private sector may be commercial businesses trying to make a profit and non-profit-making organisations, also called voluntary organisations.

If you want to go somewhere to exercise, you can use public, private or voluntary facilities. A public facility is the local leisure centre, run by the local authority and funded by the taxpayer. Better or more convenient facilities may be available in the private sector, such as private health and fitness clubs. A local athletics club belongs to the voluntary sector. You could turn up on club night and train with people of similar fitness. The Youth Hostel Association (YHA) is another voluntary organisation. If you wish to keep fit by walking or rambling, you could join the YHA, it is cheaper to stay at a youth hostel if you belong to the YHA.

Provision from the sports industry

The sports industry enables sports development at different levels: foundation, participation, performance and excellence.

See page 149 in Unit 5 for more information on development levels and strategies

Foundation level

Foundation level is where local authorities in association with clubs and schools develop basic movement and sports skills. The acquisition of good exercise habits with appropriate knowledge and understanding helps to develop a positive attitude to sports and physical activity.

Participation level

Participation level makes participation as wide as possible; for example, private clubs encourage the growth of player membership. Partnerships between different schools and local authorities can increase participation.

See page 163 in Unit 5 for more information on sports industry provision

Performance level

Performance level improves standards through coaching and training. It relates to competitive sport and encourages people to obtain fulfilment and enjoyment by improving their performance.

Excellence level

Excellence level is about reaching the top standards in sport, such as national and international competition. The sports industry can provide sponsorship, often through commercial companies such as Coca-Cola, banks and building societies.

activity

INDIVIDUAL WORK 11.3

P2

Write a report to describe the scale, structure and provision of the sports industry in the UK today. Present this report to the class and answer any questions they put to you.

How PE in schools develops provision

Physical education (PE) in schools has also contributed to the development of sport. Besides PE lessons, which encourage the development of skills used in many sports, there are many extracurricular sports activities. Examination courses in PE have raised awareness of sport in society and there are many links between schools and local sports clubs and other recreation providers.

The National Curriculum is a government list of courses that must be delivered in all state schools from primary schools to age 16 in secondary schools. One of the stated aims of the National Curriculum is to get as many children as possible to participate in sport. PE also involves learning information about health, fitness and diet.

Over the past 20 years PE has seen a huge growth in facilities such as new sports centres and all-weather playing surfaces. In a recent initiative, schools have become specialist sports colleges.

Sports colleges

Sports colleges have been created by the government's Specialist Schools Programme, along with specialist colleges in performing arts, technology and modern languages. The programme is designed to give a distinctive identity to the school. Schools must develop partnerships with the other schools, the local community and with private sector sponsors. The government gives extra funds to these specialist colleges so they can develop their specialisms.

According to what was then the Department for Education and Employment (DfEE), now the Department for Education and Skills (DfES), here are the objectives of the sports colleges initiative:

- Extend the range of opportunities available to children.
- Raise the standards of teaching and learning of PE and sport.
- Develop the school's identity.
- Benefit other schools in the area, including primary and secondary schools.
- Strengthen the links between schools and private sponsors.
- Increase participation in PE and sport for pre- and post-16 year olds and develop the potential of talented performers.

At the time of writing, sports colleges receive additional funding as a one-off grant of £100000 and an extra £120 per pupil per year for four years. So not only do schools benefit through the raised awareness of PE and sport, but they are also financially rewarded. That is why many schools are seeking to become a sports college. The YST is responsible for validating sports colleges.

Link   See page 255 of this unit for more information on the YST

National training organisations

The growth of the leisure and recreation industry over the past 20 years has created a need for high standards of training. The sport and recreation industries training organisation (SPRITO) was launched in 1995 as the national training organisation for sport, recreation and allied occupations. It offers training for leisure attractions, health and fitness, the outdoors, the caravan industry, playwork and sport and recreation.

Figure 11.9 The sports industry develops sport at different levels

Understand how contemporary issues affect sport

Contemporary issues are issues that arise from present-day culture. Contemporary issues affect sport and can influence performers, officials, organisers and spectators. This section looks at issues of funding and sponsorship, the media, government, performance-enhancing drugs, prejudice, commercialisation and globalisation.

Funding and sponsorship in sport

Sport is big business and sport sponsorship has an enormous influence. Large amounts of money are spent by commercial companies on sports participants and events. For example, Adidas may sponsor a top-class tennis player to wear its latest training shoe, or a small business may give money to a local hockey club to help buy kit for the team.

Sportswear is fashionable and this is another reason for higher sponsorship. There has been a huge increase in sales of training shoes. Many people wear trainers but would never dream of doing sport. Businesses recognise that young people see top sport stars as fashion icons, so they use them in their advertising. Many top football stars were used to advertise products during the 2006 World Cup.

The influence of the media on the development of sport

The media influences sport and sport influences the media, both need each other. Television companies in particular have spent huge amounts of money on the broadcasting rights to sports events. People pay a monthly subscription to watch the events. Sky holds the rights to many Premiership football games, which can only be viewed if you subscribe to a Sky package. Even subscribers have to pay an extra fee for some broadcasts. This practice, called pay per view, appears to be increasing. Digital TV has also had an influence. The collapse of ITV Digital in 2002 left many football teams facing financial disaster, as they did not receive the large sums of money they were expecting before the collapse.

A spate of clubs went into voluntary administration. Leicester City was one of them, but with the help of a consortium led by Gary Lineker, it was able to come out of administration in 2003 and two months later it was promoted to the Premiership. In 2004 it was relegated to the League. Some of Leicester's rivals felt that going into voluntary administration was unfair, so the League introduced a system where clubs lose 10 league points if they go into voluntary administration and there was a dramatic fall in the number of clubs choosing this option. Rotherham United was the only club to enter voluntary administration in 2006. According to the Football League, 'A lot of the worst effects of the ITV Digital collapse have been absorbed.'

Terrestrial channels such as BBC and ITV have lost many of the major sports events and sometimes BBC news cannot show a clip of a boxing match because the rights are owned by another company. There has never been so much sport on TV but much of it can only be seen by people wealthy enough to pay a subscription. Only a few sports are available to a wide audience, and of those, football receives the greatest coverage. Male sport still dominates, but there is a refreshing interest in women's football.

Sports events are often scheduled to satisfy TV companies and their viewers. Football teams may play at 6.00 p.m. on Sunday, not a traditional time slot and not always convenient for supporters who want to go to the ground. Olympic events often happen at unsuitable times for athletes, because TV companies want to screen them live to audiences in many different time zones.

Figure 11.10 Women's football is getting more media attention

Television has even influenced the rules of cricket, where the third umpire uses video replay analysis to adjudicate close run-outs and similar difficult decisions. Rugby football also uses video replays. The armchair spectator can now see an event from every angle and often has more information than the officials. That is why many argue for more technology to aid the decision-makers on the field of play.

Media involvement has brought sponsorship and advertising money to participants, clubs and other sports organisations. People have welcomed the extra money but some may say it has gone to just a small number of participants in a small number of sports and may well be a reason for decreased participation in minority sports.

The media can increase participation in sport. Look at the increased activity on municipal tennis courts during Wimbledon fortnight. People in the UK get more interested in playing a sport when top UK performers do well and are feted by the media. There was a surge of interest in curling after the GB curling team won a gold at the 2002 Winter Olympics.

Types of media involved in sport
- **Television** – BBC, ITV, Channel 4, Five, satellite, cable, digital, factual, fiction, advertising
- **Press** – broadsheets, tabloids, locals, weeklies, magazines, periodicals
- **Radio** – national, local, commercial
- **Cinema** – documentaries, movies, Hollywood, Bollywood, Pinewood.

Figure 11.11 Armchair
spectators can see events
from every angle

Anti-crime initiatives using sport

The media covers many stories about young people and crime, and the popular
press often has stories on antisocial behaviour orders (ASBOs) to combat antisocial
behaviour. Many initiatives try to deal with the root cause of *deviance* – behaviour that
is unacceptable in our society. Some of these initiatives use sport to encourage more
acceptable behaviour and to combat boredom. It is thought that many people who
commit crime in the UK have been *socially excluded*; in other words, their lifestyle falls
outside what is normally acceptable in our society. People who have a drug addiction
may turn to crime to feed their habit. Unemployed people may not have enough money
to participate in cultural and sports activities.

Sport has often been viewed as a way of helping to combat crime, particularly youth and
juvenile crime. Sports development activity has often made this assumption.

See page 147 in Unit 5 for more information on sports development activities

There is much anecdotal evidence to suggest that involvement in sport can stop general
deviant behaviour that falls short of actual crimes being committed. But there is little
evidence to show that involvement in sport has any direct link with reducing criminal
behaviour. Some people think that sport can be used as a distraction and that getting
people involved in regular sport will stop them filling their leisure time with antisocial
activities. Others feel that sport can be used as *cognitive behavioural therapy*; in
other words. socially acceptable behaviour and values can be learned through sport.
Teamwork, the values of fair play and improving a person's self-esteem are all thought to
help reduce antisocial behaviour.

case study 11.7

Two views on ASBOs

View 1

I work with young people at a pupil referral unit, many of whom have antisocial behaviour orders (ASBOs). ASBOs do very little to stop the young people carrying on as normal. More money should be spent on preventing the causes of antisocial behaviour such as poor parenting, poor education and a lack of facilities for things like sport.

View 2

I for one am happy that these ASBOs are actually being handed out. Britain is under siege by these young people who intimidate the local populace. It all stems back to poor parenthood. It is sad that we have come to a state where discipline has to be given by the law when it is the responsibility of the parent. People say the young people have nothing to do. Go to school, play a sport for a team, get a hobby. What a pitiful excuse to terrorise the neighbourhood.

activity
GROUP WORK

1. Do laws and regulations such as ASBOs help to combat crime?
2. In what ways can sport help to stop deviance?

See page 284 in Unit 16 for more information on how sport can affect behaviour, and vice versa

There are still no solutions to youth crime that have been thoroughly researched. Future academic studies are required to make causal links between possible solutions such as the provision of youth club sports activities and reductions in criminal behaviour. To establish any link between sport and control of crime, we need a clear view of why crime takes place and how sport could help. Then we need to know how to implement any policies or initiatives to reduce crime and antisocial behaviour.

Sport creates deviance

There is a view that sport may well contribute to deviance in our society. Spectators at a sports event may well be stirred to commit criminal acts by the sports spectacle. Some think that contact sports such as boxing and some martial arts may encourage violence

case study 11.8

Powerlifting

An ex-offender who spent time in a young offenders institution (YOI) got involved in powerlifting. The ex-offender trains regularly and their coach and fellow competitors are working towards the area team competition later in the year. This young person seems to be more motivated in life, has started to follow a healthier lifestyle and is now coaching younger powerlifters.

activity
INDIVIDUAL WORK

1. Look at the following ideas and say which ones occur in this case study: morals, teamwork, respect for others, increased self-esteem and self-concept, acceptance of authority, sharing of common purpose.
2. What are the possible dangers of deviance in this case study?

and antisocial behaviour. Some sports competitors use performance-enhancing drugs on the list of banned substances; this is against the rules. The desire to win tempts some sportspeople to take drugs that help them train more effectively or gain an edge over other competitors. Other competitors bend the rules or use gamesmanship to seek an unfair advantage; they also count as deviance.

Figure 11.12 Some say contact sports encourage antisocial behaviour

Some competitors cheat in a subtle way that is undesirable but difficult to control by the rules. Examples are a forward in football who dives in the penalty area hoping for a free shot on goal, a hockey player who impedes another's stick in a tackle, and an athlete who pushes another athlete in a middle-distance race. Coaches are often guilty of encouraging this behaviour and reinforcing the view that gamesmanship is a clever way to undermine your opponent and gain an advantage.

activity

GROUP WORK
11.4

P3

Using newspaper source material, discuss with others the effects of four contemporary issues on sport. Summarise your findings then present your summary.

Principles, values and ethics

A principle is a basic truth, law or policy. Principles are standards that define moral behaviour. A principle in sport might be that the officials treat all equally on the field of play. Values are ideals that form the basis of actions and beliefs. Some values in sport are enjoyment, quality of movement, fitness and health, and character building. Ethics are rules that dictate your conduct. They form a system of rules for judging groups and societies. An ethic in sport is that you stick to the rules.

Link

See page 121 in Unit 4 for more information on professional conduct

Figure 11.13 It is poor
sportsmanship to intimidate
an official

Doping offences and sporting deviance

This case study is adapted from a report in the UK Sport newsletter. After six weeks of deliberation, the Court of Arbitration for Sport (CAS) in October 2002 decided to confirm the decision of the International Olympic Committee (IOC) to disqualify Alain Baxter from the men's alpine skiing slalom at the Winter Games in Salt Lake City.

Baxter finished third in the slalom and was awarded the bronze medal, but a subsequent doping test revealed traces of methamphetamine in his urine sample, a stimulant on the IOC's list of prohibited substances.

Though Baxter maintained that the US Vicks nasal inhaler he used prior to the slalom race contained L-methamphetamine -- a non-performance-enhancing isomer of methamphetamine -- the CAS ruled that the anti-doping code of the Olympic movement prohibits all forms of methamphetamine and the presence of any prohibited substance results in automatic disqualification, whether or not ingestion was intentional.

'The panel is not without sympathy for Mr Baxter, who appears to be a sincere and honest man who did not intend to obtain a competitive advantage in the race,' the tribunal concluded.

'I'm gutted not to be getting my medal back but there's a lot of positive things to come out of this,' said Baxter. 'I also feel it's not just my loss. I'm getting things back as normal and in future maybe the policies will change a little bit.'

Baxter now falls under the British Olympic Association (BOA) doping by-law, which states that any athlete found guilty of a doping offence is ineligible to represent Great Britain at any future Olympic Games. An athlete can appeal against the by-law on the basis that there were significant mitigating circumstances and/or the offence was minor.

'Alain has paid a most severe penalty for a modest mistake and it is clear that the principle of strict liability underscored this decision,' added Simon Clegg, chief executive of the BOA.

'I know that I can continue to look Alain in the eye with confidence that he did not knowingly take the US Vick's inhaler to enhance his performance.'

activity
INDIVIDUAL WORK

1. What aspects of gamesmanship could be a feature in this case study?
2. What dangers are there by having strict rules for cheating in sport?

Racism, sexism and other discrimination

Here are some facts to consider when assessing whether sport is inclusive and lacks discrimination:

- 40% of children in London are of ethnic origin.
- Women in social group AB are 44% more likely to participate in sport than women in social group DE.
- 72% of people in social group ABC1 use local authority sports facilities compared to 50% of the population as a whole.

Figure 11.14 Sport is for people from all ethnic groups

Social groups

Table 11.1 Social groups

Social grade	Social status	Occupation
A	Upper middle class	Higher managerial, administrative or professional
B	Middle class	Intermediate managerial, administrative or professional
C1	Lower middle class	Supervisory or clerical, junior managerial, administrative or professional
C2	Skilled working class	Skilled manual workers
D	Working class	Semi-skilled and unskilled manual workers
E	Subsistence level	State pensioners or widows (no other earner), casual or lowest-grade workers

■ 13% of young people with a disability were members of a sports club in 1999 compared with 46% of non-disabled.

■ 20% of elite performers attended private schools compared to 6% of the population.

Main anti-discrimination laws in the UK

Race Relations (Amendment) Act 2001

The Race Relations (Amendment) Act 2001 makes it unlawful to discriminate directly or indirectly on the grounds of colour, race, nationality, ethnic or national origin.

Sex Discrimination Act 1986

The Sex Discrimination Act 1986 makes it unlawful to discriminate directly or indirectly on the grounds of a person's sex or marital status.

■ Section 29 – private sports clubs are exempt from provisions of the Act; many complaints are recorded about discrimination against women in private golf clubs, where they may have no voting rights on club policies.

■ Section 34 – allows for the establishment of single-sex sports clubs.

■ Section 44 – allows any sport to be restricted to one sex where the strength and stamina of the average woman would put her at a disadvantage to the average man.

Figure 11.15 Golf clubs are notorious for discriminating against women

Disability Discrimination Act 1995

The Disability Discrimination Act 1995 makes it unlawful for an employer of 15 or more staff to discriminate against current or prospective employees on the grounds of disability. Private sports clubs are exempted from the Act.

Other relevant acts

- Special Educational Needs and Disability Act 2001
- Rehabilitation of Offenders Act 1974
- Employment Protection (Consolidation) Act 1978
- Human Rights Act 1998.

Equal Opportunities Commission – detailed guidance and codes of practice are available

www.eoc.org.uk

Disability Rights Commission

www.drc-gb.org.uk

Commission for Racial Equality

www.cre.gov.uk

activity

INDIVIDUAL WORK 11.5

M2

Re-read any of the case studies in this unit and explore any influences on the individual. Write a report to explain the effects of four contemporary issues in sport.

Child protection

Child abuse by sports coaches is very rare and anyone who works with children must be cleared by the Criminal Records Bureau (CRB). Sports Coach UK, formerly the National Coaching Foundation, is also compiling a register of responsible coaches.

The Children Act 1989 had a big impact on the industry, especially playwork. The Children Act was aimed at children under age 8, but its interpretation has influenced the provision for all school-aged children. The United Nations Convention on the Rights of the Child, especially Articles 12 and 31, has also changed how workers view children. These articles encourage us to view children as a 'rightful stakeholder, rather than a needy minor'.

Every adult involved in sport – the coach, the referee, the adult helper and the club member – needs to be aware of child protection issues. To assist those working with children in sport, the National Society for the Prevention of Cruelty to Children (NSPCC) and Sport England have set up the Child Protection in Sport Unit, to assist sports bodies implement child protection policies, helping to ensure that all sporting activity is safe.

Child Protection in Sport Unit

www.thecpsu.org.uk

Globalisation and sport

Globalisation has largely occurred through new communications technology and transport. It involves different nations being more closely related. Sport can be seen as helping international relations through international competition but there are dangers with globalisation. Some see globalisation as diluting people's sense of national identity.

case study 11.10 — Keeping Children Safe in Sport

The National Society for the Prevention of Cruelty to Children (NSPCC) has designed Keeping Children Safe in Sport to help sports organisations deal appropriately with child protection issues. It will help clubs safeguard the children in their care by enabling staff and volunteers to recognise and understand their role in child protection.

Here are the key benefits outlined by the NSPCC:

- You will gain an understanding of child protection issues.
- You will be able to recognise signs that a child needs help.
- You will feel more confident to take that first vital step to get assistance.
- You can demonstrate to others that you have completed a formal programme on child protection awareness.
- You will be making an important contribution to preventing children suffering from child abuse.
- You will get a completion certificate from the NSPCC.

activity — GROUP WORK

1. Before working with young people, why is it so important to do a child protection course such as the NSPCC course?
2. When coaching your sport, how would you ensure that children are adequately protected?

Some people think that nations are losing their sense of a separate country and culture. Western values of sport tend to be dominant, and other cultures' views of sport are being lost through globalisation. The more common movement of players or competitors between countries also gives a sense of globalisation. An example is Premiership football clubs that buy clubs abroad with more lenient immigration policies so they can fast-track players into their home teams. Some UK football clubs are now owned by people in Russia or America.

case study 11.11 — Foreign players in UK clubs

Foreign domination of English football became a high-profile issue after a Premiership match when Chelsea fielded a team that had no English players. A UEFA spokesman observed that it was stifling local talent. He said, 'There are too many foreign players in teams and it is holding back young players. This is something UEFA is fighting for. The clubs themselves, well they want to win so they might not be so keen. If they go back to the old rules [that do not allow all-foreign teams] then Chelsea will have to sell some players or introduce new young players.'

activity — INDIVIDUAL WORK

1. What are the benefits of globalisation?
2. What are the drawbacks of having foreign players in our football leagues?

activity
INDIVIDUAL WORK
11.6

D1

Look at your work for Activities 11.4 and 11.5 then do some further reading. Now evaluate the effects of four contemporary issues on sport. Make some recommendations for further improvements?

Understand cultural influences and barriers that affect participation in sports activities

Cultural influences on sports participation

Culture is an important influence on sport. Some cultures do not encourage women to participate in sport, some give sport a high status and some do not value it at all.

There is still a difference in the participation levels between men and women in sport. There is a long tradition of discrimination against women in sport. Women were discouraged in the nineteenth and early twentieth century because it was thought to be dangerous to their health and childbearing potential. It is still thought by some people that being good at sport or interested in sport is unfeminine, thus reinforcing male dominance in sport and sports coverage.

Even now, media coverage of women's sport often emphasises what a woman looks like instead of what she has achieved. The prize money in women's tennis is smaller than in men's tennis. The media show lots of interest in tennis players such as Anna Kournikova because of her looks, but at the time of writing she has achieved little on the international circuit. She has a highly lucrative deal with a bra manufacturer, even though she has had relatively little success. This illustrates the continuing discrimination against women's participation in sport.

The picture is not entirely negative. More women are now involved in physical exercise than ever before; there is far more interest in health and fitness matters; women now play sports such as football and rugby and are getting at least some recognition. There is an increase in female sports presenters, which may encourage more women to take an interest in sport. There are fewer instances of open discrimination against women participating in clubs such as golf clubs.

activity
INDIVIDUAL WORK
11.7

P4

Describe three cultural influences on sports participation. Use any of the case studies in this unit or one of your own and write a description of these influences.

Other social influences on sports participation include race, social class, economic status and disability. The problems with 'access' need to be solved for each group if there is to be widening participation in sport. We shall deal with each group to explore the reasons for non-participation and possible solutions to these problems.

activity
INDIVIDUAL WORK
11.8

M3

Choose one under-represented group in sport, such as the elderly. Explain three cultural influences on the individuals within the sports group you have identified.

Figure 11.16 Is there a cultural attitude against women boxers?

Barriers to participation in sports activities

Time

Many people decide not to participate in sport because of work commitments. It is common to hear them say, 'I haven't got the time.' This is legitimate but their perception of their available time is often different from the reality. Getting home from college and watching television all evening is a way of spending your leisure time. A person who does this clearly has some leisure time but they choose to watch television instead of doing a sport.

Resources

Perhaps you have sports facilities or sports clubs nearby, but it will depend on where you live. The distance to sports facilities and sports clubs has a big effect on whether people participate. One way of increasing participation for people without facilities nearby would be to provide a good transport service to a distant sports facility.

Fitness and ability

Some people think they are not good enough to join in sports activities. This view of themselves may well have arisen from previous experiences, perhaps at school. They may have failed in an activity then felt humiliated and ever after they have seen themselves as a hopeless case. Psychologists call this feeling *learned helplessness*.

Learned helplessness

Learned helplessness is a psychological phenomenon that arises when a person fails on a task and has the failure reinforced. The person then avoids that task and may often say something like this: 'I was hopeless at sport when I was at school, so it's no good me trying again as I'll only fail.'

To overcome this feeling of helplessness and regain confidence, the person needs to experience success in some aspect of sport. After all, it's extremely unlikely they will feel a failure at every sport.

Technology

Some people think that new technology has removed the need for participation in physical activity; they prefer to use toning tables and slimming belts. Simulation games allow people to imagine they are doing a physical activity when they are playing on a computer. This can be seen as a barrier to participation.

Link See page 292 in Unit 16 for more information on the psychological barriers to sports participation

---

case study 11.12 Sports development officers

According to reports commissioned by Sport England in 2002, sport is getting youngsters away from crime and helping fight drug abuse. In Bristol there has been a 40% reduction of crime levels on the Southmead estate since the first sports development officer (SDO) was appointed.

activity
GROUP WORK

1. What might have the SDO have introduced?
2. What other strategies could be employed to reduce crime?

Health problems

Some people have health problems that prevent their participation in sport, although many medical practitioners encourage an active lifestyle as much as possible. Most rehabilitation regimes include physical exercise, and sport is an ideal way. There is an increase in obesity in the western world due to our diets and lack of exercise. Embarrassment is a powerful emotion that prevents many people taking the first step to try a sport. People that experience embarrassment need encouragement and the right environment to help them get involved. Joining clubs such as Weight Watchers can encourage some people to take exercise, which may lead to participation in a sport. Others disagree; they say that joining a weight-loss group is demeaning and only reinforces a person's lack of self-esteem. Lack of self-esteem has to be tackled before a person can gain the confidence needed to join other people and participate in sport.

See page 33 in Unit 1 for more information on healthy breathing
See page 85 in Unit 3 for more information on healthy body composition

activity
GROUP WORK
11.9

P5

Design a visual presentation that details the barriers to sports participation.

Access

Growth in sports facilities has increased access and more low-cost courses are available, but some people still do not have enough money to participate in sport. Here are the most important questions that influence access for many people:

- What is available?
- What is affordable?
- How do I feel about myself?

Here are the main issues related to access and an example:

- **Opening times** – may not be convenient for shift workers.
- **Age** – sport is often perceived as a young person's activity and the elderly may feel undignified if they participate in sport.
- **Race** – experiencing racial discrimination may be a reason for lack of confidence to get involved in a predominantly white environment such as a golf club.
- **Class** – participation in polo is often by people from the upper middle classes. It is perceived as a posh person's sport.
- **Disability** – facilities may be lacking, such as wheelchair ramps, or inadequate, such as doors that are too narrow.

activity
INDIVIDUAL WORK
11.10

M4

Give the presentation you designed in Activity 11.9. Explain the barriers and explain why some groups, such as disabled people, have lower participation.

- People on low incomes living in a disadvantaged community in the north of England demonstrate some of the lowest levels of sports participation ever measured.
- Some 71% of people from social group DE take part in at least one sport, but in Liverpool it is only 51%.
- In Bradford, the proportion of children swimming, cycling or walking is less than half the national average.
- Some 43% of British children play cricket, but in Liverpool only 3% of children play cricket.
- Yet in Bradford, Liverpool and similar areas the vast majority of children have a very positive view about the value of sport.

activity

INDIVIDUAL WORK 11.11

D2

Choose two groups that may suffer specific barriers to sports participation and compare and contrast the reasons for low participation. Write a report on your findings.

Strategies and initiatives

Strategies and initiatives to increase participation may be local or national. National initiatives often begin with national organisations such as UK Sport.

Local authorities have increased the number of sports facilities and improved their quality. The private sector has seen an explosion of health and fitness clubs, and the leisure and recreation industry is one of the most important in the UK. A larger cross section of people now visit sports facilities and more and more people regularly participate in sport. Health and fitness activities are now fashionable, and being fit and looking good is an important aspect of our culture.

Average life expectancy has increased, which means there are more older people in the population. There are more veterans teams in a variety of sports and there is a growing awareness that activity in old age can enrich a person's quality of life.

Figure 11.17 Sport can enrich life in old age

People with disabilities now have much better access to sport. Disability sport is recognised as a sport in its own right, and UK participants have achieved great success in international competition.

Figure 11.18 UK performers have been very successful in disability Olympics

The media has also played a part in changing sport in the UK. Using the latest technology, broadcasters bring sporting events from around the world live into our living rooms. Sport is often headline news, films and documentaries are made about sport, and sport is used in product promotions. This raises the profile of sport, feeds people's interest in sport and reinforces its place in society.

See page 262 in this unit for more information on how the media influences sport

activity

INDIVIDUAL WORK 11.12

P6

Using an earlier case study or an example of your own, write a description of three strategies or initiatives related to sports participation.

The government, schools, sports clubs and local authorities have introduced initiatives to encourage people to participate in sport.

Schools

The growth of specialist sports schools and colleges is intended to increase participation. These specialist schools have targets for participation; if the targets are not met, then they risk losing their specialist status and the extra funding that goes with it. The National Curriculum physical education programmes are designed to make sport as accessible as possible. Extracurricular activities, the use of sports awards and the use of external coaches and agencies are all designed to increase participation.

The Education and Standards Framework Act was passed in October 1998. Section 77 states that every decision on the disposal of a school playing field has to be taken by the education secretary. Before that, it was estimated that more than 5000 playing fields had been sold off, regardless of the purpose of the sale. The Act made it law that the proceeds for any disposal were to be invested in sports or educational provision.

Sports Coach UK – organises workshops and publishes leaflets to support coaches working with children

www.sportscoachuk.org

Game Plan

In 2002 the government's strategy unit and the DCMS published *Game Plan: A Strategy for Delivering Government's Sport and Physical Activity Objectives*.

See page 253 in this unit for more information on DCMS

It describes the government's vision and strategy for mass participation and performance up to 2020. Note that it was published before London was awarded the 2012 Olympic Games.

Game Plan deals with sports participation and inequality associated with sport. It provides a rationale or framework for plans to reduce these inequalities and to increase participation. It stated that the government perceived sport and physical activity as potential social instruments to reduce the inequalities of opportunities for people in our culture and to prevent social exclusion.

The strategy suggests that, through sport and physical activity, more people who are often marginalised could access better health, gain employment and be diverted from antisocial behaviour. There are many detailed statistics on participation in sport and physical activity broken down by socio-economic group, ethnic group, gender, disability, age, etc. It also considers the potential of sport and physical activity to help combat social exclusion.

See page 264 in this unit for more information on deviance

activity
INDIVIDUAL WORK
11.13

M5

Take the three strategies you described in Activity 11.12 and present them with full explanations to the rest of the class.

Every Child Matters

Every Child Matters is a government initiative that arises from the Children Act 2004. It seeks to develop five key aspects of well-being in childhood and later life:

- Being healthy
- Staying safe
- Enjoying and achieving
- Making a positive contribution
- Economic well-being.

The DCMS, for example, says that it is working to improve access to culture, sport and play for children and young people, so they can develop their talents and enjoy the benefits of participation. The DCMS is also a key partner in children's trusts and in contributing to children and young people's plans. There is support for families and the DCMS is promoting diversity through sport and by encouraging children and young people to be active through positive out-of-school activities.

Every Child Matters
www.everychildmatters.gov.uk

Sporting Equals

Sporting Equals is a national initiative that promotes racial equality in sport throughout England. It is a partnership between Sport England and the Commission for Racial Equality. Ethnic minorities are poorly represented at decision-making levels in most sports. They are largely excluded from various sports facilities and they are overlooked by sports development officers and coaches.

In August 1999 a survey by Sporting Equals of 62 governing bodies in sport found that they needed more guidance, support and information to help them address racial equality issues within their sport. Sporting Equals works with the governing bodies of various sports and with national organisations to develop policies and working practices that promote racial equality.

Sporting Equals has led to the development of the *Racial Equality Charter for Sport*, which has now been signed by nearly 100 sports organisations in the UK. It has also led to the development, with Sport England, of *Promoting Racial Equality through Sport*, a standard for local authority sport and leisure services published by the Local Government Association.

Sporting Equals – promotes racial equality in sport throughout England
www.sportingequals.com

Talented Athlete Scholarship Scheme

The Talented Athlete Scholarship Scheme (TASS) is a government initiative to help talented athletes who wish to progress with a formal academic programme but maintain an involvement in performance sport. It bridges the gap between junior representative levels and world-class levels for England's most talented sportspeople aged 16–25.

TASS is trying to help talented sportspeople maintain a balance between academic life or employment while training and competing as a performance athlete. TASS offers two ways to help talented sportspeople in England:

- **TASS scholarships** are for 18–25 year olds in higher or further education; there is an extended upper age limit of 35 for a scholar with a disability.

- **TASS bursaries** are for 16–19 years olds in further education or who have left education to pursue a career; there is an extended upper age limit of 35 for a bursar with a disability.

A total of 47 sports are eligible for TASS, and 15 of them are disability sports. TASS scholars receive sporting services to the value of £3000 and TASS bursars receive sporting services to the value of £1000.

Talented Athlete Scholarship Scheme

www.tass.gov.uk

TOP programmes

TOP programmes are organised by the Youth Sport Trust. They provide a sporting pathway for all young people aged 18 months to 18 years. They are designed to give young people of all abilities the chance to make the most of the opportunities that PE and sport can bring. They encourage all young people, including those with disabilities, teenage girls and gifted and talented athletes to thrive, and they provide ongoing support to teachers and others working with young children.

- **TOP Tots (18 months to 3 years)** – uses physical activity to develop communication and language techniques, coordination, cooperation and social skills.

- **TOP Start (3–5 years)** – develops basic movement and ball skills; it encourages the full integration of children with disabilities.

- **TOP Play (4–9 years)** – develops their core physical and movement skills.

- **Primary TOP** – programmes supported by Sainsbury's Active Kids (7–11 years); as well as developing skills in a range of sports for young people, they provide an enhanced set of resources and training for teachers.

- **TOP Link (14–16 years)** – encourages secondary students to organise and manage sport or dance festivals in local primary schools.

- **TOP Sportsability (all age groups)** – integrates disabled and non-disabled young people through a variety of sporting challenges.

Youth Sport Trust – more information on TOP programmes

www.youthsporttrust.org

Active Sports

The Active Sports programme was developed and set up by Sport England in 1999. Here are its objectives:

- One nationwide sports programme with all of the relevant agencies working through effective partnerships

- Wider access across the whole programme

- Improved retention in organised sport by young people

- Improved performance and talent selection processes

- Improved effectiveness and efficiency of business operations.

The programme was delivered locally through partnerships covering the whole of the country. Each partnership employed a number of core staff to liaise with local partners – local authority sports development personnel, local education authorities, national governing bodies (NGBs), funding agencies, community sports groups, etc. – to achieve the programme's outcomes. The NGBs for each of the 10 sports in the programme are athletics, basketball, cricket, girls' football, hockey, netball, rugby league, rugby union, swimming and tennis.

Sports quality marks

Sports quality marks or awards are for schools that are part of a school sport partnership, including all maintained schools in England from September 2006. They are awarded annually. Schools are automatically assessed for one of the marks through the national school sport survey, which all partnership schools take part in.

Each year, after completion of the school sport survey, a panel sets the standards that schools and partnerships have to reach in order to be awarded a quality mark. The panel includes representatives from these bodies:

- Association for Physical Education
- Youth Sport Trust
- Sport England
- Qualifications and Curriculum Authority
- Department for Culture, Media and Sport
- Department for Education and Skills.

The panel decided on these standards for 2006.

Activemark

Schools received Activemark if:

- 90% or more of pupils across the school were doing two hours of PE and sport;
- the school held a sports day; and
- the school had met or bettered the national average for the range of sports it offered or for the percentage of pupils participating in sports clubs linked to their school or school sport partnership.

Overall 50%, or about 7000, of the primary schools taking part in the annual school sport survey in 2005/6 met the standard and were awarded Activemark 2006. This includes special schools with primary-aged pupils.

Sportsmark

Schools received Sportsmark if:

- 90% or more of pupils across the school were doing two hours of PE and sport;
- the school held a sports day; and
- the school met the national average in three or more of the following areas:
  - percentage of pupils taking part in interschool competitive sport;
  - the range of sports the school offers;
  - the percentage of pupils participating in sports clubs linked to their school or school sport partnerships;
  - the percentage of pupils actively involved in sports leadership and volunteering.

Overall 16%, or about 500, of the secondary schools taking part in the annual school sport survey in 2005/6 met the standard and were awarded Sportsmark 2006. This includes special schools with secondary-aged pupils.

Sports Partnership Mark

Partnerships were awarded the Sports Partnership Mark if 50% or more of primary schools (including special schools with primary-aged pupils) within the partnership were awarded Activemark 2006 and 50% or more of secondary schools (including special schools with secondary-aged pupils) within the partnership were awarded Sportsmark 2006. Ten partnerships met the standards and were awarded Sports Partnership Mark 2006.

case study
11.13

Sportsmark

A school wishes to apply for the Sportsmark quality award to show their commitment to sport and PE. It considers it has achieved the required standard.

activity
INDIVIDUAL WORK

1. Why have quality awards such as Sportsmark been introduced?
2. What are the advantages for a school that achieves a quality award?
3. How can quality awards affect sports participation in the UK?

You can find case studies and more about these awards on the websites of Sport Development and Sport England

www.sportdevelopment.org.uk

www.sportengland.org

activity
INDIVIDUAL WORK
11.14

D3

Using the case study or example you chose in Activity 11.12, write an evaluation of three strategies or initiatives that relate to participation in your sport.

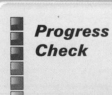
Progress Check

1. Define these three types of sports organisation: public, private and voluntary. Give one example of each type.
2. What are the characteristics of mob football?
3. When a half-day was introduced on Saturday, why was it so important for the development of sport?
4. Describe the links between transport and sports development.
5. What is the globalisation of sport?
6. Describe some recent changes in sports participation.
7. How can the media influence sport?
8. Give some reasons why sports participation rates are lower for women.
9. Explain some of the reasons for non-participation in sport.
10. Describe three current initiatives to increase participation in sport.

Psychology for Sports Performance

This unit covers:

- The effects of personality and motivation on sports performance
- The relationships between stress, anxiety, arousal and sports performance
- Group dynamics in sports teams
- Planning a psychological skills training programme to enhance sports performance

Sports psychology is an increasingly popular area for study and is useful for performers who want to get an edge by being psychologically prepared. This unit covers the important areas of personality and motivation and their effects on sports performance. To control anxiety and still be psychologically ready for action, or psyched up -- that is the crucial balance. Performers often have to compete in teams, so it is important to understand the psychological aspects of teams. The last part of the unit helps you plan a psychological skills training programme.

grading criteria

To achieve a **Pass** grade the evidence must show that the learner is able to:	To achieve a **Merit** grade the evidence must show that the learner is able to:	To achieve a **Distinction** grade the evidence must show that the learner is able to:
P1 describe personality and how it affects sports performance Pg 285	**M1** explain the effects of personality and motivation on sports performance Pg 289	**D1** evaluate the effects of personality and motivation on sports performance Pg 289
P2 describe motivation and how it affects sports performance Pg 294	**M2** explain the effects of stress, anxiety and arousal on sports performance Pg 301	**D2** analyse how group dynamics affects performance in team sports Pg 308
P3 describe stress, anxiety and arousal, their causes and their effects on sports performance Pg 300	**M3** explain how group dynamics affects performance in team sports Pg 306	**D3** justify the six-week psychological skills programme for a selected sports performer Pg 314
P4 describe group dynamics and how they affect performance in team sports Pg 304	**M4** explain the six-week psychological training programme for a selected sports performer Pg 311	

To achieve a **Pass** grade the evidence must show that the learner is able to:	To achieve a **Merit** grade the evidence must show that the learner is able to:	To achieve a **Distinction** grade the evidence must show that the learner is able to:
P5 plan a six-week psychological skills training programme to enhance sports performance for a selected performer Pg 308		

Understand the effects of personality and motivation on sports performance

Personality

Personality and performance in sport has been a popular subject for sports psychologists, but hard evidence is thin on the ground. Psychologists attempt to see links between certain types of people and success in sport. They also try to find links between types of personalities and the sports they choose to take up. Most psychologists agree there are two main theories that explain how our personalities are formed – the trait theory and the social learning theory.

Personality is widely agreed to be the total of an individual's characteristics that make anyone unique or different from their peers. Personality is thought to represent characteristics of the person that account for consistent patterns of behaviour that may show themselves in different situations. Some psychologists view personality as stable and enduring characteristics of a person's character, temperament, intellect and physique which determine how the person behaves.

Personality profiles

Sports psychologists have devoted considerable time and effort to build a picture of typical personalities of sports performers. They have attempted to show that there are major differences between successful sportspeople and unsuccessful sportspeople or people that avoid sport.

Morgan (1980) built on much previous research and found that many successful athletes had positive mental health characteristics. He investigated performers from a number of different sports using a profile of mood states (POMS), a questionnaire that assessed the moods of sports performers. Successful athletes scored higher on positive moods and lower on negative moods. Unsuccessful athletes showed the opposite. For instance, successful athletes showed high vigour and low fatigue moods. But these moods could be the result of their success, not the reason for it. When plotted on a graph, the results for successful athletes look like an iceberg, so it became known as the iceberg profile.

Research indicates that physical contact sports, such as wrestling, attract people with a different group of personality characteristics than individual sports such as gymnastics (Kroll *et al.* 1970). Team players appear to be more anxious and extroverted but lack sensitivity and imagination associated with individual sports performers. There are also links between player positions and certain personality characteristics; for instance, a midfield hockey player is likely to have a personality that gives them better concentration, more control over anxiety and greater confidence.

Fig 16.1 Iceberg personality profile

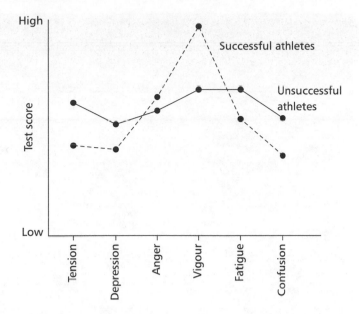

Mind Tools – self-study for essential skills

www.mindtools.com

Do some personality testing, then write a report on personality and how it affects sports performance.

Trait theory of personality

The trait theory says that we are born with personality characteristics that influence how we behave in all situations. Personality traits are *stable* – they vary little over time – and *enduring* – we are stuck with them. Psychologists have also found that traits are *generalisable*; Silva (1984) indicates that our behaviour can be predicted in different situations and there is always a predisposition to act in a particular way. Some sports performers may have an aggressive trait and this may surface in a variety of different situations.

Eysenck (1955) grouped the many personality characteristics into two dimensions or scales: **extroversion** to **introversion** and **stable** to **neurotic**. Each pair of traits should be viewed on a scale or continuum. For instance, a person may have elements of being extrovert and introvert but they are slightly more extroverted than introverted.

- **Extrovert** – seeks social situations and likes excitement; lacks concentration.
- **Introvert** – does not seek social situations and likes peace and quiet; good at concentrating.
- **Stable** – does not swing from one emotion to another.
- **Neurotic** – highly anxious and has unpredictable emotions.

The narrowband approach to personality states that personality characteristics can be grouped into type A and type B:

Figure 16.2 Some sports performers may show different traits in different situations

- **Type A** – these individuals are impatient and lack tolerance of others; they also have high levels of personal anxiety.
- **Type B** – these individuals are far more relaxed and are more tolerant towards others; they have much lower personal anxiety.

Hinkle *et al*. (1989) researched the link between the narrowband approach and sports performance. They took 96 runners, aged between 16 and 66, and identified their personalities as type A or type B. There was no significant difference between the two groups, except that when they were not motivated, type A runners did more running than type B. This research backs up the argument that one personality type is not preferable to another (Honeybourne *et al*. 2000).

People do seem to change personality over a lifetime, so the trait approach can be criticised as too inflexible. Different situations often trigger different personality characteristics. For instance, a netball player may only show signs of aggression when they are losing. Research has shown there is a link between some personality traits and the sports people do, but there is little evidence to support the view that the trait approach can predict performance.

Athletic Insight – online journal of sports psychology
www.athleticinsight.com
PsychNet-UK – mental health and psychology directory
www.psychnet-uk.com

Social learning

The **social learning** approach states that our personality characteristics are learned not genetically predetermined. Social learning involves the influences of others on a person's behaviour. We observe and imitate role models but only those who are significant to us.

The situation is an important influence in this approach, and this may explain why sports performers change their behaviour instead of showing stable traits. Reactions to situations in sport are often based on how others have reacted in similar situations. According to social learning theory, others influence us and we often copy or imitate others whose behaviour or personality we would like to emulate. People who influence us like this are often called significant others. Sports stars are more likely to be copied by others because their personalities and behaviours are seen as ideals.

Figure 16.3 Many people copy the behaviour of sports stars

case study
16.1

Role model

A junior school pupil who plays for the school team watches a Premiership football star being aggressive towards the referee. The boy will recognise the high status of the football star and will wish to copy his behaviour. According to social learning theory, the boy will imitate the footballer's aggressiveness because he sees the football star as a role model.

activity
GROUP WORK

1. In what other ways might the boy copy the football star?
2. How might inappropriate behaviour be changed?

When investigating the links between personality and sport, remember that for every piece of research that connects a personality characteristic to a type of sport, there is another that states the opposite. Yet to get the most from a performer, a coach needs to consider the performer's individual feelings, concentration levels, motives and other personality characteristics. Personality tests have been used to select sports performers but it is very dangerous to put much emphasis on personality tests for selection.

There are also research findings on how sport affects personality. It is often claimed that sport is character building and can develop team skills that may be useful at work and in everyday life. Recent research has indicated a link between sport and positive mental health.

Figure 16.4 Sport can be character building

activity
GROUP WORK
16.2

M1

Give a presentation that explains the effects of personality on sports performance; refer to relevant theories.

Interactional approach

Most sports psychologists think that the trait and social learning approaches have some value. However, the interactional or interactionist approach is popular among sports psychologists because people do appear to change personality from one interaction to another; their personality changes depending on where they are and who they are with. We are probably born with some personality characteristics that we can modify by interacting with the environment. The interactionist approach agrees that we have traits that appear consistently, but recognises that often our traits interact with a situation. The interaction between personality and situation determines our behaviour.

case study
16.2

Jekyll and Hyde

A tennis player is mild mannered off court but highly competitive on court. He shouts at the umpire and line judges when he thinks their decisions have not been fair to him. After the game, he reverts to his mild temperament. He is known to have a Jekyll and Hyde character.

activity
INDIVIDUAL WORK

1. What personality theory can be easily applied to the tennis player?
2. What other aspects of the environment may be significant in his behaviour?

activity
INDIVIDUAL WORK
16.3

D1

Evaluate the effects of personality and performance by writing a guide for a coach. Your guide should relate theories to practical examples and advise on some of the difficulties in linking sport with personality.

Motivation and sports performance

It is obviously important for sports performers to be well motivated, but some seem to be better motivated than others. You can watch two athletes of very similar ability race against each other but the one that invariably wins appears to be better motivated.

There are some people who do not seem at all interested in participating in sport, whereas others seem to be addicted to playing sport. If we could find out what actually motivates people to participate, we could encourage and enrich people's lives by involving them in sport.

Motivation can be seen as a drive for success and a wish to fulfil a need. This drive can be stimulated from within (intrinsic factors) or from external stimuli (extrinsic factors), which arouse us and dictate our behaviour.

Most psychologists agree that motivation is connected with a driving force that encourages us towards behaving in a particular way. For example, an athlete may be driven to achieve a personal best in throwing the discuss. They are driven by a strong desire for self-fulfilment – to feel they have challenged themselves and won.

Figure 16.5 Motivation is a drive to do well

Intrinsic motivation

Intrinsic motivation is the internal drive that people have to participate or to perform well in sport. Some intrinsic motives are fun, enjoyment and the satisfaction that is experienced by achieving something. Some athletes describe the intrinsic flow experienced during competition. They speak of high levels of concentration and a feeling that they are in total control.

case study 16.3 Squash player

An occasional squash player aged 45 says that, when they play, they often feel a sense of relief from the day's stresses and strains and that they enjoy the hard physical work of playing squash. This is a typical example of intrinsic motivation.

activity
INDIVIDUAL WORK

1. Why does the player have intrinsic motivation?
2. Name some potential barriers that prevent people having the drive to play a sport such as squash.

Psych Web – psychology information for students and teachers of psychology
www.psywww.com
SportsPsychology.com
www.sportpsychology.com

Figure 16.6 Sport can be a relief from everyday stresses and strains

Extrinsic motivation

Extrinsic motivation involves influences external to the performer. This is the drive that is caused by motives that are external or environmental. These motives are rewards that can be tangible or intangible.

The drive to do well in sport could come from the need to please others or to gain rewards such as medals, badges or large amounts of money. Rewards that include badges or prize money are called tangible rewards. Rewards that involve getting first place in the league or getting praise from your parents are intangible rewards.

Extrinsic motivation is very useful to encourage better performance in sport. The pleasure of receiving the reward acts as a reinforcer and the performer is more likely to repeat the actions that led to the reward. A karate performer receives a coloured belt for achieving a particular standard; the belt is a very obvious sign of that performer's standard and can motivate them to achieve even higher standards.

Extrinsic motivation can increase levels of intrinsic motivation; this is called the *additive principle*. But some research findings disagree and show that extrinsic reward can decrease intrinsic motivation. For instance, athletes' performances declined as soon as they had been signed up in contracts that paid a great deal of money.

An example of **extrinsic motivation** might be a young girl who is just starting to learn to swim. After much effort she achieves a width of the pool without any help and without armbands. She is given a badge that shows she has achieved success. This reward is pleasurable to the girl and her interest in swimming increases along with her determination. The reward has reinforced the correct behaviour.

Figure 16.7 A karate belt may be an extrinsic motivator

Achievement motivation

Your personality type may determine how motivated you are. Some people are motivated to succeed in sport, but others have personality characteristics that encourage them to avoid competition. This idea is called achievement motivation.

Sport involves trying to achieve something and this often leads to high levels of competition. If you set challenging goals for personal achievement, your performance is likely to improve. A personal achievement goal for a basketball player might be to score 80% baskets from the free throw line. This still might mean the team loses, but the player is motivated through personal achievement that may be a more powerful motivator to improve future performances.

Achievement motivation is widely recognised as arising from personality trait characteristics. Traits tend to be viewed as innate characteristics that we are born with. Athletes can be grouped into those that have a high need to achieve (Nach) and those that have a high need to avoid failure (Naf). We all probably have both types of personality characteristics but some have more Nach characteristics than Naf characteristics, and vice versa. If the performer and coach recognise what motivation drives the performer, then they can devise strategies to improve performance.

Nach

Need to achieve (Nach) is a personality type that involves the following characteristics:

- They persist on task.
- They complete the task quickly.
- They take risks.
- They like challenging situations.
- They take personal responsibility for their actions.
- They like feedback about their performance.

Naf

Need to avoid failure (Naf) is a personality type that involves the following characteristics:

- They give up on tasks easily.
- They take their time to complete the task.
- They avoid challenging situations.
- They do not take personal responsibility for their actions.
- They do not want feedback about results or performance.

How to change a Naf into a Nach

- Make goals challenging but achievable.
- Give early success.
- Show role models that have been successful.
- Be supportive and encouraging, give positive reinforcement.
- Use rewards.
- Seek to lower anxiety levels.

Attribution theory and motivation

Attributions are the perceived causes of a particular outcome. In sport they are often the reasons we give for the results we achieve. For example, a team member may cite bad weather as a reason for the team losing.

Attributions are important because of the way they affect motivation, which in turn affects future performances, future effort and whether a person continues to participate. If a young person is told that they failed because they do not have the ability to succeed, they are unlikely to try again. If the same person is given some ideas to work on, they are more likely to persevere. Sometimes people make inappropriate

case study 16.4

Running coach

The coach of a runner is interviewed on the television. He says that the runner was unsuccessful because the temperature was too high during the race. He adds that the runner has recently experienced personal problems and has done well, considering the pressure they have experienced.

activity
GROUP WORK

1. What kinds of attributions are evident here?
2. What other reasons could there be for the runner's underperformance?

attributions that need to be changed into more helpful attributions. This is known as *attribution retraining*.

Weiner (1974) identified four main reasons given for examination results: ability, effort, task difficulty and luck. He then constructed a two-dimensional model which he called the *locus of causality and stability*. The locus of causality refers to whether the attributions come from within the person (internal) or from the environment (external). Stability refers to whether the attribution is changeable or unchangeable.

Figure 16.8 Weiner's model

Locus of causality

	Internal	External
Stable	Ability	Task difficulty
Unstable	Effort	Luck

Stability (vertical axis label)

People who lose tend to attribute their failure to external causes and those who succeed usually attribute their success to internal causes. Known as the *self-serving bias*, it limits the sense of shame due to failure and highlights personal achievement in success. The stability dimension of the model will affect achievement motivation. If the reasons given for winning are stable reasons, the individual is motivated to achieve again. If failure is attributed to an unstable factor, the individual is more likely to try again because there is a good chance the outcome will change.

A third dimension, *controllability*, has recently been added to the attribution model. This refers to whether attributions are under the control of the performer or under the control of others. Coaches and teachers tend to praise effort and controllable success and punish or criticise lack of effort and controllable failures. Concentrating on uncontrollable external and stable factors is not much use if you want to turn failure into success.

Learned helplessness

Learned helplessness refers to a belief that failure is inevitable and a feeling of hopelessness when faced with a particular situation (specific learned helplessness) or groups of situations (global learned helplessness).

Low achievers often attribute their failure to uncontrollable factors, which can lead to **learned helplessnes**s. Some see high achievers as people who are oriented towards mastery, people who see failure as a learning experience and attribute failure to controllable unstable factors. This fits in well with the model of achievement motivation (page 291), where Nach performers arc not afraid of failing and will persist with a task until they succeed.

Attribution retraining

Many attributions are subjective and do not help with future progression. Attributions often need to be reassessed so a performer can succeed.

---

case study

16.5

Hockey miss

A hockey player misses a chance to score in an open goal. The player thinks they have let the rest of the side down and feels devastated and worthless. They should be encouraged to attribute to controllable unstable factors.

activity
GROUP WORK

1. What sort of attributions is the player likely to give?
2. What sort of attributions would you encourage the player to give?

To help those who have failed and are starting to experience learned helplessness, teachers and coaches should concentrate on positive attributions. If a performer feels they lack ability, they will inevitably fail, but their attribution could be changed to 'having the wrong tactics' or 'slight alteration of technique needed'. The performer may then be disappointed rather than frustrated and will persist with the task rather than avoid it altogether. The whole process is known as attribution retraining.

---

activity
INDIVIDUAL WORK
16.4

P2

Make a visual presentation that describes personality and how it affects motivation. Use a case study from your own sport.

Understand the relationships between stress, anxiety, arousal and sports performance

Stress and anxiety in sport

Much has been written about stress and its effect on sports performance. Competitors are interested in why they are anxious in certain situations and not in others. Sportspeople participate because of the buzz it gives them. They experience excitement and this can be enjoyable, especially if they can cope with the demands of the activity. In sport, performers and coaches are particularly interested in how they cope with stressful situations. When you are successful there is very little difference in the skill levels between yourself and other participants. It is the ability to handle anxiety and stress that separates the winners from the losers.

Research indicates that it is the sports performer's perceptions of a situation that can cause stress. If a player thinks they cannot cope with a situation such as the final of a big tournament, they will experience the negative aspect of stress, namely anxiety. Stress is often seen as a mixture of physiological and psychological responses occurring in situations where people perceive threats to their well-being. Anxiety is often viewed as a negative emotion caused by a situation seen as threatening. Anxiety involves feelings of apprehension that dominate a person's thought patterns.

Stress

How do we know that a performer is feeling stressed? We look for physiological and psychological symptoms.

Physiological symptoms

The physiological symptoms prepare the body for fight or flight; in other words, the body is gearing up to cope with a dramatic increase in physical action.

- Increased heart rate
- Increased breathing rate
- Increased blood pressure
- Increased adrenaline release
- Increased perspiration
- Increased blood sugar.

Psychological symptoms

Psychological symptoms are linked to physiological symptoms. The performer will notice an increase in their heart rate or their breathing rate and this can make them worry, reducing their ability to concentrate.

- Worry or apprehension
- Irritability
- Inability to concentrate
- Difficulty in making decisions
- Aggression
- Increased rate of speech.

Sources of stress

The factors that give sports performers stressed or anxious responses are called stressors. There are many stressors associated with participating in sport but here are the main ones:

- **Competition** – performers in sport are constantly being judged or evaluated by other players, coaches and spectators and in some cases millions of TV viewers. Competition is one of the most powerful stressors.
- **Frustration** – this can be caused by the performer's own mistakes, other performers' mistakes or mistakes made by officials. Injury can be psychologically stressful because of the frustration caused by not being able to play properly or at all.
- **Conflict** – there may be conflict with other players, coaches and managers or with the crowd.
- **Environment** – the climate may be uncomfortably hot or the pitch surface may be tricky to play on.
- **Outside stressors** – all performers bring baggage from their everyday or personal lives.

Once these stressors are dealt with and controlled, athletes are usually better able to control other stressors associated with their sport.

case study 16.6

Trampolinist

As a trampolinist completes her compulsory routine, she realises she will be judged by the officials but also by other performers, who can compare her routine with their own. She has noticed that the trampoline bed has a different tension to the ones she has been used to. These two observations cause her to experience a high level of stress.

activity
INDIVIDUAL WORK

1. What stressors are evident here?
2. What other sources of stress could there be?

Eustress

Eustress is a stress that can help a performer. There are some who seek stressful situations, rather than trying to avoid them. When an athlete experiences **eustress**, they are well motivated and see potentially dangerous or embarrassing situations as challenges, so their performances are helped rather than hindered.

Figure 16.9 Some people want adventure and seek stressful situations

For example, a climber with a great deal of experience has confidence in their own ability. The climber continually seeks the 'ultimate challenge' and climbs in more and more difficult situations. They decide to climb without the support of a rope because they want to experience the thrill of a potentially life-threatening activity. This is an example of eustress.

Anxiety

Anxiety is a negative stress response. It involves worry that failure might occur, and failure is always a possibility in competitive sport. Winning sometimes assumes gigantic proportions. Bill Shankly, the inspired manager of Liverpool FC, is reported to have said, 'Winning is not like life and death, it is more important than that.' Some competitors can cope with anxiety and are mainly calm. Others, including many top performers, can become extremely anxious. The anxiety experienced in sports competition is often called competitive anxiety.

Competitive anxiety

Many sports psychologists agree that there are four major factors to competitive anxiety. Anxiety arises from an interaction between the person and the situation. Some sports performers will be anxious in match situations but not in training. Anxiety can arise from a personality trait, **trait anxiety**, or by a response to a specific situation, state anxiety:

- **Trait anxiety** – this is a personality trait that is enduring in the individual. A performer with high trait anxiety has a predisposition or potential to react to situations with apprehension.

- **State anxiety** – this is the anxiety in a particular situation. There are two types of state anxiety: somatic and cognitive. Somatic anxiety is the body's response, such as tension and rapid pulse. Cognitive anxiety is the psychological worry over the situation.

Anxiety levels may vary. Those with high trait anxiety, or A trait, are likely to become anxious in highly stressful situations but they are not equally anxious in all stressful situations. Competition factors are the interaction between personality factors, trait anxiety and the situation. This interaction will affect behaviour and may cause state anxiety.

Martens (1987) developed the sport competition anxiety test, or **SCAT**, to try to identify performers who were likely to suffer from anxiety in competitive situations.

Figure 16.10 Sport has many situations that create state anxiety

Sport competition anxiety test

The sport competition anxiety test (SCAT) is a questionnaire to assess sport competition anxiety in sports participants. It is a self-reporting questionnaire and measures competitive trait anxiety. It can be useful to predict a performer's anxiety in future competitions, i.e. their state anxiety. There is a high correlation between SCAT results and pre-competition state anxiety, so the SCAT test can be seen as a valid way to predict competitive state anxiety.

case study 16.7 — Anxious hockey players

A coach decides that she would like to find out more about the players in her hockey team. She particularly wants to help team members who are very anxious in competitive situations. She administers the SCAT questionnaire and uses the results as part of her analysis of individual players.

activity
GROUP WORK

1. How could this test be a basis for team selection?
2. What other ways could be used to find out about the anxiety levels of players?

Arousal

Drive theory

High levels of stress are often caused by overanxiety to do well. Motivation is important but performance can suffer if personal drive becomes too great. Another term for a performer's motivational drive is **arousal**. High arousal can lead to high levels of stress, both physiological and psychological.

Psychologists suggest that drive theory can describe the effects of arousal on behaviour. This theory proposes a linear relationship between arousal and performance:

$$\text{Performance} = \text{arousal} \times \text{skill level}$$

In other words, the higher the arousal, the better the performance. The more emotionally driven you are to achieve a goal, the more likely you are to succeed. Behaviour that is learned is more likely to be repeated if the stakes are high.

An example of drive theory in action is when a weightlifter is well motivated to achieve their personal best. Just before they lift, the coach deliberately comes out with forceful encouragement so the performer gets angry and their arousal is very high. The 'psychological energy' created by the performer is channelled into the lift and they achieve a personal best. The higher the arousal, the better the performance.

Figure 16.11 Drive theory says the higher the arousal, the better the performance

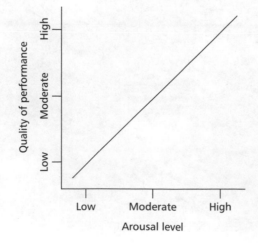

Drive theory implies that the better a skill is learned, the more likely that high arousal will lead to better performance. The problem with this theory is that even well-learned skills are often performed incorrectly under high pressure. The weightlifter may have let their anger overwhelm them and lost all their technique. Boxers can never really lose their temper because this may cloud their judgement and impair their technique. It is also difficult to define a 'well-learned task'. In sport, many skills and combinations of skills are a mixture of well-learned and novel tasks.

A Premiership side is awarded a penalty in the dying minutes of a crucial match. A prolific goal scorer steps up to take the shot. His arousal is very high because this kick could seal a win for his team. He mishits the ball. On this occasion, high arousal has led to poor performance.

Figure 16.12 High arousal can detrimentally affect performance

Inverted-U hypothesis

The inverted-U hypothesis relates arousal and performance. It proposes that performance increases as arousal increases, but only up to moderate levels of arousal. If arousal increases further, then performance falls away. Performance is poor at very low arousal and very high arousal; the best possible performance occurs at moderate arousal.

Figure 16.13 Inverted-U hypothesis – best performance occurs at moderate arousal

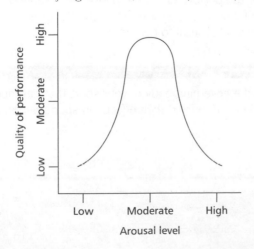

<table>
<tr><td>

case study

16.8

</td><td>

Netball player

A netball team player is well motivated and driven to win by her coach, but she keeps relatively calm and concentrates on the skills she needs to perform. Her arousal is moderate and that means she will play at her best.

</td></tr>
</table>

activity

INDIVIDUAL WORK

1. How can you apply the inverted-U theory to this case study?
2. What might make the player too aroused to maintain optimum performance?

Figure 16.14 Too much arousal could make this netballer miss

Research reveals that the required arousal in sport depends on three factors:

■ **Types of skill** – the grosser or simpler the skill, the higher the required levels of arousal; the finer or more complex the skill, the lower the required levels of arousal.

■ **Ability of the performer** – the more expert the performer, the greater their need for high levels of arousal to perform well.

■ **Personality of the performer** – if the performer is more of an extrovert, they need higher levels of arousal to perform well; if the performer is more of an introvert, they need lower levels of arousal to perform well.

activity

INDIVIDUAL WORK

16.5

P3

Write a report to the governing body of your sport that describes stress, anxiety and arousal. Include their causes and their effects on sports performance.

Catastrophe theory

As arousal increases there is often a sudden and dramatic drop in performance. We see many top sportspeople go to pieces in big events. The **inverted-U hypothesis** shows only a steady decline in performance as arousal goes from moderate to high. Catastrophe theory shows a much more dramatic decline in performance, hence its name. Anxiety can be divided into two types: **somatic anxiety**, which is experienced by the body as sweating, for example, and **cognitive anxiety**, which is anxiety experienced by the mind such as worry about failing. Catastrophe theory is a complex multidimensional theory that includes these two types of anxiety and tries to model how they interact with each other. Cognitive anxiety is more important than somatic anxiety in determining a performer's reactions to high levels of stress. According to **catastrophe theory**, increases in levels of cognitive anxiety will help performance if somatic anxiety is low. So if a performer's body is relaxed but the performer feels anxious, this anxiety can help to improve performance.

■ If a performer has high somatic anxiety and their cognitive anxiety increases, their performance will decline.

■ If a performer has high cognitive anxiety and their somatic anxiety or physiological arousal increases continuously, their performance can suddenly deteriorate in a catastrophic response.

■ If the performer's arousal decreases after this catastrophic effect, their performance will increase but not back to its optimum level before the catastrophe.

Figure 16.15 Catastrophe theory – have a relaxed body but a slightly anxious mind. Adapted from Fazey and Hardy (1988)

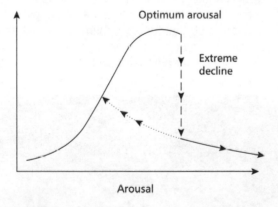

Peak flow experience

Peak flow experience is an experience where a sportsperson achieves optimum performance levels and associates them with a particular emotional response. Many top athletes describe their feelings when almost nothing can go wrong. They say they are 'in the zone', where all that matters is the performance – everything else is insignificant. A **peak flow experience** can be explained by arousal theories. All the theories related to arousal show that performance is related to the amount of inner drive and self-motivation. There are mental strategies that can help performers achieve this experience then motivate them to repeat it, driving them to achieve their very best.

activity

INDIVIDUAL WORK 16.6

M2

Write some guidelines for a player or participant in your sport. Your guidelines should explain stress, anxiety and arousal plus their causes and their effects on sports performance.

How top performers get in zone

- **Be relaxed** – top performers do not need very high levels of arousal. They need a balance between wanting to achieve their very best and being relaxed and in control.

- **Be confident** – top performers believe they have great ability. A lapse in performance will not undermine this belief. They do not show fear but they exude pride and confidence. They do not hope for success, they expect it.

- **Be completely focused** – top performers are completely absorbed in their performance. They do not dwell on what has happened in the past and what may happen in the future.

- **Activity is effortless** – top performers accomplish often complex and difficult tasks with very little effort. Body and mind are working almost perfectly together.

- **Movements are automatic** – top performers move instinctively and there seems to be little conscious thought. This can be related to motor programme theory.

- **Have fun** – top performers get immense satisfaction and fulfilment from experiencing the flow. Unless they are having fun, they seldom achieve a peak flow experience.

- **Be in control** – top performers have command over their body and emotions. They are in charge and control their own destiny.

Understand group dynamics in sports teams

Groups are of particular interest to sports psychologists because sport has many situations where participants and spectators are in groups. The most common group in sport is a *team*. It is important for team members, coaches and supporters that a team works together well and everyone plays as well as they can. A group is a collection of individuals who share similar goals and who interact. A volleyball team is a group

Figure 16.16 A cohesive team interacts well and shares the same goals

because the team members share the goals of playing and winning, plus they interact by communicating and responding to each other during volleyball games.

Team cohesion

An effective team has cohesion; the team members work well together and share similar goals. If the team members have very different goals, the team is less likely to be cohesive. For instance, if half a rugby team are principally playing to win but the other half are in it for the social life, then the team is likely to lack cohesion.

Cohesion is influenced by the motivational aspects that attract people to belong to the team and help the members resist the team breaking up. Here some factors that affect **team cohesion**:

- How the individual members of the group feel about the group as a whole.
- Reasons for being attracted to the team, e.g. social reasons or to win.
- Group performance – a winning team is more likely to be cohesive.
- Support for the team – a supportive crowd will help cohesion.
- How well team members communicate.
- Leadership – a good leader will improve team cohesion.
- Sense of identity – wearing the same kit improves a sense of identity and cohesion.
- Friendship – people who are friends off the field often make a cohesive team on the field.

Figure 16.17 Success brings cohesion

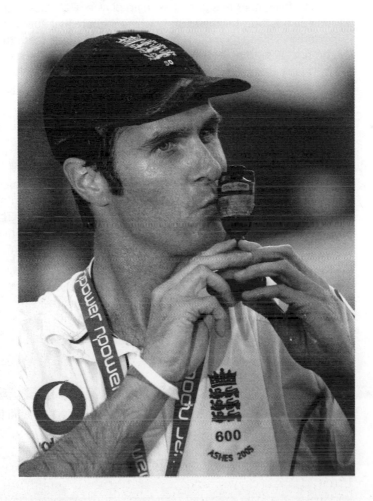

Group performance

People in teams can play extremely well together one day, but perform badly another day. Some teams have many good players and yet cannot seem to play well together, whereas some teams have no individual stars yet are very successful. The performance of a team depends on several factors. If we investigate these factors, it will help us get the most from our teams.

Steiner (1972) proposed a model for looking at the relationships between the people in a group and the group's performance:

Actual productivity = potential productivity – losses due to faulty process

Actual productivity is how the team finally performs, i.e. their results and how well they play. Potential productivity is the best possible performance of the group; it depends on the resources available and the individual abilities of the group members. Losses due to faulty processes are the problems that get in the way of the group reaching their potential. These faulty processes are mainly coordination faults and motivation faults.

Coordination faults

Coordination faults can arise from team members not connecting their play, so interaction between team members is poor. For example, a volleyball team includes players who do not connect with other players in passing sequences. Communication between players is poor and they do not play as one unit.

Motivation faults

Motivation faults can arise from individuals not trying very hard in the team, whereas others are trying hard to succeed as team players. This lack of motivation by some players can also prevent the team reaching its potential and becomes a faulty process, as indicated in Steiner's model. For example, in a rugby team there are a few players who do not seem to be trying very hard. When they get the ball, they do their own thing and invariably they lose the ball and valuable territory. One player in particular seems to disappear for long intervals in the game and does not make themselves available for the ball. This limits the options for the team in attacking play.

Social loafing and the Ringelmann effect

Social loafing is when players seem to lack motivation in team situations. Social loafers do not try hard to achieve and seem to be afraid of failure. They lack confidence and are generally highly anxious. According to psychologists, social loafers may well lack identity in the team and this may mean that they lack accountability. In other words, they can get away with doing little because no one will challenge them. This is not necessarily down to laziness; it is often because the player does not want to let the team down or feels that they cannot make any useful contribution to the team.

The **Ringelmann effect** is a **social loafing** behaviour that occurs when individual performance decreases with increase in group size. Ringelmann, a late nineteenth-century agricultural worker, found that in rope-pulling tasks, groups pulled with more force than an individual, but with not as much force as the sum of the individual pulling forces. Eight people did not pull eight times as hard as an individual, but only four times as hard.

activity
INDIVIDUAL WORK 16.7

P4

Describe group dynamics in a written report and say how it affects performance in team sports.

<table>
<tr><td>

case study

16.9

</td><td>

Mock swimming competition

Sports psychology research involved a mock swimming competition. The whole environment was designed to be as realistic as possible, with trophies, spectators, etc. In relay races, if lap times were announced, the competitor swam quicker than if the lap times were unannounced. The competitors' behaviour illustrates the Ringelmann effect.

</td></tr>
</table>

activity
GROUP WORK

1. Why did the Ringelmann effect occur?
2. What could be done to get rid of this effect?

Figure 16.18 Some group effects can impede performance

Social loafing lowers a team's performance, so coaches and players need strategies to minimise it. Here are some examples:

■ Give individual feedback rather than team feedback.

■ Ensure that each team member has their own role.

■ Make sure each team member knows their own role and the roles of all the other team members.

■ Use positive reinforcement, such as praise to encourage reluctant performers.

■ Monitor the performance of team members, e.g. on videotape.

A netball player's coach videos a match, but goes through the player's individual performance with them. The coach highlights the positive aspects but also points out areas of weakness that could be worked on for improvement.

activity
GROUP WORK 16.8

M3

Give a presentation that explains how group dynamics affects performance in team sports.

Leadership

Leaders influence behaviour in sport and leadership is very important for team performance. Here are some examples of leadership positions in sport:

- Captain
- Manager
- Director
- Coach
- Physiotherapist
- Team sports psychologist.

Leadership is often seen as behaviour that influences individuals and groups towards their own goals or targets. Effective leaders influence the people around them, and in sport this can produce better performances by individuals and teams. A good leader will have clear goals and will motivate others to achieve them.

Qualities of a good leader

Here are some qualities of a good leader:

- Good communication skills
- Enthusiastic and well motivated
- Good sports skills
- In-depth knowledge of the sport
- Charisma – they command respect
- A clear vision.

There is an ongoing debate about whether leaders are born or made. In other words, are the qualities of a good leader innate or are they learned from others by social learning? Most psychologists agree that it is probably a mixture of both. Knowledge and communication skills can be learned but an outstanding leader is probably born with charismatic qualities that cannot be learned.

Leadership styles

A sports leader's style depends on three factors. Here they are with examples of questions you could ask about them:

- **The situation** – are the team winning or losing?
- **The team members** – are they hostile?
- **The leader's personality** – is it naturally forceful?

Figure 16.19 Sports leadership comes in many styles

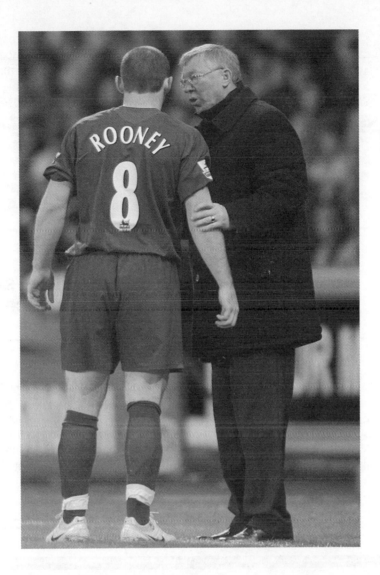

There are many different styles of leadership, but the three most common styles identified are authoritarian, democratic and laissez-faire:

- **Authoritarian style** – sometimes called task-oriented, an authoritarian leader just wants to get the job or task done. They do not have a particular interest in personal relationships and they take most of the decisions, rather than other members of the team. Leaders may use this style if they do not have time for much consultation, if they need to focus the whole team on a problem, or if they wish to instil autocratic discipline.

- **Democratic style** – sometimes called person-oriented, a democratic leader is concerned with interpersonal relationships. The leader shares out the decision-making and asks for advice from other group members. Leaders often adopt this style if their team members are experienced and have positive contributions to make.

- **Laissez-faire style** – this type of leader takes very few decisions and gives little direction to the team. The group members choose what they would like to do and how they do it with little or no input from the leader. This is usually associated with elite sport, where top performers find their own solutions, which can be creative and more effective overall.

Most successful leaders draw on a mixture of styles. A good coach may decide to be authoritarian when the team are losing a match but more democratic when the team are training. In match situations, the leader may decide to let the team get on with it, because interference might stifle the creativity of some team members.

activity
INDIVIDUAL WORK
16.9
D2

Write a report that analyses how group dynamics affects performance in team sports. Give examples from your own team sport.

Be able to plan a psychological skills training programme to enhance sports performance

Planning

Before you can plan a training programme for psychological skills, you need to assess the athlete's strengths and weaknesses in psychological skills and evaluate their psychological needs. This can be done by observations, by questionnaires or simply by having a discussion with the athlete. You also need to assess the psychological demands of the sport. Is it dangerous? Is the sport a team sport or an individual sport? What motor skills are involved? The plan should consider the current situation of the athlete and any aims and objectives for the future.

Link   See page 139 in Unit 4 for more information on planning, aims and objectives

activity
INDIVIDUAL WORK
16.10
P5

Plan a six-week psychological skills training programme to enhance sports performance for a selected sports performer.

Psychological skills to enhance performance

Stress management helps to eliminate anxiety and optimise performance. It is especially important for high-level performers: 'The most important factor which separates the very best from the good is their ability to control anxiety at crucial moments' (Jones and Hardy 1990).

Stress management techniques are widely used by sportspeople to cope with high levels of anxiety. Sport has assumed great importance for performers and for those directly associated with performance, such as coaches and managers.

Cognitive techniques for anxiety management techniques affect the mind and help control psychological anxiety. Somatic techniques, such as relaxation, work on the body directly. Cognitive anxiety can affect somatic anxiety, and vice versa. Controlling the heart rate by relaxation methods can make us feel more positive about performing. Conversely, positive thinking can control our heart rate (Honeybourne *et al.* 2000). Here are some stress management techniques that can be used as coping strategies.

Figure 16.20 Athletes try to manage their stress just before they compete

Imagery

Pictures in our minds are called **imagery**. Imagery can improve concentration and confidence. Many sports performers use mental images that capture the feeling of movement or an emotional feeling.

Imagery can also help with relaxation. When they feel anxious, a sports performer may go to 'another place' in their minds to calm down. Many top performers use this technique to lower their physiological and psychological arousal.

- **External imagery** – this is when you can picture yourself from outside your body, like watching yourself on film; for example, a racing driver may go through the route in their mind before the race.

- **Internal imagery** – this is when you imagine yourself doing the activity and can simulate the feelings of the activity, such as cornering a bobsleigh or the run-up, jump and landing in the high jump. All five senses are involved: sight, hearing, touch, taste and smell.

case study
16.10

Bobsleigh pilot

An athlete at the Winter Olympics who is responsible for steering the team's bobsleigh visualises or uses imagery to picture the track, with all its bends, twists and turns. The athlete goes through the movements they have to perform when they picture each aspect of the run in their mind. This is an example of imagery or mental rehearsal.

activity
GROUP WORK

1. What effects will this imagery have on the athlete?
2. What other mental practice could the athlete use?

Figure 16.21 A high-jumper visualises the jump before they start their run-up

Consider these points on using imagery effectively:

- Relax in a comfortable, warm setting before you practise imagery.
- To improve a skill by using imagery, practise in a real-life situation.
- Imagery exercises should be short but frequent.
- Set goals for each session; for example, have one short session to imagine the feel of a tennis serve.
- Construct a programme for your training in imagery.
- Evaluate your programme at regular intervals; use the sports imagery evaluation to help assess your training.

Self-talk

In self-talk the sports performer talks to themselves in a positive way about past performances and future efforts. It helps with self-confidence and increases levels of aspiration. Unfortunately, many performers talk to themselves in a negative way – negative **self-talk**. It is very common for sports performers to talk themselves out of winning: 'I will probably miss this penalty.'

Good performances need lots of positive self-talk and no negative self-talk. High-level performers must develop strategies to change negative thoughts into positive thoughts. Negative thoughts may be divided into five categories; here they are with an example:

- **Worry about performance** – I think she is better than me.
- **Inability to make decisions** – Shall I pass, shall I hold, shall I shoot?
- **Preoccupation with physical feelings** – I feel too tired, I'm going to give up and rest.
- **Thoughts on what will happen if they lose** – What will my coach say when I lose this point?
- **Thoughts on lack of ability to do well** – I am not good enough; he is better than me.

activity

INDIVIDUAL WORK 16.11

M4

Explain your six-week psychological skills training programme to enhance sports performance for a selected sports performer by presenting your plan to the performer.

Relaxation

Somatic anxiety can lead to cognitive anxiety, so the greater your physical relaxation, the greater your mental relaxation. But you don't want to be too laid back, as you often need to react quickly and dynamically. Performers find it very useful to do relaxation exercises before doing mental exercises such as imagery training. It helps them to be calmer and steadier. Just like any skill, relaxation skills need a lot of practice to achieve them.

Self-directed relaxation

Self-directed relaxation needs to be practised before it becomes effective. All the muscle groups are relaxed one at a time and the coach can help. The athlete then practises without direct help. Eventually it will only take a very short time for the athlete to achieve full relaxation. It is crucial that it can be done in a short time so it can be used before or during competition.

Peak Performance Sports – confidence for a competitive edge
www.peaksports.com

Progressive relaxation training

Pioneered by Jacobsen, **progressive relaxation training** (PRT) is where an athlete learns to be aware of the tension in their muscles then releases all the tension. Because the athlete is so aware of the tension in the first place, they have a more effective sense of losing that tension when it goes.

How to use PRT

1. Sit on the floor with your legs out straight in front of you.

2. With your right leg, tense the muscles by pulling your toes up towards your knee using your leg and foot muscles.

3. Develop as much tension as possible, hold it for about 5 s and concentrate on what it feels like.

4. Completely relax your leg muscles and let your foot go floppy. Now concentrate on what the relaxed muscles feel like.

5. Try to relax your muscles even more.

6. Your leg should feel far more relaxed.

case study 16.11

A gold for David Hemery

David Hemery won a gold medal in the 400 m hurdles at the Olympic Games of 1968. Here, in his own words, is what happened immediately before the race: 'I lay on the bench and the others started jogging around, while I just stayed there, because that was what my plan was, trying to bring my pulse rate down. At will, I tend to be able to relax the whole body without going through the progressive bits.'

activity
GROUP WORK

1. Why does he want to bring his pulse down?
2. In what other ways could he mentally prepare for a race?

Goal setting

Goal setting is an effective strategy that is widely used in sport for training and performance. It is a proven way of increasing motivation and confidence and controlling anxiety (Honeybourne 2006a, b). A performer or their coach can set goals without consulting the other person, but goals tend to be more effective if the coach and performer set them together.

Two types of goal are set for sportspeople:

- **Performance goals** – these goals are related directly to the performance or technique of the activity.

- **Outcome goals** – these goals are concerned with the end result, such as whether you win or lose.

Strike a good balance between performance goals and outcome goals. Too much emphasis on either can lead to demotivation and loss of confidence. A tennis player is trying to improve their speed of serve by improving their timing; this is a performance goal. Another tennis player is trying to win the grand slam by winning each open tournament; these are outcome goals. Outcome goals tend to be medium- to long-term goals and performance goals tend to be short-term goals.

There are four possible ways in which goals can affect performance (Locke and Latham 1985):

- They direct attention.

- They control the amount of effort put into an activity.

- They improve the level of effort until the goal is reached.

- They motivate a performer to develop a variety of success strategies or tactics.

See page 98 in Unit 3 for more information on goal setting
See page 129 in Unit 4 for more information on goal setting

Effective goal setting

Effective goal setting must break down the overall goal into a series of smaller goals. For instance, to win the league, a team may have to concentrate on sustaining their efforts by improving their aerobic endurance. To do this, there may be short-term goals of maintaining stamina training over future weeks. It can be more motivating to *split long-term goals* into medium-term goals and short-term goals which are more specific and manageable over a short period of time.

Effective goal setting is often called setting SMARTER targets. SMARTER targets are specific, measurable, agreed, realistic, timed, exciting and recorded:

- **Specific** – if goals are clear and unambiguous, they are more likely to be attained.
- **Measurable** – this is important for monitoring and makes you accountable.
- **Agreed** – shared goal setting is where the coach and performer agree goals together; it gives a sense of teamwork.
- **Realistic** – motivation will improve if goals can actually be reached.
- **Timed** – split goals into short-term goals that are planned and progressive.
- **Exciting** – the greater the stimulation, the greater the motivation.
- **Recorded** – records make it easier to monitor progress and are good for motivation. Once a goal has been achieved, the records can be deleted.

Goal evaluation

Goal evaluation is an essential part of making progress and improving performance. It requires measurable goals that have been clearly defined. This is easier with sports that involve objective measurements such as sprinting times. The measurements show how close the person is to their goal, which helps to motivate them and guides them in setting new goals.

Figure 16.22 Goal setting can be part of psychological preparation

Sports performers need to know how they are progressing. Most of them are highly motivated and need feedback to maintain their enthusiasm and commitment.

You are a sports psychologist. Present and justify your six-week psychological skills training programme to enhance sports performance for a selected sports performer.

D3

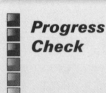

Progress Check

1. Why are personality profiles important in sport?
2. Describe the POMS.
3. Give an example from sport to illustrate interactionist theory.
4. Why is motivation important in sports performance?
5. What are the characteristics of a Nach personality?
6. What is the definition of a group or team?
7. What factors affect team cohesion in sport?
8. What is social loafing and how is it prevented in sport?
9. Give four different leadership roles in sport.
10. What factors affect leadership styles?
11. Give three physiological and three psychological symptoms of stress.
12. What are the main stressors in sport?
13. Using examples from sport, describe coping strategies that could be used to combat stress.
14. How can goal setting be effective? Illustrate you answer with examples from your own sport.

Glossary

Aerobic endurance
The ability to do continuous exercise without tiring. The more oxygen can be transported around your body and the more your muscles can use this oxygen, the greater your level of aerobic endurance.

Agility
How quickly you can change direction under control.

Anatomical position
The position of a person's body standing upright, facing forwards, arms downward, with the palms of the hand facing forward.

Anticipatory rise
A rise in heart rate before exercise begins, caused by release of the hormone adrenaline.

Arousal
The intensity of the drive experienced by an athlete when they try to achieve a goal. High arousal can lead to high levels of stress, both physiological and psychological.

ATP
Adenosine triphosphate. A complex chemical compound formed with the energy released from food and stored in all cells, particularly muscles. To carry out their functions, cells use the energy released by the breakdown of ATP.

Attribution
A perceived cause of a particular outcome. In sport, attributions are often the reasons we give for the results we achieve.

Balance
The ability to keep your body mass or centre of mass over a base of support.

Ballistic stretching
Stretching that uses bouncing movements to give the limb enough momentum to carry it through a wider range.

Bioelectric impedance
How hard it is for electric current to flow through the body. Fat has a higher bioelectric impedance than other body tissue. Measurements of bioelectric impedance can be used to estimate body composition.

Blood viscosity
Measures the resistance of the blood to flow freely. The more viscous the blood, the more it resists free flow. The amount of plasma or water in the blood affects its viscosity. A high blood plasma gives a low blood viscosity. Dehydration due to an endurance event, for example, may decrease the level of blood plasma and make the blood more viscous, which lowers the efficiency of oxygen delivery.

Body composition
The percentages of muscle, fat, bone and internal organs in a person's body. These percentages provide an overall view of your health and fitness in relation to your weight, health and age.

Cancellous bone
Bone with a honeycomb structure that is strong but very light. It consists of red bone marrow and trabeculae; trabeculae are partitions made of connective tissue. Often called spongy bone.

Cardiovascular
Relating to the heart and blood vessels.

Cartilage
Soft connective tissue between bones.

Catastrophe theory
A complex multidimensional theory that says increases in levels of cognitive anxiety will help performance if somatic anxiety is low. If a performer's body is relaxed but the performer feels anxious, this anxiety can help to improve performance.

Circuit training
A series of exercises arranged in a sequence of stations around a circuit. In one circuit, each exercise has its own number of repetitions, and a circuit can be repeated several times.

Cognitive anxiety
Psychological worry over a situation.

Command coaching
A coaching style where the coach makes all the decisions and directs the performer using an authoritarian approach.

Compact bone
Hard bone that forms the surface layers of all bones. It helps to protect bones and is surrounded by the periosteum, which is a fibrous, vascular tissue containing blood vessels.

Compound
A substance formed from two or more chemical elements in fixed proportions. For example, the elements oxygen and carbon combine to make the compound carbon dioxide.

Coordination
The ability to perform tasks accurately in a sport.

Democratic coaching
A coaching style where the performer participates in decision-making.

Discovery coaching
A coaching style where the coach encourages the performer to discover solutions to problems.

Distributed practice
Practice that has relatively long rests between trials. The rest intervals could involve tasks unrelated to the main practice activity.

Enzyme
A protein that acts as a catalyst or causes chemical reactions. Sports training can improve enzyme activity. For example, sprint interval training can improve the activity of creatine kinase.

Ergometer
A static exercise bike with alterable resistance to effort.

Eustress
Eustress is a stress that can help a performer. Some performers seek stressful situations, rather than trying to avoid them. When a performer experiences eustress, they are well motivated and see potentially dangerous or embarrassing situations as challenges, so their performances are helped rather than hindered.

Extrinsic motivation
Influences external to the performer. The drive created by motives that are external or environmental. These motives are rewards that can be tangible or intangible.

Extroversion
A personality trait where a person seeks social situations and likes excitement but lacks concentration.

Fartlek training
Also known as speed play, it is often used to maintain and improve aerobic endurance.

Flexibility
The amount or range of movement around a joint.

Flexibility training
Exercises that stretch the muscles and can help to improve performance and avoid injury. Sometimes called mobility training.

Haemoglobin
An iron-rich protein that transports oxygen in the blood. The higher the concentration of haemoglobin, the more oxygen can be carried. Haemoglobin concentration can be increased by endurance training.

Hazard
Something that has the potential to cause harm.

Imagery
Mental pictures that can improve concentration or confidence. Many sports performers use mental images that capture the feeling of movement or an emotional feeling.

Insertion
The end of the muscle attached to the bone that actively moves; for example, the biceps insertion is on the radius.

Introversion
A personality trait where a person does not seek social situations, likes peace and quiet and is good at concentrating.

Inverted-U hypothesis
A hypothesis that relates arousal and performance. It proposes that performance increases as arousal increases, but only up to moderate levels of arousal. If arousal increases further, then performance falls away.

Karvonen principle
A formula that identifies correct training intensities as a percentage of the sum of the maximum heart rate reserve and resting heart rate. It is a valid measure because it takes account of the stress on the heart and the athlete's V_{O_2max}. The maximum heart rate reserve is calculated by subtracting an individual's resting heart rate from their maximum heart rate. The maximum heart rate can be calculated by subtracting the athlete's age from 220. It is suggested that average athletes should train at an intensity equal to 60–75% of their maximal heart rate reserve.

Learned helplessness
A belief that failure is inevitable and a feeling of hopelessness when faced with a particular situation (specific learned helplessness) or groups of situations (global learned helplessness).

Massed practice
A continuous practice period.

Metabolic activity
The rate of metabolism.

Modelling
A coaching technique that uses demonstrations or models of performance, so the person being coached can see what is required then attempt to copy it.

Muscular endurance
The ability of a muscle or group of muscles to contract repeatedly without rest.

Neurotic
Adjective that describes a person who is highly anxious and has unpredictable emotions.

Notational analysis
Taking notes about a person's performance or a team's performance during an activity. The notes give important information to assess what went well and what needs improvement.

Objective performance data
Results you have achieved or performance outcomes such as goals scored or shots saved in team sports, distance thrown or distance jumped in individual sports.

Origin
The end of the muscle attached to a bone that is stable, e.g. the scapula. The point of origin remains still when contraction occurs. Some muscles have two or more origins; for example, the biceps muscle has two heads that pull on one insertion to lift the lower arm.

Osteoporosis
A condition that causes bones to become fragile and increases the likelihood they will fracture. It occurs when the body fails to form enough new bone, when it reabsorbs too much old bone, or both.

Outcome goal
A goal concerned with the end result of an activity, such as winning and losing.

Passive stretching
Stretching where another person pushes or pulls your limb to stretch the appropriate muscles.

Peak flow experience
An experience where a sportsperson achieves optimum performance levels and associates them with a particular emotional response.

Performance goal
A goal related directly to the performance or technique in an activity.

Phosphocreatine
A chemical compound stored in muscle. It is used to generate ATP from ADP, forming creatine.

Plyometrics
Training designed to improve dynamic strength. It improves muscles' speed of contraction and therefore affects power.

Power
A combination of strength and speed, it is the amount of work that can be done per unit time. Power is often known as fast strength.

Progressive relaxation training
Training where an athlete learns to be aware of the tension in their muscles then releases all the tension. Because the athlete is so aware of the tension in the first place, they have a more effective sense of losing that tension when it goes. It was pioneered by Jacobsen and is sometimes called the Jacobsen technique.

Proprioceptive neuromuscular facilitation
Training that tries to decrease the reflex shortening of the muscle being stretched, when the muscle is at its limit of stretch.

ProZone
A technique for collecting objective video evidence on player performance and statistics, used by most Premiership football clubs. It collects footage using specially placed cameras around the football stadium.

Reaction time
The time it takes someone to make a decision to move.

Reciprocal coaching
A coaching style where groups of performers learn from each other.

Ringelmann effect
A phenomenon which may be the cause of social loafing, whereby individual performance decreases with increasing group size.

Risk
The likelihood of harm from a particular hazard. Estimate risk by estimating the severity of the harm caused by the hazard and the likelihood that the hazard will occur.

Risk assessment
A process for estimating risks. According to the British Safety Council, it is a technique by which you estimate the chances of an accident happening, anticipate what the consequences may be and plan any actions to prevent it.

SCAT
Sport competition anxiety test. A questionnaire to assess competition anxiety in sports participants. It is a self-reporting questionnaire and measures competitive trait anxiety. It can be useful to predict a performer's anxiety in future competitions, i.e. their state anxiety.

Self-talk
A technique where a sports performer talks to themselves in a positive way about past performances and future efforts. It helps with self-confidence and raises levels of aspiration.

Shaping
A coaching technique where reward or praise is given when the performer's behaviour or technique is correct.

Socialisation
Adoption of a culture's norms and values.

Social learning
An approach to sports psychology that says our personalities have characteristics that are learned rather than genetically predetermined.

Social loafing
Describes the behaviour of players who seem to lack motivation in team situations.

Somatic anxiety
The body's response to a situation, such as tension and rapid pulse rate.

Speed
The ability of the body to move quickly. It can be seen as a person's maximum rate of movement over a specific distance or it can be measured for individual body parts.

Speed training
Training that uses shorter intervals of more intense training to improve anaerobic fitness needed for speed.

Sports development continuum
The framework for sports development is called the sports development continuum. It is actually a four-level progression from foundation to excellence via participation and performance.

Sports development officer
A person whose job is to improve access to sport and physical activity and to develop interest in them among people from all cultures in society. Sports development officers organise sporting projects, provide information and training for competitive athletes and leisure participants to increase levels of participation.

Sports equity
An idea that promotes fairness in sport and equality of access to sport, and requires people to recognise inequalities and take steps to eliminate them.

Stable
Adjective that describes a person who does not swing from one emotion to another.

Strength
The ability of a muscle to exert force for a short period of time.

Subjective observation
Assessment where an observer, usually the coach, makes judgements about what they see.

Team cohesion
The tendency for members of a team to stay together and resist breaking up. It is influenced by motivational factors.

Tendon
Attaches muscle to bone. Tendons pull the muscle to the bone and help with the power of muscle contractions. Tendons are attached to the periosteum of the bone through tough tissue called Sharpey's fibres.

Trait anxiety
A personality trait that endures in a performer. A performer with high trait anxiety is predisposed to react to situations by showing apprehension.

Vasoconstriction
Constriction of blood vessels which decreases their diameter and increases blood pressure.

Vasodilation
Dilation of blood vessels which increases their diameter and decreases blood pressure.

V_{O_2max}
The maximum amount of oxygen an individual can take in and use in 1 min.

Whole, part, whole
A coaching technique that teaches a whole skill, teaches its separate parts, then reteaches the whole skill.

Bibliography

Allport, G. W. (1935) *Attitudes*. Clarke University Press.

Atkinson, J. W. (1964) *An Introduction to Motivation*. Van Nostrand.

Bandura, A. (1977) *Social Learning Theory*. Prentice Hall.

Baron, R. A. (1977) *Human Aggression*. Plenum.

Barrow, J. C. (1977) The variables of leadership: a review and conceptual framework. *Academy of Management Review*, April, 231–251.

Berkowitz, L. (1974) Some determinants of impulsive aggression: role of mediated associations with reinforcements for aggression. *Psychological Review*, **81**, 165–176.

Bernstein, S. and Bernstein, R. (1998) *Elements of Statistics: Descriptive Statistics and Probability*. McGraw-Hill.

Bryman, A. and Cramer, D. (1999) *Quantitative Data Analysis for Social Scientists*. Routledge.

Bull, S. J. (1991) *Sport Psychology: A Self-Help Guide*. Crowood.

Burns, R. B. (2000) *Introduction to Research Methods*. Sage.

Carron, A. V. (1980) *Social Psychology of Sport*. Mouvement Publications.

Chelladurai, P. (1984) Multidimensional model of leadership. In Silva, J. M. and Weinberg, R. S. (eds) *Psychological Foundations of Sport*. Human Kinetics.

Coon, D. (1983) *Introduction to Psychology*. West Publishing.

Cottrell, N. B. (1968) *Performance in the Presence of Other Human Beings*. Allyn & Bacon.

Cox, R. H. (1998) *Sport Psychology: Concepts and Applications*. McGraw-Hill.

Cratty, B. J. (1981) *Social Psychology in Athletics*. Prentice Hall.

Csikszentmihalyi, M. (1975) *Beyond Boredom and Anxiety*. Jossey-Bass.

Davis, D., Kimmet, T. and Auty, M. (1986) *Physical Education: Theory and Practice*. Macmillan.

Deci, F. L. (1985) *Intrinsic Motivation and Self-determination in Human Behaviour*. Plenum Press.

Dollard, J. (1939) *Frustration and Aggression*. Yale University Press.

Duda, J. L. (1989) The relationship between task and ego orientation and the perceived purpose of sport among male and female high school athletes. *Journal of Sport & Exercise Psychology*, **11**, 148–165.

Dweck, S. (1980) *Learned Helplessness in Sport*. Human Kinetics.

Eysenck, H. J. (1970) *The Structure and Measurement of Personality*. Routledge.

Fazey, J. and Hardy, L. (1988) *The Inverted-U Hypothesis: A Catastrophe for Sport Psychology?* British Association of Sports Sciences.

Festinger, L. (1963) *Social Pressures in Informal Groups*. Harper & Row.

Festinger, L. A. (1957) *A Theory of Cognitive Dissonance*. Harper & Row.

Fiedler, F. E. A. (1967) *Theory of Leadership Effectiveness*. McGraw-Hill.

Fitts, P. M. (1967) *Human Performance*. Brooks-Cole.

Flick, U. (1998) *An Introduction to Qualitative Research*. Sage.

Gibbs, G. (1988) *Learning By Doing*. Further Education Unit, London.

Gill, D. L. (1986) *Psychological Dynamics of Sport*. Human Kinetics.

Gill, D. L. and Deeter, T. E. (1988) Development of the sport orientation questionnaire. *Research Quarterly for Exercise and Sport*, **59**, 191–202.

Hinkle, J. S. *et al*. (1989) Running behaviour. *Journal of Sport Behaviour*, **15**, 263–271.

Hogg, R. V. and Craig, A. T. (1994) *Introduction to Mathematical Statistics*. Prentice Hall.

Hollander, E. R. (1971) *Principles and Methods of Social Psychology*, 2nd edn. Oxford University Press.

Honeybourne, J. (2006a) *BTEC First Sport*. Nelson Thornes.

Honeybourne, J. (2006b) *Acquiring Skill in Sport: An Introduction*. Routledge.

Honeybourne, J., Hill, M. and Moors, H. (2000) *Advanced Physical Education and Sport*, 3rd edn. Nelson Thornes.

Honeybourne, J., Hill, M. and Wyse, J. (1998) *PE for You*. Stanley Thornes.

Howitt, D. and Cramer, D. (2000) *An Introduction to Statistics in Psychology*. Prentice Hall.

Hull, C. L. (1943) *Principles of Behaviour*. Appleton-Century-Crofts.

Ingham, A. G. *et al.* (1974) The Ringlemann effect. *Journal of Experimental Social Psychology*, **10**, 371–384.

Jarvis, M. (1999) *Sports Psychology*. Routledge.

Jones, J. G. and Hardy, L. (eds) (1990) *Stress and Performance in Sport*. Wiley.

Knapp, B. (1965) *Skill in Sport*. Routledge.

Kroll, W. *et al.* (1970) Multivariate personality profile analysis of four athletic groups. In Cox, R. (ed.) *Sport Psychology*. WCB/McGraw-Hill.

Latane, B. *et al.* (1980) Many hands make light work. *Journal of Personality and Social Psychology*, **37**, 822–832.

Levitt, E. E. (1980) *The Psychology of Anxiety*. Erlbaum.

Lewin, K. (1935) *A Dynamic Theory of Personality*. McGraw-Hill.

Lewin, K. (1951) *Psychological Theory*. Macmillan.

Locke, E. A. and Latham, G. P. (1985) The application of goal setting to sports. *Journal of Sports Psychology*, **7**, 205–222.

Lorenz, K. (1966) *On Aggression*. Brace & World.

Magill, R. A. (1993) *Motor Learning: Concepts and Applications*. Brown and Benchmark.

Martens, R. (1987) Science and sport psychology. *The Sport Psychologist*, **1**, 29–55.

Martens, R., Vealey, R. S. and Burton, D. (1990) *Competitive Anxiety in Sport*. Human Kinetics.

Moore, D. S. and McCabe, G. P. (1998) *Introduction to the Practice of Statistics*. Freeman.

Morgan, W. P. (1980) *Sport Personology*. Mouvement.

Mosston, M. and Ashworth, S. (1986) *Teaching Physical Education*. Merrill.

Nolan, B. (1994) *Data Analysis: An Introduction*. Cambridge.

Ott, L. R. and Longnecker, M. (2001) *An Introduction to Statistical Methods and Data Analysis*. Duxbury.

Pervin, L. (1993) *Personality Theory and Research*. Wiley.

Punch, K. F. (1998) *Introduction to Social Research*. Sage.

Radford, J. and Govier, E. (eds) (1991) *A Textbook of Psychology*. Routledge.

Rice, J. A. (1995) *Mathematical Statistics and Data Analysis*. Wadsworth.

Robb, M. (1972) *The Dynamics of Skill Acquisition*. Prentice Hall.

Roberts, C. G., Spink, K. S. and Pemberton, C. L. (1986) *Learning Experiences in Sport Psychology*. Human Kinetics.

Roberts, G. C. (ed.) (1992) *Motivation in Sport and Exercise*. Human Kinetics.

Roberts, K. C. and Pascuzzi, D. (1979) Causal attributions in sport. *Journal of Sport Psychology*, **1**, 203–211.

Rohatgi, V. K. (2000) *An Introduction to Probability and Statistics*. Wiley.

Sage, G. H. (1974) *Sport and American Society*. Addison-Wesley.

Schmidt, R. A. (1991) *Motor Learning and Performance*. Human Kinetics.

Schurr, K. T. *et al.* (1977) A multivariate analysis of athlete characteristics. *Multivariate Experimental Clinical Research*, **3**, 53–68.

Sharp, R. (1992) *Acquiring Skill in Sport*. Sports Dynamics.

Shaw, M. E. (1976) *Group Dynamics*. McGraw-Hill.

Silva, J. M. and Weinberg, R. S. (eds) (1984) *Psychological Foundations of Sport*. Human Kinetics.

Skinner, B. F. (1953) *Science and Human Behaviour*. Macmillan.

Smoll, F. L. and Shutz, R. W. (1980) Children's attitudes towards physical activity. *Journal of Sport Psychology*, **4**, 321–344.

Steiner, I. D. (1972) *Group Process and Productivity*. Academic Press.

Thorndike, E. L. (1914) *Educational Psychology: Briefer Course*. Columbia University Press.

Triandis, H. C. (1977) *Interpersonal Behaviour*. Brooks-Cole.

Weinberg, R. S. (1984) The relationship between extrinsic rewards and intrinsic motivation. In Silva, J. M. and Weinberg, R. S. (eds) *Psychological Foundations of Sport*. Human Kinetics.

Weiner, B. (1974) *Achievement Motivation and Attribution Theory*. General Learning Press.

Wesson, K. *et al.* (1998) *Sport and PE*. Hodder & Stoughton.

Willis, J. D. and Campbell, L. F. (1992) *Exercise Psychology*. Human Kinetics.

Wilmore, J. H. and Costill, D. L. (2005) *Physiology of Sport Exercise*, 3rd edn. Human Kinetics.

Wood, B. (1998) *Applying Psychology to Sport*. Hodder & Stoughton.

Yerkes, R. M. and Dodson, J. D. (1908) The relation of strength of stimulus to rapidity of habit formation. *Journal of Comparative Neurology and Psychology*, 18, 459–482.

Websites

www.baalpe.org – British Association of Advisers and Lecturers in Physical Education

www.cre.gov.uk – Commission for Racial Equality

www.homeoffice.gov.uk – Home Office

www.dfes.gov.uk – Department for Education and Skills

www.doh.gov.uk – Department of Health

www.defra.gov.uk – Department for the Environment, Food and Rural Affairs

www.efds.co.uk – English Federation of Disability Sport

www.sportscoachuk.org – Sports Coach UK

www.npfa.co.uk – National Playing Fields Association

www.sportengland.org – Sport England

www.pea.uk.com – Physical Education Association of the United Kingdom

www.sportscotland.org.uk – Scottish Sports Council

www.wsf.org.uk – Women's Sports Foundation

www.sportni.org – Sports Council for Northern Ireland

www.uksport.gov.uk – UK Sport

www.sports-council-wales.org.uk – Sports Council for Wales

Sites for practical sports

Athletics
www.iaaf.org – International Association of Athletics Federations

Basketball
www.fiba.com – International Basketball Federation
www.bbl.org.uk – BBL website

Cricket
www.cricinfo.com
www.lords.org

Football
www.fa-premier.com
www.uefa.com
www.fifa.com

Golf
www.foreteevideo.co.uk – history of golf

Rugby league
www.therfl.co.uk
www.rleague.com

Rugby union
www.rfu.com – England RFU site
www.wru.co.uk – Wales RFU site
www.sru.org.uk – Scotland RFU site
www.scrum.com
www.planet-rugby.com

Show jumping
www.bsja.co.uk

Skiing
www.fis-ski.com

Skating
www.isu.org

Index